Poetry and Language Writing

Poetry & ...

Also in this series

Poetry and Displacement Stan Smith

Poetry and Language Writing

Objective and Surreal

David Arnold

LIVERPOOL UNIVERSITY PRESS

First published 2007 by
Liverpool University Press
4 Cambridge Street
Liverpool L69 7ZU

Copyright © 2007 David Arnold

The right of David Arnold to be identified as the author of this work
has been asserted by him in accordance with the Copyright, Designs
and Patents Act 1988.

British Library Cataloguing-in-Publication data
A British Library CIP record is available

ISBN 978-1-84631-115-4 cased

Typeset in Stone Serif and Stone Sans by R. J. Footring Ltd, Derby
Printed and bound in the European Union by Biddles Ltd, King's Lynn

For my children, William and Frances

Contents

Acknowledgements

Like every piece of writing, this book has multiple points of origin, some of which even now may be lying dormant and undisclosed. Nonetheless, I thank without hesitation or reserve my first and inspirational tutor in poetry, Professor John Henderson of King's College, Cambridge. I also thank Professor Peter Nicholls of the University of Sussex, for his patient supervision of the doctoral dissertation from which the initial argument of the book was derived, and my colleagues at the University of Worcester, for their tolerance and support. I am also grateful to my home institution for granting me a period of research leave in which to complete the manuscript. Professor Judith Elkin's support has been invaluable in this respect and I warmly thank her. I would also like to thank my readers at LUP for their astute and supportive comments on the manuscript, Dr Phillippa Bennett for handling the permissions, and Ralph Footring for his meticulous scrutiny of the final draft.

Despite the rhetorical modes and formal conventions of scholarly discourse, literary criticism is a deeply personal business. In my case, the connection between my critical voice and my personal voice lay so deep that I missed it for years. It is in this context that I offer my heartfelt thanks to Elizabeth Hewitt for helping me to bring that connection to light. 'Acknowledgement' does not cover the breadth of my gratitude to my partner, Jill, nor does it span the range of ways in which her generous spirit has shaped this book and made it buoyant. Other words will do for that, in other places.

Permissions

Baudelaire:
- 'Correspondances' (quoted here on pp. 126–27, 185), taken from *Baudelaire* (pp. 36–37), introduced and edited by Francis Scarfe (Penguin Books, 1961), ©Francis Scarfe, reproduced by permission of Penguin Books Ltd.

Charles Bernstein:
- 'Interview with Tom Beckett' (p. 19), by Charles Bernstein, reprinted in *Content's Dream* (Sun and Moon Press, 1986), ©Charles Bernstein, reproduced by kind permission of the author.
- '"Passed by Examination": Paragraphs for Susan Howe' (p. 118) and 'The Revenge of the Poet-Critic' (p. 120), by Charles Bernstein, reprinted in *My Way: Speeches and Poems* (University of Chicago Press, 1999), ©Charles Bernstein, reproduced by kind permission of the author.

André Breton:
- *Mad Love* (p. 128), reprinted from *Mad Love* by André Breton, translated by Mary Ann Caws, by permission of the University of Nebraska Press, ©1987 University of Nebraska Press, ©1937 Éditions Gallimard.
- *Les Champs Magnétiques* (pp. 27, 28), by André Breton and Philippe Soupault, ©Editions Gallimard, Paris, reproduced by kind permission of Editions Gallimard, Paris.
- *The Magnetic Fields* (pp. 27–28), by André Breton and Philippe Soupault (Atlas Press, 1985), translation ©1985, David Gascoyne, reproduced by kind permission of Atlas Press.
- *Manifestoes of Surrealism* (pp. 44–46), by André Breton, trans. Richard Seaver and Helen R. Lane (University of Michigan Press, 1969), ©University of Michigan Press, reproduced by permission of University of Michigan Press.

Barrett Watten:
- *Frame* (Sun and Moon Press, 1997) (pp. 147ff), by Barrett Watten, ©Barrett Watten, reproduced by kind permission of the author.
- *Total Syntax* (Southern Illinois University Press, 1985) (p. 139), by Barrett Watten, ©Barrett Watten, reproduced by kind permission of the author.

William Carlos Williams:
- *A Novelette* (pp. 47–49), *Spring and All* (p. 38), *The Descent of Winter* (p. 37), *The Great American Novel* (pp. 39–43), by William Carlos Williams, from *Imaginations*, reproduced by permission of New Directions Publishing Corp.
- *Kora in Hell* (pp. 37, 38), by William Carlos Williams, from *Imaginations*, ©1970 Florence H. Williams, reproduced by permission of New Directions Publishing Corp.

Louis Zukofsky:
- *Prepositions* (pp. 69, 70–71, 73, 77, 83) and 'My One Voice' (p. 88), by Louis Zukofsky (Wesleyan University Press, 2001), ©2001 Paul Zukofsky, reproduced by kind permission of Wesleyan University Press. All Louis Zukofsky material ©Paul Zukofsky; the material may not be reproduced, quoted, or used in any manner whatsoever without the explicit and specific permission of the copyright holder.

CHAPTER 1

The Scholarly Life of Language Writing

It has been variously labelled 'Language poetry', 'Language writing', 'L=A=N=G=U=A=G=E writing' (after the magazine that ran from 1978 to 1981) and 'Language-centred writing'. It has been variously defined as non-referential or of diminished reference, as textual poetry or a critique of expressivism, as a reaction against the 'workshop' poetry enshrined in creative writing departments across the United States. It has been variously described as non-academic, theory conscious, avant-garde, postmodern and oppositional. It has been placed according to its geographical positions, on east or west coasts of the United States; its venues in small magazines, independent presses and performance spaces; and its descent from historical precursors, be they the Objectivists, the composers-by-field of the Black Mountain school, the Russian Constructivists or American modernism *à la* William Carlos Williams and Gertrude Stein. Indeed, one of the few statements that can be made about it with little qualification is that 'it' has both fostered and endured a crisis in representation more or less since it first became visible in the 1970s.

As far as period is concerned, it currently occupies a liminal space between past and present. For a start, most of the writers involved are still alive, and writing. That said, the positions from which they write, not to mention the audiences for and the contexts of their writing, have changed dramatically since the 1970s. Language writing – for this is what I am going to call 'it' – now features in university syllabuses on both sides of the Atlantic, and several of those involved have accepted academic appointments.[1] Critics have registered these shifts in different ways. For example, when Hank Lazer revised his 1988 essay 'Radical Collages' for publication in volume 2 of his *Opposing Poetries* (1996), he changed the title to 'Outlaw to Classic: The Poetry of Charles Bernstein and Ron Silliman'.[2] 'Classic' is, no doubt, being used somewhat ironically in the context of the oppositional stance of these two writers but the preposition signals the difficulty of classifying careers and practices that remain in formation.

If Language writing is achieving 'classic' status of a heterodox kind, we should not be surprised to find a certain amount of anxiety surrounding its influence over contemporary American poetry. In their introduction to *Telling It Slant: Avant-Garde Poetics in the 1990s*,[3] produced within the series 'Modern and Contemporary Poetics' by University of Alabama Press, Mark Wallace and Steven Marks acknowledge the success of what they call 'L=A=N=G=U=A=G=E writing' in helping to expand the arena for 'avant-garde poetries' (pp. 1–2). At the same time, their collection of recent interventions in the field of poetics is motivated partly by a desire to answer those who feel 'that no new and significant directions in avant-garde poetry have developed after those poets' (p. 2). The fact that the 'past' of Language writing is so recent, and not co-terminous with the lives of 'those poets' themselves, generates a certain amount of qualification on the part of the editors. When they account for the absence from their collection of essays by Language writers, they cite 'the greater level of exposure' that these writers have received, though they swiftly note thereafter that this exposure remains 'undoubtedly insufficient' (p. 2).

Such qualification is particularly understandable in light of the ongoing careers of writers like Barrett Watten, Charles Bernstein, Lyn Hejinian, Bob Perelman and Susan Howe.[4] It becomes even more so when one considers that only four years earlier, and in the same series, Christopher Beach edited a similar anthology, *Artifice and Indeterminacy*, in which the 'new poetics' of its subtitle were almost exclusively represented by the Language writers.[5] To some extent, the collision between Beach's newness and that of Wallace and Marks is softened by the fact that Beach presents his selection as an anthology that is overdue; a search through publications from the late 1990s, he suggests, returns numerous collections of poetry by these writers but discloses 'no comparably wide-ranging anthology of their poetics' (p. ix). Interestingly, whereas Wallace and Marks offer no appeal to the academy in their rationale, Beach implies, rather problematically, that 'the coming of age of the poetic avant-garde in the 1990s' is defined by the growing attention of professional scholars (p. vii). Such a view turns Lazer's earlier celebration of the extra-curricular status of Language writing on its head.

Even this brief comparison of two perspectives illustrates the difficult terrain that must be crossed by anyone who wants to give an account of Language writing. Questions of definition and period are currently unresolved and are likely to remain so. In the present work, I have no desire to petrify Language writing with definitive fixity, nor to allocate it a niche in some official archive of the literary past. If there is a point to discussing any aspect of what has come before, it is surely to create some kind of significance in the present. My early encounters with Language writing first took the cast of research when I began to think that this amorphous and heterogeneous body of work had been only partially interpreted by critics who sought to frame it as ideology critique. In this respect, although my discussion is undeniably informed by theories of society, the psyche and signification, it lodges most comfortably with those attempts to place Language writing in relation to its literary precursors. For me, the 'present' significance of such a project has a lot to do with a re-evaluation of the legacies of post-structuralism. These legacies continue to slide through the discipline of literary studies like the glowing effluvia of a giant volcano that blew its top some time ago but still demands our vigilance and, perhaps, our respect.

From this point of view, it is no coincidence that my scepticism over the blanket description of Language writing as ideology critique goes hand in hand with an enthusiasm to raise the profile of Surrealism in the context of twentieth-century American poetry. It is fair to say that, in general, Language writers have been reluctant to claim Surrealism as a positive influence. As will become apparent, this wariness is not unrelated to the keenness for continental theory shown by many Language writers, since, Jacques Lacan and Walter Benjamin apart, these theorists did not have much time for Surrealism, at least as far as Language writing's aspirations to theoretical rigour were concerned. What I hope to demonstrate in the chapters that follow is that the reluctance to acknowledge positive comparisons with Surrealism is often based on a reduced account of the poetics *and* the politics of the European movement. Lift this limiting frame and novel correspondences, unlooked-for affinities arise. It is to this end that many of my readings are directed.

Language writing as ideology critique

For those not familiar with the early reception of Language writing, an account is in order. I have suggested that early academic responses to the work focused on its oppositional credentials as ideology critique. Key texts here are Jerome McGann's article 'Contemporary Poetry, Alternate Routes' and George Hartley's monograph *Textual Politics and the Language Poets*, both from the late 1980s.[6] Against the backdrop of the 'dramatic shift to the political right' which occurred in the United States at the end of the Vietnam War, McGann reads the project as an 'antithetical venture' to the dominant forces of capitalism (pp. 625 and 629). The oppositional character of this venture is established through an appeal to Marxist ideas of commodity fetishism. Just like anything else in capitalist culture, language is subject to reification; hence, in McGann's view, the task of writing 'must be to set language free, to return it from the domains of the abstract and the conventional ... to a world of human beings and human uses' (pp. 634–35). Despite his concession that not all Language writers share a single political perspective, Hartley's interest is also in the ways in which individuals associated with the movement seek to disclose and resist capital's appropriation of language.

Drawing on the work of Georg Lukács, Hartley was one of the first to discuss the 'analogy' drawn by some Language writers between Lukács' definition of reification and 'the production of language and poetry'. As Hartley succinctly puts it (p. 34), 'signifiers here replace the commodity and reference replaces surplus value'. Since reference obscures its origins in social relations, it also exhibits the 'phantom objectivity' that is the defining feature of reification. To extend the analogy, this illusion manifests itself in capitalist culture as the assumption that the meaning of words is fixed independently of context and language's own material dimension.

The argument continues that much early Language writing sought to expose the illusory character of this objectivity through an increased attention to the materiality of language, to what Charles Bernstein has described as 'the fact of wordness'.[7] Take, for example, the following extract from P. Inman's 'OCKER', a piece sampled in the 1986 anthology *In the American Tree* (p. 336):[8]

> debris clud
>
>> (sbrim
>> m,nce
>
> (nome,id
>
>> (armb,jor,
>
> (droit,cur.

And on the next page:

> cocone, emble blems
> off diller apiece
>
>> andn'ts,
>
>> bed unes
>
> meanglence,
>
> coat qol
>> field jah

Inman here uses two strategies to keep the materiality of language at the forefront of our attention. The first is to adopt a sparse typographical layout such that the higher ordering of words into lines, stanzas or paragraphs is not allowed to take hold. The second is to disrupt the semantic force of individual words, either by juxtaposing the familiar with the strange – 'coat qol' – or by subjecting them to various kinds of graphic mutilation and phonic ambiguity. So, writing's conventional abbreviation for 'not' is saddled with an 's' that seems more appropriate to a plural noun and harnessed to a common conjunction – 'andn'ts'. Of course, the designation of a plural ultimately makes sense if we are paying attention at a graphemic rather than a semantic level. In a similar vein, the word 'emblems', itself a metaphor for 'sign', is not allowed to take its customary shape but is visited by a distorting reduplication – 'emble blems'. In its similarity to 'blah blah' this embellished repetition makes a mockery of the semantic order while at the same time reminding us that words are material in their sounds as well as in their graphic forms.[9] Reference would seem to be at stake in the hybrid word 'meanglence', but we receive only a glimpse at how we might invest in this signifier. For the abstract value of meaning is doubly undermined, firstly by the suggestion of the particularity of a concrete and embodied look (reading 'glance' for '-glence') and secondly by the fact that this suggestion is not confirmed one way or the other by the letters on the page; it is, after all, 'meanglence', not 'meanglance'. Inman's text is one example of a method by which some Language writers sought to defamiliarize language at 'the submorphemic level'.[10] The difficulty of making sense of this piece helps to explain how the assumption came about that 'the foregrounding of the referential dimension of language' within Language writing could be interpreted – often negatively – only as 'non-referential poetry'.[11]

To some extent, following Hartley's detailed analysis, in which he draws heavily on Louis Althusser, it became *de rigueur* amongst critics to think about Language writing in terms of its interrogation of the ideological ramifications of linguistic reference.[12] This critique is further contextualized by commentators in their recognition that it took shape at a time when 'workshop' poetry in the United States was characterized by a narrow orthodoxy. Here the norm was to place the personal 'voice' at the centre of the poem, to accept and exploit its ability to represent both subjective states and objective conditions.[13] By contrast, Michael Greer sees as 'one of the fundamental impulses in Language poetry' a 'complex, ambivalent desire to problematize "speech" and "voice" as the locus of poetic expression'. Lee Bartlett notes the shared commitment to the 'ongoing critique of the "workshop poem"', while for Hank Lazer the 'critique of referentiality' is itself targeted at 'the heart of the workshop craft'.[14] Like a number of other commentators, Lazer believes that the value of Language writing is not only in its critique of referentiality but also in the positive alternative it offers: in resisting 'habitual reading' it 'invites the reader to become a producer of the text rather than remain its consumer'.[15] Similarly, in discussing Lyn Hejinian's influential essay 'The Rejection of Closure', Hartley notes that:

> meaning exists within an active inter-agential process rather than as an object or product existing outside of language, just as value results from a social process rather than from some inherent quality of the object.[16]

Take, for example, another piece included in *In the American Tree* (p. 70), this one by Bob Perelman:

My One Voice

At the sound of my voice
I spoke and, egged on
By the discrepancy, wrote
The rest out as poetry.

Read the books, duets
From nowhere say they speak;
Why not let them. Habitual stares
Leave trees in rearview mirrors.

I came from a neutral point
In space, far from the inside
Of any one head. O say can I
Still see the tabula rasa outshining

That rosy dawn on the near side
Of the genetic code. Doubt,
Thy name is certainty. Generations
Of recordings of the sunrise

Picture the light until the page
Is white and I predict
The present, hearing a future
In the syllables' erasing fade.

The title of this conventional-looking poem, 'My One Voice', declares the univocality of the individual subject.[17] But this security is immediately dissolved by the suggestion, illogical in itself, that the subject speaks not *ex origine* but in response to another voice that is also his. This absurd situation could be recovered if the first 'voice' were read as a metaphor for 'thought' itself, the second voice then following on as its material representation. But Perelman's terms do not allow us to settle into this 'habitual' reading, since the two voices do not match each other but are linked through 'discrepancy'. Contrary to expectation, this discrepancy does not get in the way of poetry but is its driving force. At stake here is the generic sanctity of the lyric voice. Despite the form of the piece, despite the references to 'rosy dawn' and 'sunrise', this poem challenges the convention that the voice is the 'essence' of poetry.[18] Divided within itself, it cannot participate in those exemplary qualities of the lyric, namely 'its honesty, its directness, its authenticity, its artlessness, its sincerity, its spontaneity, its personal expressiveness; in short, its naturalness'.[19] Hence the subjective associations that are imminent and familiar in 'That rosy dawn' are blocked by the impersonal determinism of 'the genetic code'.[20]

Hence the direct address of the conventional apostrophe is short-circuited by the fact that the communication appears to be between the voice and its own imperative to speak – 'O say'.[21]

Direct communication between poem and reader is equally called into question; with the traditional qualities of lyric bracketed as they are, readers are in no position to trust the voice they hear. How many voices are there, anyway, and what *exactly* are they trying to say? Such discomfiture seems appropriate in this disturbed lyric landscape. We might compare our expectation that poetry will be representational to the 'Habitual stares' that 'Leave trees in rearview mirrors'. According to this analogy, the reader is a passive, disengaged spectator, while the writing itself is always no more than a belated ('rearview') image of something other than itself.[22] In the face of this atrophied scene, the same stanza allows the possibility for alternative – 'Why not let them' – situations in which there are two, equally active, partners making their way in 'duets' through the same 'books'. These two models of reading subsequently compete for the lyrical terrain of the poem. On the one hand, 'Generations / Of recordings of the sunrise' can be read as an ironic put-down of Romantic expressiveness. Through its commitment to the *same* treatment of the *same* subjects, the lyric voice has not demonstrated personal uniqueness but has generated the kind of serial repetition that one expects from the 'genetic code', weakening in the process the force of its own expression ('Picture the light until the page / Is white'). On the other hand, the reader is in a position to generate a more unconventional image of the sunrise, one in which the words of the poem do not represent the visual effects of the event so much as gesture towards the iconic relationship between those effects and the word*less* spaces of the printed poem. In allowing for this 'duet', the poetic 'I' envisages the co-productive combination of two subjects and two temporalities. Since this combination can take place any number of times, the poem's 'future' is bright and plural, enabled as it is by the 'erasing' of 'my one voice'.

In the eyes of some, however, Language writing is hardly an outlaw project. Vernon Shetley, for example, has suggested that the critical repu-tation of these writers has grown out of a reciprocal relationship between academics and poets. Just as the latter rely on 'academic boosters' like McGann to establish them at the centre of the literary scene, so do the academics need to gesture towards radical poets in order to demonstrate their own politicization and 'ideological self-awareness'.[23] Few would con-test that there is a community of interest amongst some academics and some Language writers but Shetley is out on a limb to suggest that this relationship works only for the ideological status quo.[24] Nonetheless, put side by side, the accounts of Hartley and Shetley illustrate that, for both the boosters and the detractors, Language writing has been repeatedly characterized in terms of its political contours. As Perelman himself has put it, 'the political remarks have gotten more attention than the declara-tions of poetic heritage'.[25] Hartley's remarks are instructive in this respect, since they suggest both that 'the anti-referentialist stereotype' started early and that it was not a case of simple misconstrual by the critics:

> They themselves [Language poets], of course, are largely responsible for such a characterization because of their earlier realism-equals-reification argument and their participation in symposia such as 'The Politics of the Referent' (1977) and 'The Death of the Referent?' (1981).[26]

With hindsight, the collective forum of the symposium looks like a double-edged sword, under which an emergent and dynamic community of interests could be made to look like a doctrinaire and unswerving cadre.

Over time, commentators have taken a broader perspective on the critique of referentiality. Ever vigilant against the pitfalls of general classifications of poetry, Marjorie Perloff has taken time to point out that the anti-referentialist phase of Language writing was short-lived, as some of its most strident adherents quite quickly began to moderate their views.[27] In an interview with Perelman, Peter Nicholls also acknowledges that the Language project has apparently moved on from the disclosure of language as 'primarily an ideological medium' to a consideration of ways in which specifically poetic language might be 'refigured as a place of social connection'.[28] The critique of referentiality has also been challenged according to its own terms. One line of argument has been to suggest that the disclosure of language's ideological dimension makes for a limited project. John Koethe, for one, suggests that Language writing has been 'too content to merely illustrate the ways in which meaning is conventionally constructed'.[29] At stake here is the implication that any particular poem is always in the service of a general rule. This is a point made explicitly by Peter Middleton. In his opinion, to yoke poetry to the 'broad determinisms of Althusserian and related theories' is to deny it the specificity it needs to have any social consequences.[30] Restricted in this way, actual poems run the risk of becoming nothing more than repeated instances of the same proposition, mere 'exempla of the functioning and disruption of the symbolic realm'.[31] In his by now familiar reading of Perelman's poem 'China', Fredric Jameson is even less optimistic, interpreting the anti-referentialist features of Language writing as more symptomatic of the capitalist order than disruptions of it. For him, the kind of 'discrepancy' of voice to be found in this writing signals not a liberation from the constrictions of expressiveness but the 'schizophrenic fragmentation' that is the condition of the postmodern subject.[32]

The status of the reader as 'co-producer' has also come under interrogation. If Koethe's and Middleton's challenge holds good, there would appear to be no room for co-production in the first place. Like Punch responding to Judy's club, the reader can react to repeated disclosure only with repeated recognition *of* disclosure. In Jameson's scenario, the reader cannot even get this far: waves of 'wordness' do not prompt recognition but keep the subject in a perpetual state of fragmentation. In Michael

Davidson's opinion, the balance of power between writer, text and reader belies claims to the equality of co-production. Pointing out that the idea of the reader as co-producer relies on the assumption 'that there be some interplay between poem and reception', he suggests that this dynamic is limited (if not prevented) by the reliance on 'formal design'.[33] This is to say that, at its most extreme, the very foregrounding of artifice that is supposed to enable interaction between the poem and its reception often results in a rhetorical manipulation of the reader: 'The reader becomes a voyeur upon an artful attempt to seduce him or her into playing by the rules'.[34]

It would be a misrepresentation to suggest that all of the early critical responses to Language writing concentrated on its status as ideology critique, or that they employed only continental theory in their readings of it. In their work, Perloff, Nicholls and others confirm the need for more blended accounts of literary production.[35] 'Influence' is a category that demands some attention in this respect. Post-structuralist critiques of causality and linear time have made this object of scrutiny a hot potato for literary historians. On the other hand, it is liberating to think that the study of influence is no longer confined to establishing the verifiable impact or imprint of one generation/writer/period on another. For influence no longer necessarily obeys a linear temporality. For example, when Barrett Watten elaborates his formulation of the 'Constructivist moment' in his book of the same name, he asserts that it 'is informed by the historical experience of social construction' but also 'depends on the way that meaning is constructed through retrospective determination or *Nachträglichkeit'*.[36] This Freudian concept, which can also be translated as 'deferred action', is important for my own reading of Surrealism. It also inflects my thinking about influence, allowing it to flow backwards in time as well as forwards. From this perspective, the present significance that one attaches to the past is not a secondary quality overlaying the historical object but a primary quality of that object as it is constructed in the present moment. Put simply, there might be Surrealisms, Objectivisms, even Language writings that have yet to be built. This is not to say, however, that such future constructions have *no* causal relation to the past. The translation of *Nachträglichkeit* as 'deferred action' conveys more clearly than Watten's rendering of it the implication that the new meanings we give to the past were always already there, *potentially*, if not realized, recognized or represented. *Nachträglichkeit* is not, then, at odds with Watten's emphasis on 'historical experience'. In *The Constructivist Moment*, he relates his own use of cultural poetics to the New Historicism of Stephen Greenblatt, albeit with some reservations (pp. xxv ff.).

The Objectivist Nexus is a collection of essays that is also important for my view of the relationship between Language writers and the work of earlier poets.[37] Its editors – Rachel Blau DuPlessis and Peter Quartermain – similarly acknowledge Greenblatt's work as influential for their collection of 'culturalist interpretations of poetry, readings inflected with sociopolitical concerns' (p. 20). They draw on Foucauldian theory to support their proposal of 'nexus' as a term which has the potential to change our understanding of literary history. Against traditional notions of the 'literary movement', thinking in terms of the nexus allows the critic to dispense with the methodological demand for 'conformity of the literary materials or producers'. Equally unnecessary is 'a temporal and philosophical consistency of application' (p. 22). When these constraints – particularly the latter – are relaxed, DuPlessis and Quartermain argue (p. 22) that it becomes possible to articulate a model of literary history in which the critical act entails more than a simple reconstruction of the past:

> Hence, 'nexus' could be a term for a literary history written under the rubric of Foucault's observation that the problem in the study of literature 'is no longer one of tradition, of tracing a line, but one of division, of limits; it is no longer one of lasting foundations but of transformations that serve as new foundations' – a literary history that remains a shifting place of dialogue, debate, and reconfiguration.

This expanded notion of literary history is very relevant to a project like this one, which seeks to challenge the received wisdom about the relationship between apparently established literary movements. So helpful is it that I have coined the title 'the Surreal-O-bjectivist nexus' (Chapter 4) to designate my discussion of Surrealism and Objectivism.

Language writing, Objectivism and Surrealism

Also relevant is what can be described as the ethical turn in literary studies. Ethics is, of course, one branch of 'sociopolitical concern' to which a cultural poetics might attend. My own understanding of Language writing has been significantly guided in this respect by Tim Woods's book *The Poetics of the Limit: Ethics and Politics in Modern and Contemporary American Poetry*.[38] Drawing on the aesthetic philosophy of Theodor Adorno, and the ethical philosophy of Emmanuel Lévinas, Woods links the Objectivism of Louis Zukofsky and George Oppen with Language writing in what he calls a 'discourse of responsibility' (p. 1). In his Introduction, he suggests that this discourse has been neglected for two reasons: firstly, it was overwhelmed by the 'vehement antihumanist outburst' issued by 'the early twentieth century modernists'; secondly, 'some subsequent critics and historians of modernist poetry, often swayed too heavily by poststructuralist edicts, have been too disconcerted by the humanist overtones of this discourse to give this ethical dimension the concentration it demands' (p. 2). Central to Woods's thesis is what he calls 'a fidelity to otherness' (p. 8). This fidelity helps to define the continuity between Objectivism and Language writing. For my discussion, it also provides a frame for extending this continuity to include Surrealism, albeit in qualified terms.

Extremely welcome, in my view, is Woods's suggestion that critics also have a stake in ethics. In this respect, the 'ethical turn' that succeeded the 'linguistic turn' in literary studies in the late 1980s and early 1990s itself contributes to the discourse of responsibility shared by Objectivist and Language writers. Crucially, fidelity to otherness does not occur at the expense of subjectivity, a concept that came in for some heavy bombardment while the linguistic turn was in full momentum: 'the "ethical turn" is part of an attempt to *preserve* the role of the subject in view while respecting the difference of the (other) object', according to Woods (p. 11). This kind of stance might also serve as a measure of influence, according to which a writer corresponds with precursor texts and writers in terms that neither declare the identity of the past with the present nor overwhelm the past with the 'interpretative violence' of the present (p. 11). I have found this measure valuable in thinking about the relationship between Michael Palmer and William Carlos Williams, as well as that between Barrett Watten and George Oppen. It has also been enabling in thinking about Susan Howe, whose heterodox writing often traces a narrow line between fidelity to the other and absorption by it.

The scholar whose work is on the 'avant-garde' risks more than most committing the violence of interpretation. Watten's critical writings are again instructive here. As a point of reference for his account of the Language school, in which he has played such a key role, Watten takes Paul Mann's provocative book *The Theory-Death of the Avant-Garde*. From Mann's perspective, scholarly interpretation participates in this demise. In *The Constructivist Moment*, Watten summarizes (p. 46) thus:

> The avant-garde dies into theory simultaneously when its political critique turns into an empty circularity of discourse, and when its radical forms are reduced to commodities and collected by museums.

In fact, interpretation belongs not so much with this first death as with 'a second death' whereby the agency of the avant-garde is dispersed by 'ancillary phenomena', such as 'academic analysis' (p. 47). The result of this 'surplus of interpretation' is that 'the potential for agency' that accrues to the material text is always 'short-circuited', limited to the discursive realm (p. 48). Watten is in an interesting position to reflect and comment on Mann's diagnosis of academic activity. On the one hand, he is committed to the critical potential of the avant-garde and continues to produce oppositional writing. On the other hand, as Professor of English at Wayne State University, he is also a member of an interpretative community that Mann would expect to manage difference and dilute opposition to hegemonic institutions such as the academy. Watten seems confident, however, that the contradiction between these two positions can be resolved (p. 49):

> In proposing a matrix of theory as consequence of the death of the avant-garde, however, Mann actually works to preserve the agency of the avant-garde, whose negativity (either radical form or political agency) may now be distributed throughout the social totality as a critical force.

In a sense, this declaration is performative as well as descriptive, since it makes avant-garde agency available to the same discourse that it represents. In this respect, it is hard to say that Watten's criticism is 'just' discourse, since it makes something happen.

Watten's suggestion that theory might disseminate avant-garde negativity *throughout* the social totality sounds a little optimistic but it prompts some interesting reflections for anyone currently working in the British system of higher education. With the commitment of the New Labour administration to a national rate of 50 per cent participation in higher education, it would seem that the potential for academics to affect the social totality is also likely to rise. And yet there is evidence to suggest that many academics in Britain are concerned more than ever that their critical agency is under threat from policy makers, funding bodies and university managers alike. Relative to the curricular regimentation of secondary education, the scope for critical thinking is extensive; relative to the 'Dissenting Academies' of the eighteenth century or the communitarian visions of plate-glass universities in the 1960s, the managerial culture and marketization that dominate higher education now really do threaten to make critical enquiry an extinct formation. From this point of view, the identification of the academy with the institutions that host its members is increasingly invalid. In the eyes of our chief executives, a book about poetry is at best an exotic remnant of an era almost banished; at worst it is an aberration that only gets in the way of genuine entrepreneurial attempts to 'grow the institution'. From Watten's more optimistic perspective, however, perhaps the scholarly monograph is now an example of 'radical form'.

If not entirely in line with the institutional imperatives of higher education, my reassessment of the relationship between Language writing and Surrealism is sanctioned by the broadening horizons of cultural poetics. At stake, on the one hand, are the historical affiliations, encounters, brush-offs and departures that have shaped the reception of Surrealism in the United States. Beckoning, on the other, is the dissolution of temporal and poetic divisions between practices and writers. I have in mind here the idea that Surrealism might persist, or emerge, in the work of specific writers associated with the Language school, and in my readings of this work. In the light of Watten's suggestion that meaning is determined retrospectively, critics gain a licence for creativity that they did not have before. Of course, with this licence comes responsibility; at the close of their introduction, Duplessis and Quartermain remind us that 'critical acts ... form reception', and that critics will have their own 'investments' in the literary nexus.[39] Mann might argue that the primary investment of the institutionalized critic is to keep the wheel of discourse in motion. Across Watten's activist landscape, however, avant-garde agency retains the power to animate critical discourse. If this state is an example of the 'deferred action' of *Nachträglichkeit*, it also entails a 'retrospective determination' in which modernism itself is still coming to pass. In what he describes as 'an avowed polemic that addresses the situation of avant-garde poetry and poetics in the mid-1990s', Watten argues that:

> modernism is best imagined not retrospectively, as a politics of form, but prospectively, as the site of an emerging cultural order that structures ways of feeling, thinking, and imagining differences within modernity.[40]

Watten is reacting here against what he perceives as Charles Altieri's misleading account of modernism as lacking 'social reflexivity'. Viewed retrospectively, Surrealism has often been considered in these terms, as 'a critique of representation presumed "to exemplify ways of feeling, thinking and imaginatively projecting investments *not bound to dominant social structures*"'.[41] Watten is not writing about Surrealism specifically here but, as we shall see, he and other Language writers have discussed the movement in terms that do not depart radically from Altieri's view. From this sceptical position, Surrealism's critique of representation by way of automatism and a poetics of the dream leads to the transcendent self rather than the transformation of social conditions. When Surrealism appears in the writings of Language's 'poet-critics', it often features as a well meaning but compromised enthusiasm which touched upon some useful techniques without realizing their true import. Portrayed in this fashion, it usually merits brief mention rather than extended discussion.[42]

Despite these qualifications, Surrealism is already on the critical map as a positive force in the development of twentieth-century American poetry. Specifically, I have in mind here Nicholls's extended mapping of an American tradition that does not derive from the image but grounds itself in the material character of language and its contexts. As Nicholls reads it, the accommodation of Surrealism by American poets turns on a distinction between those who followed André Breton in an 'orthodox' fashion – yielding primarily to its allure as a poetics of the inner life – and those whose unorthodox interpretation led to its absorption as a 'practice of writing'. It is as a 'practice of writing' that, Nicholls says, the European movement informs 'an alternative non-image based poetics in America running from Gertrude Stein to the Language writers'.[43] As far as early modernism is concerned, the orthodox American congregation would include Kenneth Patchen, Charles Henri Ford and Parker Tyler.[44] William Carlos Williams's wresting of Surrealism into an American context sets him at the springs of the unorthodox tendency. Zukofsky is out of reach altogether, 'lining up' with George Oppen, Carl Rakosi and Charles Olson 'against Surrealism'.[45] The Surrealism that emerges from my readings does not, however, divide quite so neatly. Surrealism in America was subject to many mediations, such that the division between orthodox and unorthodox is not an easy one to sustain.[46] Timing is important, too. If the division is a historical fact, at what point was it achieved? My reading of the poetic production of the late 1920s and early 1930s suggests that there is an alternative to the view that Surrealism was by then already a known quantity against which the emerging formation of Objectivism might define itself. Further, the dialogue that I hear taking place in the magazine *Blues* (Chapter 3) and the Objectivist edition of *Poetry* (Chapter 4) is, I believe, ongoing in the work of Palmer and Watten (discussed in Chapters 5 and 7).

This is a good point at which to mention Walter Benjamin. Benjamin is important for my discussion because he took seriously the political claims of Surrealism in his own project to develop what Margaret Cohen has called, in *Profane Illumination*,[47] 'Gothic Marxism'. By contrast with 'mainstream Marxism', Benjamin's variant is 'fascinated with the irrational aspects of social processes'. Equally, it 'investigates how the irrational pervades existing society and dreams of using it to effect social change' (pp. 1–2). Just as the image was important for the emergence of different poetic formations in modern and contemporary America, so was it a crux for Benjamin's Gothic Marxism. For writers whose convictions and practice tended towards materialism, the image was, not surprisingly, suspect for the priority it appeared to give to registering subjective processes rather than objective relations. In his efforts to think of the relationship between base and superstructure in psychoanalytical terms, Benjamin built a platform on which the *dialectical* image might be sustained in a materialist poetics. This image does not float free or withdraw from objective conditions but, as Cohen puts it (p. 42), it fulfils 'a collective symbolic need: the need to give the new imagistic form'. Benjamin famously got into deep water with his colleague Theodor Adorno for mixing Marxism with psychoanalysis and Cohen's book is invaluable for its detailed account of a debate in which the image was central. For Benjamin, the dialectical image was associated with consciousness, in the form of 'dream'. Adorno, by contrast, felt that this association 'mires dialectics in that murky realm between objective forces and subjective experience'; for him, the dialectical image must be thought of 'as a fragment of objective relations'.[48] What is so provocative about Cohen's discussion for this study are the parallels it prompts between this disagreement and the reception of Surrealism amongst American poets. For it seems to be the same 'murky realm' between objectivity and subjectivity that leads American poets from the 1920s onwards to resist Surrealism as a 'poetics of the inner life'. In this respect, Cohen's book also offers an important reminder that Bretonian Surrealism should not be reduced to the 'period of dreams' but acknowledged as a developing and ongoing debate with Marxism from 1925 onwards. As a result of this sustained interrogation, the range of concepts privileged by Breton and those around him was extended from the dream to include the *rencontre*, the *trouvaille* and interpretative desire. All of these concepts appear, more or less substantially, in the chapters that follow.

To the extent that Language writers are 'theory conscious', this consciousness should bear some of the responsibility for their abbreviated accounts of Surrealism. Again, Cohen's work is illuminating in this respect. In justifying her project to re-open the discussion of Surrealism and Marxism, she gives (p. 12) a narrative that is not without consequence for an understanding of the intellectual scene of Language writing:

> Not only Breton's modern materialism but high surrealism more generally has been a dead letter in the theoretical ferment of the past thirty years. Above all, high surrealism was dismissed by the French theoretical avant-garde that came to dominance in the sixties and seventies and that has been so influential in shaping the current critical scene.

Debates like the 'Politics of the Referent' may have taken place outside the academy but the early zeal for political accounts of signification was without question fired by the theoretical work of Roland Barthes, Louis Althusser and others. In this furnace of engagement, high Surrealism could not stand the heat of what we would now call high theory. Also worth noting is that the bias Cohen points to, towards 'dissident' Surrealism, still holds true. Wallace and Marks's anthology includes an essay by Charles Borkhuis explicitly implicating Surrealism and Language writing. But true to Cohen's observation, Borkhuis argues that the validity of this connection rests on a distinction between the 'orthodox' Surrealism of Breton and the work of 'later or tangential writers, influenced by surrealism but antithetical to its orthodoxy'.[49] Breton is rendered conservative in his commitment to 'stiff, rhetorical prose style' and 'high lyricism', while the dissidents deserve positive comparison with the Language group precisely by virtue of their recognition that language constitutes rather than represents reality. Indeed, Borkhuis cites Barthes in the act of differentiating Werner Sollers' *Event* from automatic writing, on the grounds that Sollers' text shows an 'emphasis on the grammatical' that is lacking in Surrealist practice.[50]

Borkhuis's essay sits nicely towards the end of this Introduction, since the reduced version it offers of Bretonian Surrealism suggests that there is space and cause to consider the redemption of 'high Surrealism' for Language writing and its precedents in American modernism. At stake here is not the recovery of obscured affiliations, lost manuscripts or missing diaries. In rattling the categorical fixities that have corralled Surrealism within a narrow compass as far as American poetry is concerned, I am salvaging both what might have been and what might still be in the enchanted place that writing works and weaves.

Overview

In the chapter that follows, I begin by discussing the part played by Surrealism as a negative exemplum for the early poetics of Language writing. In this context, Surrealism stands routinely accused of expressivism, of leaving writing at the service of the subjective interior. The problem

15

with this charge is that it engages with Surrealism only at the level of its aspirations. Breton did, indeed, hope for the ultimate unification of the self but, as more than one critic has observed, this hope inevitably came up against the materiality of the language. My attempt to align Language writing and Surrealism in this respect draws on Peter Nicholls's account of a modernist 'poetics of negation'. From this perspective, the two tendencies share a mode in which the gap between language and the world becomes a space for critique and opposition. In my argument, this space serves, in turn, as the ground for a positive comparison between Surrealism and Objectivism, both of which negotiate in their protean poetics the 'murky realm' between objective forces and subjective experience. Fredric Jameson and Hal Foster have also drawn attention to the conflicted poetics of Surrealism and their work helps to contextualize my discussion further. Particularly valuable for my purposes is Foster's understanding of automatism as a technique that tends as much to the dissolution of the subject as it does to its unification. The tension discerned by Foster feeds into my own interpretation of *Nachträglichkeit* as a kind of aberrant principle of automatic writing. To read the automatic texts of Surrealism in the light of this concept is to bring them within an interpretative frame where they might sit more congenially alongside Language texts. The chapter ends with one such reading of a section of *The Magnetic Fields* by André Breton and Philippe Soupault.

Continuing in this revisionary vein, Chapter 3 turns to the improvisations of William Carlos Williams. Williams is an important figure for many Language writers and their reception of his work has often been at odds with canonical representations of it. My aim in Chapter 3 is to show that Williams's positive engagement with Surrealism has been unnecessarily muted, in discussions both of his own poetics and of his 'influence' on subsequent phases of oppositional writing in the United States. In my view, what links Williams, Surrealism and Language writing is precisely a sensitivity to the intractability of language, tending towards a poetics of negation. The normative function of genre is also at stake in this connection and a substantial section of the chapter is given over to reading Williams's *The Great American Novel* in relation to Breton's *Soluble Fish* as an example of a Surrealist 'false novel'. After some extended close reading, I begin to explore the broader prospects for the links I am making. *Blues* is the anchor for this section. As a small magazine, it offers a more finely calibrated, albeit partial, measurement of the protean poetics characterizing the shift from first- to second-wave literary modernism. To read the contributions to *Blues* of Williams, Charles Henri Ford and Parker Tyler is, in my view, to discern no clear boundary between the orthodox American followers of Surrealism and its renegade dissidents.

In Chapter 4, I expand the field still further by proposing a Surreal-Objectivist nexus. As this coinage implies, I am working backwards as well as forwards here, unpicking, where I can, the definitive fixity with which criticism has absorbed these two groupings over the years. Clear definition was part of Louis Zukofsky's aspirations for poetry at the beginning of the 1930s but it is one inevitably snagged in the field of desire. It is on this field, I suggest, that Surrealism and Objectivism draw close, close to the point where, once again, clear distinctions between the two begin to dissolve. I pursue this dissolution through Zukofsky's contributions to *Blues* and into the 'symposium' he stages with Tyler and Ford, towards the end of the supposedly foundational Objectivist edition of *Poetry* in 1931.

As far as the concept of nexus resists closure, in both categorical and temporal terms, it allows me to conjecture the persistence of a Surreal-O-bjectivist nexus into more recent American poetry. In Chapter 5, it is my contention that the work of Michael Palmer can be read in these terms. In his commitment to what I call a poetics of witness, he willingly steps into the 'murky realm' between subjective experience and objective forces. Specifically, he opens up the subjective side of Objectivism by stressing the need for an 'unrelenting exposure' of the self. The sensitivity to otherness that results links the poetics of witness to the disjunctive temporality of Surrealism, as well as to the discourse of responsibility that Woods identifies as an important ethical continuity between Objectivism and Language writing. For Palmer, the voice of poetry is often engaged with a re-articulation that cannot be reduced to simple repetition. As I show, Bretonian Surrealism is one touchstone for this aspect of Palmer's poetics. Nowhere, perhaps, is the ethics of poetry more urgent than in the representation of war, which accounts partly for my concentration on Palmer's sequence 'Seven Poems Within a Matrix for War'. Also alive in this discussion of the poetic 'theatre' of war is Benjamin's image sphere, rocked as it is by the contemporary face of the informational image.

Like that of Palmer, the writing career of Susan Howe is somewhat *en avant* of the emergence of 'Language' as a cultural signifier in the late 1970s. It is in her concern for the 'dark side' of American history that she connects with the themes of the present work. If Palmer's writing bears witness to the more recent traumas of America's violent history, Howe's reaches back still further, to the ungovernable and silenced relics of the Puritan settlement. As with Palmer, her respect for the abject of this settlement leads her writing into a re-articulation that simultaneously opens horizons on to past and future. Her work is already familiar to scholarship in these terms but the suggestion that her project of recovery also has a stake in the Surreal-O-bjectivist nexus is, I think, a new one. Williams is a hinge figure in this respect. In simple terms, *In the American Grain* is a precursor text for Howe's *My Emily Dickinson*. In terms of *Nachträglichkeit*, however, her writing determines retrospectively Williams's reception of Surrealism. According to the way Howe understands Puritan attitudes to reality, there already existed an American poetics of negation to which Surrealism could be accommodated by a modernist writer so inclined. My discussion of Howe's work also departs from some recent scholarship in seeking to blur the boundary between her 'praxis of writing' and her 'inner life'. The shift is prompted by Howe's decision to add prefaces to new collections of earlier works. By no means generically orthodox, these texts invite the reader to the junctions between the national history of the United States and the life of Susan Howe.

In the final chapter, I turn my attention to the writing of Barrett Watten. As poet, editor, theorist and, more recently, tenured scholar, Watten has been pivotal in the life of Language writing. As well as doing much to foster the significance of Objectivism for contemporary American poetry, he has considered explicitly and in some detail the relationship between Surrealism and what he now calls the 'Language school'. I reflect on Watten's early account of Surrealism as a defence of the self and move on to consider his serial poem *Complete Thought* as a text in which the Surreal-O-bjectivist nexus becomes once again a possibility. The image sphere is active in this discussion, since it allows for a comparison of Surrealist poetics with Watten's commitment to the integrity of his 'materials'. This term in turn hinges the poem to George Oppen's collection *The Materials* (1962), wherein, I argue, the writer is equally exercised by the reciprocity of subjective and objective states. To read these two texts in relation to each other is not just a critical convenience but respects Watten's Constructivist method. As I have already noted, this method itself relies partially on the concept of *Nachträglichkeit*. Watten looks to Russian precursors much more positively than he does to Surrealist ones but it is nonetheless telling that a concept active in Surrealism has become integral to his method.

CHAPTER TWO

Surrealism: An Excommunicated Vessel?

Uncertain influence

When Charles Bernstein critiques expressiveness in his essay 'Stray Straws and Straw Men', Surrealism does feature, but only to illustrate the flawed 'Modernist assumption' that 'consciousness existed prior to – aside from – language and had to be put into it'.[1] Bernstein gives more attention to Surrealism in an interview with Tom Beckett, published in Bernstein's *Content's Dream*.[2] He is most positive when he acknowledges Surrealist innovation at the formal and technical level (p. 392):

> Surrealism is to be credited with opening up new possibilities for images and perhaps more crucially for the transition from image to image (unit to unit) within the total organization of the poem – opening up, that is, the domain within which we now work.

But this advance came about, in Bernstein's view, despite rather than because of 'the underlying psychologism and the reliance on symbolic, allegoric, or "deep" images' (p. 389). Indeed, Bernstein's desire to substitute the technical term 'unit' for the inherited term 'image' illustrates well Nicholls's contention that Surrealism was valuable to Language writing as a practice of writing rather than as a poetics of the inner life. In its parenthetic form, this substitution declares rather than rehearses the departure of one tradition from another.

A similar departure is announced during the course of Ron Silliman's essay 'The New Sentence'.[3] This text has been a touchstone for discussions of the poetics of Language writing, not least because it sets out quite categorically the formal distinctions that differentiate the *new* sentence from its superseded precursors. Referentiality is at stake in this formal revolution, since it is Silliman's belief that the historical failure of linguistics to consider the sentence is related to the general tendency under late capitalism to ignore the materiality of language and writing. Targeted by Silliman are all those forms of writing that assume 'integration above the level of the sentence' (p. 79). Such integration serves referentiality by offering a window on the world at the expense of the materiality of language. 'Hypotactic logic' is crucial to this process; hypotaxis organizes the sentence into 'completeness' through the governance of grammar and syntax and, by means of the 'syllogistic leap', promotes integration at the higher level (p. 79). Silliman pushes the analysis further by claiming that the control exercised at the level of the sentence participates in the restrictive organization of society as a whole. In ideological terms, we are told, 'the sentence, hypotactic and complete, was and still is an index of class in society' (p. 79). Silliman's opposition to such control consists in the effort to maintain the sentence as the focus of attention. Syllogism is to be kept primarily 'limited' to the domain of a few local sentences.[4] In place of hypotaxis, then, we have parataxis. This mode is not new in itself: Silliman cites (p. 79) as precursors the 'fragmented' sentences of Gertrude Stein's *Tender Buttons* and the 'minimal syllogistic shift' which characterizes the individual entries in Willliam Carlos Williams's *Kora in Hell*.

Surrealism forms part of the definition of the 'new sentence' but, as with Bernstein, it plays the part of negative exemplum. In the first version of Silliman's essay, published in *Talks: Hills* in 1980 and excerpted in *In the American Tree* (1986), Silliman states that the 'new sentence' 'has to do with prose poems, but only some prose poems'. Those excluded are, on the one hand, 'surrealist prose poems, whether of the European or American variety' and, on the other, 'the non-surrealist prose poems of the middle-American variety'.[5] Surrealists are disqualified specifically for the reason that their attention is not kept at the level of the sentence; rather, they 'manipulate meaning only at the higher or outer layers'.[6] At stake here is something akin to what Michael Davidson describes as the '*paysage moralise*' of the 'conventional prose poem', by which he has in mind the projection of 'a landscape upon which is grafted a series of psychological speculations'.[7] If, as Silliman's terms imply, Surrealism also aims to integrate writing at the level of psychology, it falls into the trap of expressivism, despite appearances to the contrary. To borrow Davidson's terms, 'disjunctions at the level of the sentence are expressive; they dramatize the emotional state of the author'.[8] Language and its syntactical organization are not viewed 'anew' as exterior materials, units of composition, but remain at the disposal of the subjective interior.

Silliman does not address automatism but his critique of the prose poem seems, on the face of it, to be just as applicable to texts generated by this technique. In 'The Automatic Message' of 1933, for example, Breton makes it clear that the method has always been oriented towards the 'higher' or 'outer' layers of meaning. Defining Surrealism against spiritualism, he states categorically that where the latter proposes 'the dissociation of the subject's psychological personality – surrealism proposes nothing less than the *unification* of that personality'.[9] Recent work on the poetics of Surrealism suggests, however, that automatism was compromised in its attempts at such unification. Peter Nicholls's analysis is instructive here and helps to explain how Surrealism became available to American poets as 'a practice of writing'. In his book *Modernisms: A Literary Guide*, Nicholls identifies the aspiration of Surrealism in terms that suggest the expressivist model about which Bernstein and Silliman are so suspicious. For the constitutive role of language appears as a blind-spot in the ambition of Breton and others to unify thought and expression. As Nicholls writes (p. 285), 'the Surrealist objective is always to be present at the moment of creation, when thought takes shape'. He goes on to suggest, however, that something stands between Surrealism and its poetic horizons. For its ambitions are 'haunted by the fear that writing will reveal itself as the mimesis of an unconscious which has *already* presented itself in figurative form'. Language itself is at the root of this problem. The unification to which Surrealism aspires has, in writing, to be achieved through 'a system of signs whose very mode of operation entails a certain *negation* and separation' (p. 285). Language, then, is not *successfully* overlooked by the Surrealists but remains to 'constitute' the conditions in which the subject encounters both thought and the external world.

Nicholls (p. 41) situates Surrealism in relation to a specific strand of modernism. This strand is characterized by its 'negative poetics' and links writers such as Stéphane Mallarmé, Paul Valéry, Giuseppe Ungaretti, Pierre Reverdy, Franz Kafka and Samuel Beckett. Although the mediation of language forecloses the Surrealist aspiration to unify thought and expression, it opens up an alternative path along which the subject's search for personal freedom is bound up with a critique of the world around him or her. In Nicholls's terms (p. 286):

> language's negation of the real, the absence which always echoes within it, is potentially a rejection of reality-as-it-is, that world which, codified by law and logic, exists by exiling what-is-not to the fantastic realms of art and the imaginary.

Framed in these oppositional terms, the critical dimension of Surrealist poetics looks much more promising from the point of view of ideology critique, particularly when the rationale for negation sits so well alongside post-structuralist accounts of signification. Also provocative is Nicholls's suggestion that the gap between language and the world may prompt the Surrealist 'not to a mourning of the real ... but to an incessant work of *interpretation* in which desire proves legible in its objects' (p. 288). In Nicholls's view, the activity of interpretation provides 'the very medium of the self's engagement with the world' (p. 288). For many Language writers, the lack of fit between language and the world is similarly animating, and meaningful. As Lyn Hejinian puts it in the published version of her talk 'The Rejection of Closure':

> the incapacity of language to match the world permits us to distin-
> guish our ideas and ourselves from the world and things in it from
> each other. The undifferentiated is one mass, the differentiated is
> multiple. The (unimaginable) complete text, the text that contains
> everything, would in fact be a closed text. It would be insufferable.[10]

The gap between language and the real also has consequences for
the 'murky realm between objective forces and subjective experience'
(Chapter 1). Given that linguistic signs are not identical to their referents,
Nicholls says (p. 288) that a 'residual opacity clings to the object, preventing its complete assimilation to discourse'. In respect of the suspicions
of Surrealist expressivism, it is important to note the possibility that the
object remains intractable by consciousness as well as by discourse. From
this perspective, there is scope for the suggestion that Surrealism shares
with Objectivism a *respect* for the objective world. To be sure, this attitude may well be in tension with the goal to unify the self but it is also,
at crucial points, part of the same aspiration. To recognize this shared
regard is to open a further nexus, in which Language writers and post-
structuralist thinkers also have a stake. In this book, I argue that one of
the ways Language writers continue and extend Objectivist poetics is to
consider the consequences for the subject of a practice in which the integrity of exterior materials is a high priority. So, Barrett Watten points to the
necessity for a 'reflexive' self (Chapter 7), while Michael Palmer commits
his writing to a demanding exposure of the self (Chapter 5). This idea of
exposure, and the risk that attends it, chimes with Jacques Lacan's account
of subjectivity. Malcolm Bowie's description of Lacanian subjectivity is
provocative here. As he puts it, the Lacanian subject is 'other-infested'
and 'possesses no other destiny than that of successive disappearance and
return, entity and non-entity, sense and nonsense, concentration and
dispersal, being there and being gone'.[11]

The nexus I am sketching here is not, however, a settled, harmonious
place. If post-structuralist constructions of subjectivity have influenced
the response of Language writers to the poetics of Objectivism, they
may also have opened, inadvertently, a back-channel to Surrealism. But
there is, nonetheless, a world of *ethical* difference between an attitude
in which the integrity of the object deserves respect and one in which
the separateness of the object is viewed with suspicion and dread.[12] Some
would argue that the Surrealist response to the objective world veers not
between respect and dread but between fascination and anxiety, both of
which privilege the subject's condition. This structure issues, of course,
from the paradigm of psychoanalysis. While this paradigm has not been
part of the legacy passed on from Objectivism to Language writing, it may
well have seeped into the nexus via Lacan. In which case, we should not
be surprised to find that the 'discourse of responsibility' identified and
heralded by Woods (see Chapter 1) does not always run smooth.

In his willingness to theorize Surrealist poetics as interventionist,
Nicholls sets his account in relation to Benjamin's perspective on the

movement. Where Benjamin's motivation is directly political, Nicholls's stance is more scholarly. Somewhere between the two, perhaps, is Fredric Jameson. As we have seen, Jameson tended to regard Language writing's complex relationship to reference as symptomatic rather than critical of the postmodern condition. His analysis of Surrealism in *Marxism and Form* provides a valuable context for this position.[13] If his scepticism of Language writing echoes Adorno's view of Surrealism, his regard for the modern-ist movement has more in common with Benjamin's optimism for it.[14] Like Nicholls, Jameson reads Surrealism as interventionist, distinguishing it in this respect from earlier, Romantic forms that functioned only as 'defense mechanisms' against 'that stupendous, total, and unprecedented transformation of the world into the henceforth barren and materialistic environment of middle-class capitalism' (pp. 94–95). Jameson also shares with Nicholls the view that the revolutionary challenge of Surrealism lies in its ability to mobilize desire, to re-open the communication between subject and object such that we might be 'reminded' of ourselves in ways which exceed and unsettle our conventional self-representations (p. 99). Such release is, once again, achieved through a rejection of reality-as-it-is. Celebrating the Surrealists' 'theory of narration', he notes their commit-ment to excavating the object-language of the unconscious (p. 97). Their tenacious pursuit of this end means that they exploit 'description' and 'character' in such a way that both things and people are allowed the 'second life' that they embrace in our fantasies but that is banished from the conventional narratives of the novel (p. 100).

One possible link between Jameson's celebration of Surrealist interven-tion and his less optimistic appraisal of Language writing is in the privilege he grants to the Surrealist object. He ends his discussion of Surrealism in *Marxism and Form* by comparing the movement's historical moment with that of contemporary America. Directing our attention towards 'the gasoline stations along American superhighways, the glossy photographs in the magazines, or the cellophane paradise of an American drugstore', he invites us to conclude (p. 105) that 'the objects of Surrealism are gone without trace':

> Henceforth, in what we call postindustrial capitalism, the prod-ucts with which we are furnished are utterly without depth: their plastic content is totally incapable as serving as a conductor of psychic energy, if we may express ourselves that way.

The implications of this position for the present discussion are worth noting. To offer a contrast in terms of materialism: Jameson's materialism would deny the possibility that postmodern writing can unite subject and object in a critical way, on the grounds that postmodern objects are not *objective* enough. 'Plastic' as they are, they have subjective manipulation 'built in'. Conversely, the materialism of Bernstein, Watten and others precludes Surrealist writing from critique on the grounds that it fails to register the substance of language and the materiality of writing.

Although Jameson's reading has much in common with Nicholls's account of Surrealist intervention, it is not as sensitive to the compromised character of Surrealist poetics. In Jameson's view, it is not so much the dialectic of conscious and unconscious towards which Surrealism strives but rather 'nothing less than the reconstruction of the primal continuity of the unconscious itself' (p. 98). He discusses the unconscious in terms of figuration but, unlike Nicholls, does not appear to view the relationship as a source of anxiety for the Surrealists. The materiality of Surrealist writing is addressed in a consideration of Breton's prose style. Jameson notes the hyperbolic state to which 'the rhetorical apparatus' is stretched in automatic writing but treats this form merely as a 'surface' feature of the technique. The ultimate goal is framed in terms of 'some deeper logic, some buried yet irresistible continuity of thought underground, to which the [rhetorical] devices themselves make fateful allusion, and on which they are carried relentlessly forward' (p. 98, n34). It is precisely this hierarchical, depth model to which Bernstein and Silliman object, since it overlooks the ways in which language constitutes reality. More engaging is the subsidiary point that Breton's overblown rhetoric also activates 'the twin claim on the reader's attention of both past and future as an interlocking syntactical system within the sequence of sentences' (p. 98, n34). On the one hand, Jameson seems much closer here to recognizing the constitutive power of language. On the other, his idea that past and future interlock in the sequence of sentences raises the opportunity to discuss automatic writing in terms of *Nachträglichkeit*. I want to take this opportunity in the paragraphs that follow.

Deferred action

In his book *Compulsive Beauty*, Hal Foster also assumes there is a conflicted poetics at the heart of Surrealism. Like Nicholls, he acknowledges the drive towards unification in Surrealism and recognizes the importance for this endeavour of prising the unconscious away from its definition in therapy.[15] In Foster's terms it could then be reconstituted and 'revalued as synthetic end rather than dissociative means' (p. 4). In this account, the 'problem' to be overcome is described precisely as one of 'authenticity', that is, 'the threat posed by calculation and correction to the pure presence of the automatist psyche' (p. 4). But, as Foster suggests, Surrealist authenticity is endangered not only by calculation and correction but also by the unconscious itself. The risk here is that automatism may not lead to liberation, 'not because it voided the control of the (super)ego (such was its express purpose) but because it decentered the subject too radically in relation to the unconscious' (pp. 4–5). The consequent confusion of 'decentering with liberation' resulted in an aporia, according to which the first term is both 'desired' and 'feared'. Foster sums up the tension as follows (p. 5):

For automatism revealed a compulsive mechanism that threatened a literal *désegregation* of the subject, and in doing so it pointed to a different unconscious from the one projected by Bretonian surrealism – an unconscious not unitary or liberatory at all but primally conflicted, instinctually repetitive.[16]

Nachträglichkeit presents one aspect of the desegregated subject. The concept was introduced by Freud in his investigations into trauma and was subsequently reworked by Lacan. A good account of the term is given in John Forrester's book *The Seductions of Psychoanalysis*.[17] Here we learn that Lacan's contribution was to build on Freud's own recognition that the lag between the cause and symptom of trauma is itself causal. Forrester notes that Freud describes this traumatic structure in letters to Wilhelm Fliess as involving, in some way, both a 'retranscription' and a 'failure of translation'. Trauma becomes, as it were, an attempt to retranscribe events that could not previously be fully translated. In this way, the past ceases to be a closed book and is rendered open to manipulation. This fluidity in turn becomes the basis for Lacan's own version of 'deferred action', as what Forrester describes as 'the articulation of two moments with a time of delay' (p. 206). This formulation makes it clear that what Lacan had in mind was not simply a revision of the past from the point of view of the present but a form of dual temporality in which the subject is, as it were, in two times at once.

Deferred action waits in the wings of Breton's First Manifesto, of 1924. The context is a comparison between dream and waking states, in which Breton treats 'normal' memory disparagingly as a privative operation:

> man, when he ceases to sleep, is above all the plaything of his memory, and in its normal state memory takes pleasure in weakly retracing for him the circumstances of the dream, in stripping it of any real importance.[18]

Breton here presents 'normal memory' as simple recollection. Its goal is to maintain the subject's 'impression of continuing something worthwhile'. In so doing the dream is shrunk to 'a mere parenthesis'. In its exercise of 'correction', memory pays no heed to 'transitions' within the dream. Instead it *re*-presents a 'series' of dreams, not the 'dream itself'.[19] Normality, he implies, involves not a synthetic resolution of dreaming and waking states but a subordination of one to the other. As the word 'parenthesis' suggests, Breton's thinking about memory here is hard to separate from his thinking about writing. Just as waking subordinates dreaming, so does hypotaxis overwhelm parataxis; the conjunction of 'series' triumphs over the disjunction of 'transitions'.

If recollection is 'normal memory', deferred action might be 'abnormal memory'. In this shift, hypotaxis itself transmutes into the 'articulation of two moments with a time of delay'. Sequent sentences (or even the sentence itself) do not simply recollect or represent a prior state of consciousness but reconfigure in their very movement the relationship between past, present and future. As Forrester comments in his discussion of Lacan (p. 363, n137), the 'temporal structure of deferred action is of a higher order than the reversible time of discourse in which meaning is created only with the last term of the phrase'.

In common with the 'new sentence', then, deferred action breaks free from the completeness to which hypotaxis tends. The fact that regular syntax persists in automatic writing allows the technique to generate a parody of realistic narrative. Automatism has a further stake in the 'politics of the referent' in this respect. Of those who joined in this debate, Steve McCaffery was one of the most vociferous critics of the commodification of language. For him, 'classical narrative' treats meaning like surplus value; it 'is frequently "achieved"' only 'to be reinvested in the extending chain of significations'.[20] Automatic writing, it might be argued, renders this transaction hyperbolic. Automatic texts often exhibit a bewildering alternation of narrative suspense and resolution. So rapid and intensely contrasted are the shifts that meaning is not allowed to accumulate into the complexity of plot or the fullness of character. In this way – like a film sped up – does automatism lay bare the device of classical narrative. From a different point of view, however, this 'shallow' reference can be understood in relation to what Nicholls describes as the 'incessant work of interpretation'. As a representation, automatic writing dramatizes this work; as an activity pursued both by the writer and the reader, it is this work itself. To bring *Nachträglichkeit* back into the frame, as a 'failure of translation', it participates in negation by unseating conventional representations of reality-as-it-is. But we need to remember that *Nachträglichkeit* might also lead to a retranscription. In Forrester's words (p. 205), 'articulation will come to depend upon a transferential function in which the past dissolves the present such that the future becomes once again an open question'. Incessantly open, at the tip of the pen.

A reading of automatic writing

To test this claim, I want to look at a section from *Les Champs Magnétiques*. This collection of automatic pieces, produced by Breton and Philippe Soupault in 1919, was subsequently identified by the former as 'indisputably the first surrealist (and in no sense dada) work, since it is the fruit of the first systematic use of automatic writing'.[21] In the First Manifesto Breton claims that the experiment came about as a result of his medico-psychiatric training in the First World War and he devotes some time to demonstrating how 'the forms of Surrealist language' relate to certain 'pathological states of mind'.[22] The point, however, is to show not that automatic writing is mad writing but that expressive forms usually interpreted as indicative of insanity can be deliberately produced in controlled conditions. Central to the automatic method is the concept of distraction, a state that is brought about by writing at speed.[23] The sections of *Les Champs Magnétiques* were written at different speeds, a factor that is constitutive of their final form. The section that I want to look at – 'En 80 Jours' ('In 80 Days') – was composed at slightly less than medium speed. At the time of its composition, the concept of 'deferred action' was not explicitly available but Breton's later comment that 'In 80 Days' relates to 'the memories of a man seeking escape from his memories' suggests that there might be some point to reading the section in terms of *Nachträglichkeit*.[24] Here goes, then:

> Un agent de police du VIe arrondissement rencontra un homme qui sortait d'un café et qui courait. Un carnet tomba de sa poche mais l'homme avait disparu. A la lumière d'un haut réverbre, il lut ces quelques lignes crites au crayon:
>
> *La rougeur des crépuscules ne peut effrayer que les mortels. J'ai préféré la cruauté.*
> *Les manufactures anatomiques et les habitations á bon marché détruiront les villes les plus hautes.*
> *A travers les vitres des hublots, j'ai vu toujours les mêmes visages: c'étaient des vagues échappées.*
> *La fièvre tourne doucement dans ma poitrine; on dirait ke bruit plus lointain des villes vers onze heures du soir.*
>
> L'homme courait á perdre haleine. Il ne s'arrêta que lorsqu'il aperçut une place. Héros des grandes expéditions, il oubliait toute prudence. Mais les vagissements d'un nouveau-né lui firent comprendre la gravité de l'heure. Il sonna á une petite porte et aussitôt la fenêtre qu'il regardait s'ouvrit. Il parla, attendant en vain une réponse. Il n'y avait plus personne sur la place. Il reconnut son ami et les souvenirs frappèrent ses oreilles. Comètes postiches, éruptions falsifiées, clefs des songes, charlatanismes obscurs. Il comprit la lueur des symboles et les monstrueuses évocations. Une sueur régulière et déprimante n'est pas plus atroce que cette vision aiguë des baudruches soi-disant créées.[25]

A policeman of the 6th arrondissement met a man who was coming out of a café and running. A notebook fell from his pocket but the man had disappeared. By the light of a high street-lamp, he read these few lines written in pencil:

> *The redness of twilight can scare only mortals. I have preferred cruelty.*
> *Anatomical manufactories and cheap dwellings destroy the highest towns.*
> *Through the glass of the portholes, I always saw the same faces: they were escaped waves.*
> *Fever is turning round gently in my breast: you might say it is like the more distant sound of towns about eleven o'clock at night.*

> The man ran away fast enough to lose breath. He stopped only
> when he noticed a square. Hero of many a great expedition, he
> forgot all caution. But the pulings of a new-born child made him
> realize the gravity of the hour. He rang the bell of a little door and
> immediately the window he was watching opened. He spoke, wait-
> ing in vain for a reply. There was no longer anybody in the square.
> He recognised his friend and memories hit his ear. Superfluous
> comets, falsified eruptions, keys to dreams, obscure charlatanisms.
> He understood the gleam of symbols and the monstrous evoca-
> tions. Even a regular and distressing sweat is not more atrocious
> than this acute vision of allegedly created gold-beater's skins.[26]

Given its title and the repeated reference to the 'character' of the
traveller, this section appears to fit the bill of *'paysage moralise'*. We could
certainly read the disjunct sentences written in the notebook as expressive representations of the fragmented emotional state of the automatic
writer. Such a reading would also explain why the allegorical potential
of natural phenomena is invoked only to be frustrated. Nonetheless, the
passage also manifests features of the 'local' integration required by the
'new sentence'. So:

> Le vide est sans doute moins étourdissant que ces danses acro-
> batiques. Des paroles passaient: c'était un vol triangulaire et furtif:
> il n'y avait donc plus rien á faire qu' á marcher sans but: les asiles
> d'aliénes sont peoples de ces fragments de rêves qui conduisent les
> homes devant un mur inexistent.[27]

> The void is no doubt less deafening than these acrobatic dances.
> There was an exchange of words: it was a triangular and furtive
> flight: so there was nothing left to do but proceed aimlessly: luna-
> tic asylums are populated by these dream fragments which lead
> men in front of a non-existent wall.[28]

The second sentence immediately offers itself as syntactically ordered but
irregularly so in its triple use of the colon. This repeated feature shifts the
'exchange of words' out of its narrative context and into a literal one: in
completing the meaning of the first half of the expression, the second half
is, in a sense, exchanged for it. But if we look at the first colonic combination, we notice that the second half does not complete the meaning of the
first half in any straightforward way. Instead of giving us the *content* of the
exchange, it appears to describe the *manner* of it. Nor are the terms of this
description prescribed by the narrative context but by metonymic association with the 'acrobatic dances' of the previous sentence. This seems to
me a good example of what Silliman describes as 'torquing', that is, 'the
projection of the principle of equivalence from the axis of selection into
that of combination'.[29]

In this acrobatic display, language appears to be departing its subject,
giving way to deferred action. We might read the unusual repetition of

the colon as 'compulsive' – a traumatic combination of punctuation with puncture. The colon literally articulates the two moments that it defines. But this articulation threatens a 'failure of translation', since the axis of combination, to which the logical development of hypotaxis clings, has been usurped by the potentially indefinite deferral of substitution. In an instance of the hyperbolic closure I mentioned earlier, the threat is apparently lifted with the adversative 'But' which opens the next paragraph:

> But the wind had blown the windows wide open and they fled into the clay night. They saw beyond the mists. A flame licking the clouds rose and sank back.[30]

With windows blown 'wide open' and vision reaching 'beyond the mists', revelation once again appears within the reach of the sentence. Nonetheless, my 'local' reading of this passage suggests that Silliman sets up a false distinction between Surrealism's 'systematic distortion of the maximum or highest order of meaning' and writing in which 'each sentence plays with the preceding and following sentence'.[31] Taken as 'deferred action', the juxtapositional mode of automatic writing entails such 'play' both within and between sentences.

But if the syntagmic chain has the potential for the indefinite deferral of substitution, what is to stop automatic writing from breaking down into a chaos of signifiers, an omen of the inert postmodern condition identified by Jameson, a precursor of the 'homogenized meaninglessness' recognized by Bruce Andrews as a possible risk for 'an experimentalism of diminished or obliterated reference'?[32] Silliman may have had just such a concern in mind when he allowed syllogism a limited purchase in the dispensation of the 'new sentence'. An example is also to be found in Breton's piece under discussion. A 'square' is a public space where the statues of great men might be erected. Our character is a man in contact with a square and, therefore, appears to qualify as a 'hero'. This thread continues in the third sentence in a phrase resonant with the solemnity of military annals ('the gravity of the hour'). But by now, the dominant motif is also under serious threat. If our 'hero' stands on the verge of yet another glorious campaign, how come his realizations are determined by the cries of a new-born child and not those from the battlefield? How are we to account for the fact that this sentence proposes the parallel contradictions of the man who is both father and fighter, and the sounds of new life swaddled in the tropes of violence and death?[33] Juxtaposing 'square' and 'expedition' raises another paradox: war is easier to justify when it takes place 'out there', in the colonies, than it is when the disputed territories are the very space which should embody social harmony and national pride.

Read in this way, the initial syllogism produces a challenge to reality-as-it-is, reminding us that the safe and civilized spaces of home are achieved and preserved through the execution of violent imperial projects in 'other' countries.[34] Deferred action also has a stake in this critique, for the abolition of the distinction between man-as-fighter and man-as-father is immediately followed by a bizarre recognition scene – bizarre because it seems to take place in the presence of only himself: the man recognizes his friend, but there is no one in the square and he has not received a reply to his ring on the bell. Perhaps, then, this is a moment of self-recognition. If so, it is not a moment of self-identity; the man is caught between the present of his recognition and the past of his infancy. What delays him, what keeps him waiting is none other than the sentence itself. The anaphoric cluster of 'comets ... eruptions ... dreams ... charlatanisms' does not bring the final clarity of recollection but perpetuates the paralysis of symbolic redundancy, falsification and mystification. Retranscription is possible but it is for the reader to see, perhaps, that aspirations to heroic status are only the 'ophthalmias of sterile youthful days', that the natural place for dreams of fame and glory is really the 'lunatic asylum', since, in their assimilation of ideological imperatives, they construct barriers and constraints that need not be there at all ('non-existent walls').

In this chapter, I have tried to open the way for a more positive discussion of Surrealism and Language writing than has hitherto prevailed. I have depended heavily on formal analysis and theoretical concepts. True to the idea of 'nexus', however, and to cultural poetics in general, I have no desire for this discussion to float free from history. The encounters, as well as the missed encounters, between Language writing and Surrealism are historically as well as formally and theoretically determined. If the 'new sentence' has a lineage, William Carlos Williams is an important figure in it. Silliman's reference to *Kora in Hell* points both to this disclosed continuity and to an undisclosed linkage. For the period in the 1920s when Williams was exploring improvisatory form was also the time of his greatest enthusiasm for Surrealism. Although his interest in the European movement has been long noted, accounts of it have tended to be overly coloured by his ultimate rejection of it. After all, the story usually goes that the Williams of the improvisations is superseded not by the Surrealist Williams but by the Objectivist Williams. In the two chapters that follow, we will become increasingly aware of what a Surrealist Williams and a Surreal-O-bjectivism might look like.

CHAPTER THREE

Under the Sign of Negation: William Carlos Williams and Surrealism

Which Williams?

When Ron Silliman cites *Kora in Hell* as a formal precursor to the 'new sentence' (see Chapter 2), he intervenes in the politics of canon formation, for the Williams of the improvisations is not the same writer as the Williams known and celebrated for his exemplary American voice. As Hank Lazer points out, to understand the 'particular traditions' of Language writing we need to acknowledge the ways in which its participants have engaged in 'a deliberate act of rewriting literary history'.[1] Despite the playful title of the essay in which he makes this claim – 'Language Writing; or Literary History and the Strange Case of the Two Dr. Williamses' – Lazer makes clear that this act has entailed a battle over the representation of Williams. This battle has not taken place on a level playing field; by the time that Ron Silliman and Charles Bernstein joined the fray in the 1980s, there already existed a hegemonic version of Williams as 'the poet of common objects, immediate description, and common life'.[2] By the 1980s, this characterization had come to sponsor both the appearance of his work in anthologies and a preferred aesthetic in poetry workshops across the nation.[3]

Against this academically sanctioned version of Williams, both Silliman and Bernstein stress the oppositional bite and drive of his work. For Silliman, the 'critical element of oppositionality' shared by Williams with Gertrude Stein, Louis Zukofsky, Charles Olson and Robert Creeley was 'the identification of method with content'.[4] From this perspective, the virtues championed in the hegemonic version of Williams were mere 'surface features'.[5] Similarly zealous, Bernstein presents Williams as exemplary amongst his peers for his 'activist position in respect of the place of poetry'.[6] Williams is an activist in two senses: firstly, because of his refusal to accept the subservience of writing to the coercive regimes of any academic discipline, be it philosophy, literature or science; secondly, because of his own project to make writing itself active. These two senses are clearly related. As long as it was in thrall to 'conventional education and rational scholarship', writing was simply being '*used*' to represent intellectual and emotional states, and was not 'allowed to enact them'.[7] For both Silliman and Bernstein, then, an important feature of Williams's oppositionality is his commitment to writing as practice, by which it might be understood both to *be* something in its own right and to *do* something.

In a similar way, perhaps, Language writing's project to rewrite literary history has done something to criticism. In his important book *Poet's Prose: The Crisis in American Verse*, the Williams that Stephen Fredman reads – and reads so sensitively – has much in common with the activist Williams recovered by Silliman and Bernstein.[8] Indeed, in the preface to the second edition he is keen to emphasize that his enquiry into the use of prose by American poets grew out of 'the context of the poetry scene in San Francisco in the seventies' (p. vii). The scene that he has in mind is the emerging network of talks, performances and small publications that helped to shape Language writing on the west coast.[9] In flexing the reach of his enquiry back to Ralph Waldo Emerson, Williams, Robert Creeley and John Ashbery, Fredman is himself rewriting literary history, from the perspective of a recent phase in which Language writing has made all the running in poetic innovation. His intervention is relevant both to a sounding of the poetics of the improvisations and to an understanding of the neglect to which Williams's Surrealist side has been subjected. In this respect, Fredman's narrative is founded on a scepticism over French forms that chimes with the suspicion of Silliman and Bernstein. So, in the preface to the first edition, he advances his coining of the term 'poet's prose' partly on the basis that 'the more common "prose poem"' has been debased through its association with 'the atmospheric sentiment of French Symbolism' (p. xiii). In his subsequent discussion of Ashbery's relationship to the French prose poem, Surrealism also comes under attack. Taking issue with Michael Benedikt's view that the prose poem is 'a virtual ink blotter for the unconscious', Fredman goes on to berate 'classic Surrealism' for its commitment to an image-based poetics which, although 'startling', nonetheless adheres generally to 'very static verse forms or classically constructed sentences' (pp. 131–32).

The Ashbery that Fredman reads is to be set apart from this counter-tradition that is not counter enough. In a move that we have already seen, Ashbery is aligned with French writers who are 'fringe figures' as far as Surrealism is concerned (p. 132). At the same time, Fredman seems to reproduce Benedikt's conflation of prose poem and automatic writing, citing Ashbery's own expression of 'boredom' with 'the automatic writing of orthodox surrealism' (p. 132). A small host of assumptions get away scot-free in Fredman's efforts to delineate an American tradition of 'poet's prose', one that actively engages grammar and syntax 'in order to investigate language at a much deeper level' (p. 132). Why should Benedikt be allowed to represent 'the poetry of Surrealism', just because he compiled an anthology of the same name?[10] Why, in a work so intent on specifying the characteristics of literary forms, do the distinctions between prose poetry and automatic writing go unexamined? In defence of Fredman, his is not a book about Surrealism, but it is surely fair to expect a degree of vigilance when the movement is invoked as antithetical to the tendency that he is seeking to establish.

To return to Williams and his place in this tendency, Fredman situates the improvisations of *Kora in Hell* in relation to an Emersonian stance, according to which the priority for the American writer is 'to represent experience and not tradition' (p. 7). The exploratory practice that results is active without being domineering:

> Proceeding, as any modern poet does, from an initial position
> of alienation, the American poet uses prose not to give evidence
> of genius and the ability to impose order but instead to create,
> through attentive receptivity, a space of permission through which
> the world is allowed to appear through language. (p. 8)[11]

Williams's special contribution to poet's prose is what Fredman describes as the 'generative sentence'. This active form is close to the 'enactment' that Bernstein celebrates in Williams's writing, and the terms in which it is elaborated resonate with those employed by Silliman in 'The New Sentence'. For Fredman, Emerson is a writer of 'wholeness' rather than of 'completeness'. The difference is described thus:

> The contrary notions of wholeness and completeness can be em-
> ployed to symbolize various meanings that the word 'sentence'
> has acquired during its history; throughout the rest of this study,
> *wholeness* will represent organic, implicit, or generative forms of
> the sentence (often employing parataxis), and *completeness* will
> represent normative, explicit, or preconceived forms of the sen-
> tence (often exhibiting hypotaxis). (p. 30)

Fredman goes on to distinguish between the hypotactic sentence as one that can be 'diagrammed hierarchically; it has a logical order' and the paratactic sentence, which 'works by a continual sidewise displacement' (p. 31). The alternative forms of the sentence also, in Fredman's view, suggest different models of interaction between subject and world. The former may function as a kind of 'measuring rod of thought and reality' while the latter may act as 'itself a way of thinking' (p. 32). Building on this second model, Fredman traces the etymology of the word 'sentence' back through the Latin *sententia* ('way of thinking, opinion') and *sentire* ('to feel, sense'), in order to argue for the sentence as 'a perceiving, generating entity' (p. 32).

The generative sentence opens more than one avenue for thinking about Language writing. In resisting 'normative ... preconceived forms of the sentence', it appears to offer the chance for a kind of reference that slips the grip of reification. Crucially, this alternative not only acknowledges the materiality of language but makes of it a virtue; like other objects, language is something that we encounter in the world and which helps us to make the world mean. Fredman's analysis is invaluable, I think, for anyone who wants to address Language writing in phenomenological terms. Given his account of Surrealism, however, we should not be surprised to find no positive comparison between the generative sentence and automatic writing or the Surrealist prose poem. As close as it comes to 'classically constructed' sentences, the regular syntax of Surrealist prose forms must be judged as normative rather than alternative, in Fredman's terms. The importance of the image in these forms further declares, it would seem, a commitment to 'measure' reality, however bizarre and 'startling' that reality is.

Improvisation and the unconscious

Poet's prose seems to lead into a cul-de-sac as far as a positive comparison between Surrealism and Williams's improvisations are concerned. But what of other perspectives? When *The Iowa Review* published a facsimile version of *Rome* – an unpublished manuscript that Williams began while on sabbatical in Europe in 1924 – it included an essay on improvisation by Gerald Bruns.[12] From one point of view, the signs are good for an alignment between improvisation and Surrealism. Just as automatism aspires to be present at the moment of creation, the 'teleology' of improvisation is, according to Bruns, 'entirely in the present' (p. 66). For Bruns, however, the temporality of improvisation is not related to a higher goal of unifying the personality. He is interested in this heterogeneous form as *discourse* above all else. For him, the 'defining categories' of improvisation derive from rhetoric rather than psychology: 'Improvisation is the performance of a composition in the moment of its composition' (p. 66). Subsequently, however, Bruns considers the relationship between this 'species of unforeseen discourse' and the unconscious (p. 66). Although 'the improvisator' may often appeal to the unconscious to sanction an utterance, he or she ought really to consider it an 'enemy':

> It is clear ... that what we call the unconscious is, quite as much as tradition or learning, a natural enemy of improvisational desire. The unconscious is full of artful subterfuge; it shapes our unplanned utterances with unforeseen forethoughts – or foreforms, if one permits such things, for the mind is a repository of hidden and ready formations, a dark library of grammars whose nature is to make possible the inspired and the rash: dreams, talk, solemn unbreakable vows. The unconscious is the great beforehand where everything is in rehearsal. It is made up of quotations waiting for words. (p. 67)

This scepticism maps directly onto the 'fear' haunting Surrealism's aspiration to be present at the moment of creation; if 'quotations' precede the words that express them, writing is indeed reduced to 'the mimesis of an unconscious that has *already* presented itself in figurative form'.

For a more positive outlook, and one which bears directly on the links between improvisation and automatic writing, we can turn to Tim Armstrong's notion of 'distracted writing'. In his cultural study *Modernism, Technology and the Body,* he refers automatic writing to a 'dialectic of attention and distraction' (p. 193). There is an unexpected link here with Bruns's concentration on improvisation as discourse, since Armstrong's analysis builds on Friedrick Kittler's book *Discourse Networks,* in which Kittler 'traces a recurrent fascination with language as pure product, examined through psychological experiments which typically treated the production of discourse as a motor activity' (p. 193). As itself an aspect of modernity, this fascination is a transatlantic one. In this respect, Armstrong focuses primarily on an original comparative reading of automatic writing and the verbal experiments of Gertrude Stein. In line with other comparisons of American poetics and Surrealism, he notes the difference between Stein's emphasis on 'exteriority and the mechanics of language' and André Breton's desire to ground automatism in 'the spontaneous values of the "true" self' (p. 202). Important, however, for my thesis is Armstrong's recognition that, as his thought develops, Breton struggles to fit the unconscious into the logic of unification. In fact, he goes so far as to suggest that the shift to prioritize writing over the integration of the self happens in Surrealism *alongside* its American counterparts:

> Sidestepping the issue of the nature of the unconscious, Breton privileges the technique and casts doubts on the idea of a secondary personality, in the end joining Stein in the pursuit of writing. (p. 203)

It is in relation to his approval of Stein's writing that Williams appears; it is her ability to keep her attention mobile 'across the process of writing' that he finds so beneficial (p. 203). Armstrong records that Williams himself 'borrowed' automatic techniques from Surrealism over a fairly lengthy period, between 1918 and 1932 (p. 203). Shared by these American and French writers is the belief that distraction is worth cultivating in writing. For the Surrealists, it was meant to allow for the emergence of a pre-reflective self that could be reconciled in the writing with its rational partner; for Williams, it allowed him to become absorbed in writing *per se,* rather than as a handmaid to all those rational disciplines that commanded his attention.

The hand of negation

In his 'cultural' approach, Armstrong does much to loosen the constraints of more 'literary' accounts of modernism, and his willingness to consider positively the links between Williams's improvisations and automatic writing is an incentive for my explorations of American poetry. The Williams I want to represent is the writer whose improvisations share the conflicted poetics of Surrealism, to the extent that the aspiration to unify the subject in expression vies with the recognition that language has its own plans for reality. That said, if Williams has this problem in common with Surrealism, he also comes to see the opportunity it presents to prise writing away from the alien discourses that are parasites on it. To liberate writing in this way is simultaneously to negate reality-as-it-is. At this point of opposition does 'my' Williams make contact with the Williams that Bernstein, Silliman and other Language writers think they read.

The oppositional mode of the improvisations is, not surprisingly, bound up with the circumstances of Williams's life when he wrote them. Although they are now regarded by some as the most innovative and valuable works of his career – the product of what Fredman (p. 14) has described as 'a remarkably fruitful decade of experimentation' – it should be remembered that they were written during a difficult phase. During the late 1910s and early 1920s in particular, Williams struggled to find both outlets for his writing and a literary peer group that would remain consistent in its aims and physically accessible. In this situation, he appears to have felt acutely the 'expense' of his commitment to writing. Not only could it literally and paradoxically 'separate' him from the 'contact' that was its goal but it also threatened simply to remove him from the conventions of family and profession, with no compensatory transcendence into a community of writers.[13] Williams's biographer, Paul Mariani, sums up the bleakness of his literary isolation in 1921:

> He felt stranded, like someone who had come to a picnic only to learn that it was being held somewhere else ... yesterday. The Chicago renaissance was dead, and the awakening he'd sensed in New York in 1915 had proved illusory, moribund. At thirty-eight Williams had had to come face to face with the bitter realization of what it had cost to stay at home, to try and grow prize flowers in that volcanic ash.[14]

The frustration of this phase sheds new light on the 'energetic disgust' that Marianne Moore found in Williams's first improvisation, *Kora in Hell*. Fredman (pp. 41–47) reads this disgust as the means by which Williams broke through the Puritan censor he had partly internalized, to make contact with his turbulent and unpredictable emotions. But more than emotions is at stake: Williams is also gesturing against the rigid compartmentalization of social and professional identity, the inhibitions of categorization that render the different facets of his life antagonistic to each other. At any rate, Moore's assessment is telling in the broader context of a poetics of negation, since for her, according to Fredman (p. 42), the relevant comparison is with 'a kind of intellectual hauteur which one usually associates with the French'.

The hand of negation is everywhere upon the improvisations but it would take another book to trace its imprint in full. Instead, I will content myself with establishing such a poetics as one thread through a volatile period in Williams's writing career. This leaves me free to read in parallel and in some detail two passages: one from Williams's improvisation of 1923, *The Great American Novel*, and one from *Soluble Fish*, published by André Breton in 1924. These works have been chosen for their contemporaneous assaults on the conventions of the novel form. In this respect, they are both works that identify 'method with content'. This is despite the fact that *Soluble Fish* could easily be read as an example of the kind of European prose poem that has nothing to offer the counter-poetic tradition of the United States, as a specimen of that deceitful expressivism the fragmented form of which is, in the end, only a new form of mimesis.

I will begin, however, by situating the improvisations in relation to Surrealism's goal of unification. The urge to unify inner life and expression appears in Williams's earliest published improvisation, *Kora in Hell*. (Quotations here and below are taken from the posthumous collection *Imaginations*.[15]) In the prologue (p. 16) we read:

> By the brokenness of his composition the poet makes himself master of a certain weapon which he could possess himself of in no other way. The speed of the emotions is sometimes such that thrashing about in a thin exaltation or despair many matters are touched but not held, more often broken by the contact.

This aspiration resurfaces in 'chapter' XI of *Spring and All* (1922, also reprinted in *Imaginations*). Discussing the state of 'imaginative suspense', Williams proposes that the aim of writing in this condition is 'to perfect the ability to record at the moment when the consciousness is enlarged by the sympathies and the unity of understanding which the imagination gives'. Important here is not '"fit" but a unification of experience' (p. 120). Notwithstanding the benefits of imaginative suspense and improvisation's disjunctive mode, the operation of the imagination is bound up from the beginning with a kind of negation. Also in the prologue to *Kora*, Williams apparently cautions that 'Rich as are the gifts of the imagination, bitterness of world's loss is not replaced thereby' (p. 18). The concern for the gap between imagination and the world is tied specifically to a discussion of poetry in *The Descent of Winter* (1928, likewise collected in *Imaginations*). In the delayed 'Introduction' to this hybrid text, Williams starts by remarking that the figures used in verse (be it his or anyone else's) are 'vague.... The truth of the object is somehow hazed over, dulled'. Significantly, the vagueness of the figure is likened to 'a soft second light of dreaming' (p. 247). Surrealism may well have been in Williams's mind at this point. If so, it is as a negative exemplum, its dependency on dream imagery to be unfavourably compared with the emergent Objectivist concern for 'the truth of the object'. As it stands, he sees no prospect of the dream being integrated with the reality of waking life, characterizing it as only a poor substitute for 'observation' (p. 247). This is not, however, the clinically detached and belated observation of the scientist or the naturalist. The examples offered are the sagas, which 'seem to have been made on the spot'. He goes on to link this positive model of poetry with 'vividness', the realization of which 'has its own internal fire that is "like" nothing'. Through this exposition, Williams believes he has disclosed the 'bastardy' of the simile (p. 147). Simile is the outcome of a union between situation and rhetorical order, which is now considered to be illegitimate. For Williams, the union between life and writing will have no embarrassing offspring to misrepresent and deflect attention away from the primary moment of that union.

But observation, however reformulated, is not the way out of the problem, since it remains enmeshed in a system of signs that separates it from its source. In this passage Williams attempts to bypass the difficulty in Rousseauistic fashion, by making language part of nature rather than culture. But in the prologue to *Kora in Hell* he had been more accepting of the gap between imagination and the world. Indeed, in the passage already cited he continues his discussion of 'loss' in terms that suggest both a critique of reality-as-it-is and the mobilization of desire:

> Rich as are the gifts of the imagination, bitterness of world's loss is not replaced thereby. On the contrary, it is intensified, resembling thus possession itself. But he who has no power of the imagination cannot even know the full of his injury. (p. 18)

An echo of this formulation is also to be found in 'chapter' XI of *Spring and All*. The discussion here lays down the theme that *The Descent of Winter* will subsequently take up. Writing, we read, 'is not a searching about in the daily experience for apt similes and pretty thoughts and images'. Conventional observation is challenged for its appropriation of 'things' in the interests 'of writing them down later' (pp. 120–21). The question of desire is raised most suggestively in the following paragraph (p. 121):

> A world detached from the necessity of recording it, sufficient to itself, removed from him (as it most certainly is) with which he has bitter and delicious relations and from which he is independent – moving at will from one thing to another – as he pleases, unbound – complete.

Despite its dynamism, its propulsive enthusiasm, this is a tortuous bit of thinking. The phrase, 'bitter and delicious relations' suggests the reciprocity of self and world through desire. But at the beginning and the end of the paragraph, Williams is tempted to view this reciprocity as something optional rather than functional, a relationship to be indulged at times in a writerly way but always surmountable by the poet's will. The emphatic parenthesis, together with the word 'unbound', suggests, however, how hard Williams is straining to maintain simultaneously both the integrity of self and world and their interconnectedness. At the same time, 'A world detached from the necessity of recording it' would also be a world free from the fatal touch of language.

The Great American Novel

Begun in the autumn of 1921, *The Great American Novel* issued out of what Mariani has described as 'the nexus of near-despair' in which Williams found himself at that time.[16] In this biographical respect, at least, it is perhaps not surprising that the urge to unify life and writing often gives way in this text to an insistent and intense exasperation. Part of Williams's frustration is with dominant literary forms; the text is haunted from the first sentence by the conventional novel's commitment to 'progress'. Is it only this development, this advance that will qualify the novel as 'great'? Is it possible to write a novel that does not progress? In which case, the practice might be considered as genuinely disinterested, detached from dominant discourses that would drive the culture forward in directions that have nothing to do with writing. To explore these questions, I will read a passage that accounts for more or less the second half of the first chapter of *The Great American Novel* (with quotations below taken from *Imaginations*). In accordance with this extract's concentration on words, I shall follow Stephen Fredman's example by carrying out a 'disjointed, microscopic reading', and shall attempt to keep faith with his laudable commitment to 'a heuristic rather than explanatory voice'.[17] Unlike Fredman, I shall take the liberty of passing over parts of the chapter.

> One must begin with words if one is to write. But what then of smell? What then of the hair on the trees or the golden brown cherries under the black cliffs. What of the weakness of smiles that leaves dimples as much to say: forgive me – I am slipping, slipping, slipping into nothing at all. Now I am not what I was when the word was forming to say what I am. (p. 158)

At stake is the gap between words and the world, a gap both in kind and time. But what to make of 'slipping, slipping, slipping'? The dash makes the sense ambiguous: slippage belongs both to the described scene, as the reason for the appeal for forgiveness, and the self-reflexive attitude of the narrator. But then in what sense is the narrator slipping into nothing at all? By falling for the temptation to interpret, the temptation to transform a physical phenomenon ('dimples') into an expression ('as much to say'). By such gestures do writers both lose the world and rob it.

> Progress is to get. (p. 159)

The meditation subsequently links progress with acquisition, suggesting perhaps the promise of fulfilment that comes with referentiality:

> But how can words get. Let them get drunk. Bah. Words are words.
> (p. 159)

This assumption is immediately challenged. The only acceptable answer is to shift from the possessive to the predicative sense of the verb. The predicate deployed has the advantage of negating the power of the next period to represent, and to progress syntactically. In Fredman's terms, the writing is developing organically, allowing itself to generate meaning out of grammatical possibilities rather than the will to interpret.

> Fog of words. The car runs through it. The words take up the smell of the car. Petrol. Face powder, arm pits, food-grease in the hair, foul breath, clean musk. (p. 159)

We are into a paratactic formation here that befits the scene of the moving car. The scene of the moving car befits the paratactic formation. Priority has been at issue from the start of this great American novel. The 'real' car might be moving through a 'real' fog but it is a 'Fog of words'. The true novelty of this text is that it is prepared to accept the atmospheric conditions in which language itself rematerializes in a way along which the world might pass but not with the transparent ease readers have come to expect. Then, 'through' is a preposition both of place and means. Consequently, the words do not acquire a scene that is already out there, in the world, but 'take up' its sensory details and move them along.

The movement has to be paratactic, since Williams is working at this stage below the level of the sentence. Freed from the obligation to represent a scene, parataxis draws the sensory phenomena into a new arrangement in which the anima of the automobile is juxtaposed with the human 'Face', the cosmetic appeal of which is immediately undermined by its collocation with 'arm pits'.

> Words. Words cannot progress. (p. 159)

But in its status as a list, defined along the axis of substitution, this new arrangement cannot go anywhere without, it seems, hypotaxis. This despite the fact that the apparently innocent and undiscriminating list offers us at least one example of a surreal syllogism that works at a very local level: 'Petrol. Face powder' (p. 159).[18] Out of this clash between technology and the human, the third word is the term that results. 'Powder' now hovers at the threshold of animate and inanimate: cosmetic complement to the individuated human form, on the one hand; by-product of technology, on the other.[19]

> Yes, one can break them. One can make words. (p. 160)

But Williams opts neither to extend this local syllogistic movement nor to return to hypotaxis. Progress at this stage means more disjunction, a fracturing of the words themselves. But in the spirit of constructive negation, a loss of sense brings with it a gain in sound; 'make' can once again take the place of 'break' in even a politely impersonal sentence. In this sound-scape, syntax re-emerges but not hypotaxis. Patterned by sound, the two verbs no longer require a particle of connection to explain or justify an alignment that is paradoxical only in semantic terms.

At this point in the meditation, the subject seems to have found progress. Progress not in the literal sense of a step forward, however, but in terms of a poetics. This is not quite the poetics of negation as we have come to expect it, since out of the destruction of the semantic property of words Williams considers the possibility that he can now unify self and expression; divorced from their public context as a means to communicate, words become the literal 'pushing out' of their individual creator. The problem now, however, is that he has severely curtailed the power of words to mean through differentiation. To take an earlier example, the similarity in sound of 'make' and 'break' achieves most meaning against the dissimilarity in sense between the two words. In this situation, Williams cannot get beyond 'One big word', be it 'splurging', 'blurb' or 'bah' (p. 160).

The drive for a great American novel seems to have reached a cul-de-sac. To 'take' words as they are given to him will make his text no different from the average American novel; he might just as well 'catch up a dozen good smelly names and find some reason for murder, it will do' (p. 160). On the other hand, to 'make' words is to reduce all expression to a personal gesture without content; Williams is back to 'bah'. The subsequent paragraph explores a new way out of the dead-end of words in terms of genre. Here the fantastic and metamorphic realms of the fairy tale are the model. Creation out of destruction is now back on track, as is the power of words to differentiate between both the things of the world and each other. Williams begins the paragraph by visualizing the words that make up a novel not as a progression towards something new but as a physical mass which is itself a metaphor for the murder that words do to things:

> There cannot be a novel. There can only be pyramids, pyramids of words, tombs. Their warm breasts heave up and down calling for a head to progress toward them, to fly onward, upon a word that was a pumpkin, now a fairy chariot, and all the time the thing was rolling backward to the time when one believed. (p. 160)

This visualization suddenly propels the writing from death into a kind of life. Through resemblance, the shape of the pyramids suggests the breasts of a woman, a shift in scene across the 'pyriod' that is aided by the assonance of both 'words' and 'tombs' with 'warm'. The metamorphic impulse – which owes as much to Ovid as it does to Hans Christian Andersen – is by now building up a 'head' of steam that Williams seems reluctant to relinquish. The second half of the paragraph apparently recapitulates the earlier stages of verbal fragmentation. This time, however, it is not so much 'union' that is achieved as 'union-with-a-difference':

> Hans Anderson [*sic*] didn't believe. He had to pretend to believe. It is a conspiracy against childhood. It runs backward. Words are the reverse motion. Words are the flesh of yesterday. Words roll, spin, flare up, rumble, trickle, foam – Slowly they lose momentum. Slowly they cease to stir. At last they break up into their letters – Out of them jumps the worm that was – His hairy feet tremble upon them. (p. 160)

What emerges out of the rubble of letters is a warm and wordy 'worm'. A generic hybrid that is part real, part fairy tale; part human, part God; part monster, part poet. Exactly the kind of creature, in fact, that naturalistic writing would want to 'exterminate', along with that other agent of hybridity, the mosquito.

The remainder of Chapter 1 of *The Great American Novel* reads like a serious attempt at a conventional novel. It abounds in observational detail while also presenting a narrative that restores a referential scene to the earlier 'fog'. The fog is now encountered not in words but 'On the highway' and materializes not in the passage of the writing but 'all the way home' (p. 161). That said, these five paragraphs have not convincingly blocked themselves off from the fantastic mode that precedes. The 'Mosquito Extermination Commission' is eccentric in itself, coming as it does immediately after the fantastic worm and beginning as it does *in medias res* (or even later than that). But at least readers have the peg of some proper nouns upon which to hang their expectations. More unsettling is the appearance of another voice in the narrative:

> They walked around the side of the old-fashioned wooden building – constructed in the style of the fine residences of sixty years ago and coming to the car he said: Go around that side as I will have to get in here by the wheel. (p. 160)

For a start, the speech of this 'character' is deprived of the quotation marks that would make it an example of straightforward novelistic mimesis, clearly distinguished from the voice of the narrator. At the same time, the utterance itself is oddly without tone, strangely mechanical. Mechanical, indeed, to the point of absurdity. Is the passenger so unfamiliar with the topography of the automobile that he does not know that the driver needs to sit behind the wheel? Or so lacking in common sense that he does not see the benefit of getting into it on the side where he is to sit? Or perhaps this is a mode of address to fit the man addressed. We learn subsequently that the passenger is 'a mechanic in a certain sense', one who would value the instrumentality of a handkerchief over its ornamental status (p. 161). When the driver talks for the first time, then, a transformation begins to take place, in which the naturalistic content of the narrative begins to infest the realism of the representation.

> The windshield was opaque with the water in minute droplets on it – through which the moon shone with its inadequate light. That is, our eyes being used to the sun the moon's light is inadequate to see by. But certain bats and owls find it even too strong, preferring the starlight. The stars also were out. (pp. 160–61)

The shift is even more marked two sentences later, when an unproblematic description is immediately followed by an overextended scientific explanation of why the moon's light is 'inadequate'. Explanation shifts back into description via the reference to 'starlight' but, coming after such naturalistic hyperbole, the final sentence is again absurdly mechanical and toneless in its simplicity.

But generic infestation cuts both ways. The more the rationalistic explanation gets its teeth into the question of luminary preferences, the more it raises the spectre of the vampire. Held under curfew in the explanation itself, the monster breaks loose in the next paragraph, making its ghostly presence felt in three simple words: 'which looked *a good deal* like a handkerchief' (p. 161, my emphasis). Only a character in a fantastic novel would be concerned to make sure that the undulant shape in the moonlight was a handkerchief and not a 'bat'. In this moment of generic hybridity, Williams has picked on the definitive feature of the literary fantastic, at least as defined by Tzvetan Todorov, as 'that hesitation by a person who knows only the laws of nature, confronting an apparently supernatural event'.[20] But the mechanic does not belong in the literary fantastic; he does not hesitate and, indeed, 'doesn't care' (p. 161).

This mini-plot is looking less and less like a successful attempt at a conventional novel and this suspicion is confirmed by its equivocal denouement. The driver's arrival home brings with it the suggestion of a more romantic scenario:

> And so it went all the way home, sometimes clearer, sometimes so thick he had to stop, nearly – ending in his own bed-room with his wife's head on the pillow in the perfectly clear electric light. The light shone brightest on the corner of her right eye, which was nearest it, also on the prominences of her face.
>
> Her right arm was under her head. She had been reading. The magazine Vanity Fair, which he had bought thinking of her, lay open on the coverlet. He looked at her and she at him. He smiled and she, from long practice, began to read to him, progressing rapidly until she said: You can't fool me. (p. 161)

The magazine appears to signal their wordless entry into a familiar romantic game: 'He looked at her and she at him'. But the game itself is not wordless and leads ultimately out of the soft focus of the bedroom scene and back to the conclusion that 'there cannot be a novel'. The writing runs on to the end of the chapter with this short paragraph:

> He became very angry but understood at once that she had penetrated his mystery, that she saw he was stealing in order to write words. She smiled again knowingly. He became furious. (p. 161)

To write, then, is to risk both appropriating unfairly (and 'vainly') the substance of one's life with others and prostituting that life as hypocritical and commercial pap. But bitterness of the world's loss is a force in itself; 'fury' drives the great American novel on to Chapter 2.

Mariani describes *The Great American Novel* as an 'antinovel really', the adverb suggesting, perhaps, a certain reluctance to commit to the description.[21] Perhaps Breton's classification of 'false novel' would be even better. In the First Manifesto, he devotes a whole section to instructing the reader on how 'To write false novels'. Here Breton makes it clear that automatic writing has a practical application as a critique of the commercial novel.[22] In the 'false novel', writing itself takes the place of the usual characters, and the conventional novelistic techniques of 'observation, reflection and ... generalization' are displaced by the automatic message itself.[23] These techniques have indeed proved of no help to Williams. At least, not according to the standard model. On the one hand, naturalistic observation could not be divorced from fantastic speculation; on the other, it threatened to become so over-extended (how much detail is enough?) as to disrupt the plausibility of the depicted scene. In a similar vein, generalization cut a swathe through the uniqueness of the narrative, leaving the reader uncertain whose 'eyes' 'ours' were. Reflection is discounted from the start. Belated, signed and sealed, it precludes the spontaneity and the sinuousness of the meditation. Hovering in some timeless, some immaterial zone, reflection is beyond the temporality of the subject, able neither to dash forward in haste nor 'run through' the fog of unknowing.

Soluble Fish

To compare, I shall offer a brief interpretation of section 26 of *Soluble Fish* by André Breton (with quotations taken from the collection *Manifestoes of Surrealism*).[24] Published in 1924, this text came at a time ripe for intervention in the institution of French letters. Armand Hoog sums up the literary scene as follows:

> A novel by the lamentable Thierry Sandre had just received the Goncourt prize. The French academy was bestowing its literary award on Abel Bonnard's affected descriptions. An amusing reporter, who for a long time imagined himself a novelist, Paul Morand, had been granted the Priz de la Renaissance. Anatole France, and Barrès, and Loti had just died at the height of their fame; three enemies of surrealism, really three number one enemies, since they were of equal importance.[25]

Amidst these shining lights of the status quo, the Surrealist novel radiated an explosive brilliance: 'In French literary history, no imagery in fiction has shown such demiurgical enthusiasm, such joyous and shattering will to change the conditions of existence.'[26]

To navigate my way through a portion of this chimerical territory, I shall again employ Fredman's method of the 'disjointed, microscopic reading'. The heuristic impulse is in evidence once more, but this time the reading finds it increasingly difficult to keep apart method and (my)self.

> The woman with breasts of ermine was standing at the entrance of the passage Jouffroy in the light of songs. She readily consented to follow me. (p. 89)

The definite article declares that the narrative is once again beginning *in medias res*. I feel I ought to know this woman already. Unsettled, perhaps, by her 'breasts of ermine', I am reassured by the reference to an actual place, just as I was more or less content with the plausibility of the Extermination Commission.[27] Tropically speaking, I am also at home with the stages of an amorous encounter: the sight of the woman in an in-between zone; the request; the consent (perhaps offered with more than the customary readiness but, then again, he seems to have met her before). The writing runs on:

> I flung the chauffeur the address of Rendezvous, Rendezvous in person, who was an early acquaintance. Neither young nor old, Rendezvous ran a little broken-glass shop near the porte de Neuilly.
> 'Who are you?'
> 'One of the stabbing pains of the mortal lyre that vibrates at the edge of capitals. Forgive me the pain that I shall cause you.'
> She also told me that she had *broken* her hand on a mirror on which the usual inscriptions were gilded and silvered and blued. I took this hand in mine; raising it to my lips I suddenly noticed that it was transparent and that through it one could see the great garden where the most experienced divine creatures go to live.
> The spell ended when we stepped out of the car.... (p. 89)

If my narrative expectations are stirring, they are also frustrated here by the transformation of a structural element of the plot into one of its characters. Breton jauntily announces such 'false' characterization in the First Manifesto:

> Here are some characters rather different in appearance; their names in your handwriting are a question of capital letters, and they will conduct themselves with the same ease with respect to active verbs as does the impersonal pronoun 'it' with regard to words such as 'is raining,' 'is,' 'must,' etc.[28]

'Rendezvous' returns the narrative to the grammar, as it were, of its own genre, and in this respect reminds me of Williams's tale, where the detail of the naturalistic mode takes over and makes a little absurd the speech of the driver. At stake in Breton's skewing of genre is a specific rendezvous between bourgeois readers and their expectations, which are subsequently parodied in the absurd details of Rendezvous's age (which adds nothing to his personal character), his profession (which can hardly be lucrative) and the site of his business.

'Who are you?'

Returning us (we?) to the allure and enticement of the amorous liaison, the 'lead' character asks the question on all of my lips. I am part of a community of readers. Of course, I always was but now, in Williams's terms, I 'know the fullness of my injury', if not the boundaries of my identity; who am I anyway? 'One of the stabbing pains of the mortal lyre that vibrates at the edge of capitals. Forgive me the pain that I shall cause you.' One who is now prepared to acknowledge the departure from bourgeois expectations of the woman's reply; to accept the pain of the knowledge that the metropolis, the hub of culture and profit, can push to the margins but never expel the mortality of all persons. In fact, this woman's identity is only fulfilling the potential of the puncture that already awaits me in the over-determined image of the 'little broken-glass shop'. The residual 'small' businesses that hang on in the capital are reminders of the history that is 'the other' of consumerism's timeless 'now', the *broken* glass on sale there a shocking *aide memoire* that commodities, too, are subject to time and its contingencies. But what an appropriate product to make me see these things! How delicious the pain that transforms and 'brokers' this locale into the figure of desire its…! A figure formed brokenly for both the eye and the ear, that hums in the words of its own realization. That's who we are!

> She also told me that she had *broken* her hand on a mirror on
> which the usual inscriptions were gilded and silvered and blued.

But we are so in breach of genre now that we have no norm against which to fulfil the apparent expectation of the narrator that we will understand *exactly* what is meant by 'the usual inscriptions'. This mirror is both the privileged object of some fantastic revelation – predictably deferred across a full stop and a semi-colon – and just another piece of commercial junk that ages and changes state rapidly towards the end of the sentence, despite the sameness of the grammatical connective that repeats to bind the adjectives together. But, of course, to read these inscriptions is not to make sense of what is definitively 'out there' anyway but to trace open-endedly (how long have I got?) one's desire in the lineaments of a world partly and partly not given by genre. Any other offers?

> I took this hand in mine; raising it to my lips I suddenly noticed
> that it was transparent and that through it one could see the great
> garden where the most experienced divine creatures go to live.

As romantic lead, I once again attempt to take hold of the generic reins. But the figure of desire disdains to objectify itself as the usual reader might expect (so I set myself off at last!), refiguring as a further horizon of transcendent allure.

> The spell ended when we stepped out of the car.

Not so (I'll be led by this yarn no longer), since I will never again be able to distinguish this iconic object of modernity from the elusive form with which and whom I shared this brief journey. Both of whom have got me to where and who I am today. As Breton writes in a subsequent section (32): 'Nothing, certainly, is simpler than saying to a woman, to a taxi: "Take care of me"' (p. 106).

A Novellete

What I hope to have shown above all in this comparison is that, contrary to the views of Davidson, Silliman and others (see Chapter 2), it is not necessary to read Surrealist texts as expressive only. The 'false' novel's dramatization of structural elements hijacked from its 'true' counterparts surely merits praise for its 'identification of method with content'. Support for this view comes from a neglected area of criticism. 'Straight' structuralism is rarely called upon these days to elucidate texts, but in the case of Surrealism a structuralist analysis is worth considering as an antidote to 'the expressivist fallacy'. Michael Riffaterre discusses *Soluble Fish* in his *Semiotics of Poetry*. Under the heading 'Nonsense: intertextual scrambling', he suggests that the cumulative absurdity of this text makes it 'impossible to read it referentially'.[29] What is at stake here for Riffaterre is not the disturbed psychological state of the narrator or the writer but a technique whereby the text lays bare its own devices:

> What makes even the absurd thus acceptable is the fact that the text is a series of events unfolding out of a given whose truth is tolerable for the simple reason that it is grammatical.[30]

A little later, he draws a structuralist lesson from automatic writing:

> the poem's significance lies in its very semantic emptiness, in the lesson surrealists meant to teach by their automatic writing – that beneath the words there is nothing but more words.[31]

To suggest that this lesson was an intended one is to mute the Surrealist aspiration for the unification of thought and expression. On the other hand, there are enough examples of 'intertextual scrambling' to support the claim that automatic writing is also *about* writing.

Although he probably did not know it, Riffaterre's understanding of Surrealism comes uncannily close to that of Williams. Published in 1932, *A Novelette* presented the occasion for Williams's most enthusiastic response to Surrealism. His expression comes closest to Riffaterre's in the following brief paragraph (again, quoted from *Imaginations*): 'Surrealism does not lie. It is the single truth. It is an epidemic. It is. It is just words' (p. 281).

The context for Williams's discussion of Surrealism is a hybrid one, mixing his anxiety for the state of modern writing with his experience of the 1929 flu epidemic. In keeping with a text generated in part by the dynamic but difficult reciprocity between the personae of doctor and writer, Williams introduces Surrealism as a kind of prescription, beginning his discussion, 'Take the surrealists, take Soupault's *Les Dernières Nuits de Paris*, take –' (p. 280).[32] The curative effect of this prescription is nothing less than the renewal of language, by which Williams has in mind the end of its servitude to alien discourses and its return to writing:

> Language is in its January. How shall I say it? The surrealists are French. It appears to them to knock off every accretion from the

> stones of composition. To them it is a way to realize the classical
> excellences of language, so that it becomes writing again, and not
> an adjunct to science, philosophy and religion. (p. 280)

French medicine should, however, be taken with care in the United States; alongside comments about the general state of language, Williams makes it clear that the specific insights of Surrealism are the products of French experience. The particular discovery of the Surrealists, according to Williams, is the recognition that language is 'in constant revolution' (p. 281). While the substance of the claim appears universal, its wording suggests that France's dense history of violent political turmoil has paved the way for the radical analyses of Soupault and others. In emphasizing these local conditions of Surrealist writing, Williams reasserts the concept of 'contact' first elaborated with Robert McAlmon during the early 1920s. The acknowledgement of French history that tempers Williams's drive towards generalization is a good example of 'the conviction that art which attains is indigenous of experience and relations'.[33] In seeking to wrench writing away from its subservience to 'science, philosophy and religion', Williams is nonetheless in sympathy with the Surrealist urge to undermine the institutionalized discourses of 'law and logic'. Crucial to this project, it seems, is a poetics of negation, since the Surrealists liberate language by making words 'into sentences that will have a fantastic reality which is false' (p. 280). At risk from this shake-up is the unholy alliance of science and philosophy with commodity culture, since by the construction of a 'false reality', the Surrealists make manifest 'the falseness of the piecemeal (when language is made subservient to the sale of old clothes and ideas and the formulas for the synthetic manufacture of rubber)' (pp. 280–81).

If *A Novelette* is surreal at this point, it is, in its own use of words, to make a 'fantastic reality which is false'. The 'classical excellences of language' Williams has in mind are precisely those properties which discourses founded on the 'classics' have sought to ignore and exclude. Williams lays his words alongside those of the Surrealists in a wilful attempt to re-inscribe this excluded material. Hence, the efforts of the 'idea venders' [*sic*] to transcend language are described in terms that remain unusually mired in the material world. Of the four terms used, one transforms a noun into a verb ('slimed') while another ('Merded') has become grammatically 'entangled' between the first and second languages of translation. The pun which results from this Franco-American hybrid thus 'soundly kills' the very abstract concept which it calls to mind (p. 281).[34]

In fact, the governing motif of *A Novelette*, the epidemic, figures the conflict between medicine and writing precisely in the paradoxical terms of a negative poetics.[35] On the one hand, the demands of the sick seem simply to stand in the way of Dr Williams's literary interests. At times the demands on his attention seem so acute that those with lesser ailments must simply be ignored:

> You think I take no interest in you? It is not so. I avoid your eye merely to avoid interruption. Gladly, were I able, would I serve you and listen to you talk of your sore toe. (p. 280)

On the other hand, the urgency and intensity of the epidemic negates that 'service' which is a kind of slavery. The sore toe would be a minor cross to bear in any circumstances, one that the doctor might treat only out of professional obligation. The epidemic has similar results when it comes to thought:

> It has the same effect – the epidemic – as clear thought. It is like the modern advent of an old category supplanting a stalemate of information. A world of irrelevancies in the doing of one thing. But the intense haste is raised, wholly unforeseen, to a higher power: the birth of a female baby (colored) under a mustard-colored ceiling, by a cracked wall, to a turkey wishbone, in the shivering cold. (p. 279)

In this passage, which immediately precedes the treatment of Surrealism, the haste of attending to a problematic birth might be read as analogous to the haste of automatic writing. Armstrong's concept of 'distraction' is very apt here. It is precisely the subjective haste with which Williams is working that allows him to break free from the logic of realist representations. So, the designation of an event in the world then slides into a paratactic formation of subordinate clauses. Distraction here supports an ambiguous composition: in what sense is the birth of a female baby 'to a turkey wishbone'? At the same time, the emphasis in these clauses on sensory experience illustrates nicely Fredman's view of the generative sentence as a 'perceiving entity'. Armstrong's cultural perspective has more to offer, perhaps. It clearly has more to offer my argument, since it readily sets the improvisations alongside automatic writing. More importantly, it represents a productive tension between modernism and modernity that Williams both lived and wrote.

'Superrealism'?

To compare a piece of improvisation with some automatic writing is revealing but it does not exploit to the full the reach of 'nexus' as a critical concept. It is possible to situate Williams's strong enthusiasm for Surrealism at the end of the 1920s and the beginning of the 1930s in relation to broader currents within American literary modernism. One of the issues at stake at this point in time was the validity of Imagism as an aesthetic response to the material crisis of the Depression. Useful here is Marjorie Perloff's work on what she calls 'The "New American Poetry," 1930–32'.[36] Perloff has focused on this phase in order to tease out an 'aesthetic that has been insufficiently distinguished from its modernist past and its postmodernist future'.[37] She characterizes this aesthetic in terms that invoke a comparison with the Surrealist critique of reality-as-it-is:

> The shift that takes place at the turn of the decade is one from the modernist preoccupation with *form* – in the sense of imagistic or symbolic structure, dominated by a lyric 'I' – to the questioning of *representation* itself. Discourse now becomes increasingly referential, but reference does not go hand in hand with the expected mimesis. Rather, the boundaries between the 'real' and the 'fantastic' become oddly blurred.[38]

As Perloff is herself aware, the blurring of the distinction between the real and the fantastic clearly resonates with notions of the surreal. Indeed, she reads Erskine Caldwell's prose poem 'Hours before Eternity' very much in terms of an 'equivocation between surrealism and naturalism'.[39] But Perloff also takes pains to point out that we should not conflate European Surrealism with American Superrealism, since the latter is less 'programmatic' and less 'Freudian', on the one hand, and very much grounded in 'Depression America', on the other.[40] My reading of the problematic birth 'to a turkey wishbone' suggests that *A Novelette* qualifies as an example of 'equivocation between surrealism and naturalism'. The reference to disease and poverty invokes those members of the population who were most at risk during the Depression but the semantic ambiguity that attends the representation does indeed undercut the 'expected mimesis'.

My reading of the improvisations nonetheless provokes two qualifications to Perloff's account of this 'threshold' aesthetic. On the one hand, the generic indeterminacy of *The Great American Novel* is evidence for the claim that Williams was exploring the boundaries between the real and the fantastic as early as 1924. On the other hand, Breton's contemporary interest in the 'false novel' suggests that Surrealism and Superrealism have more in common than Perloff allows. Surrealist texts are not completely determined by their commitment to the ideas of Freud.

In his book on Williams, Mike Weaver devotes a whole chapter to the 'Americanization' of Surrealism and his account shares features with Perloff's. Although his starting point is American popular culture, he too regards Surrealism as opening up a fissure in the naturalistic order of the nation's prose. He says of Nathanael West, for example, that he 'combined the radical techniques of the popular arts with the naturalistic tradition of John Dos Passos, James T. Farrell, and the early Edward Dahlberg'.[41] Even more revealing is Weaver's discussion of an article by historian Henry Bamford Parkes: 'Notes on Dadaism and Super-realism' appeared in 1932 and was, according to Weaver, 'the first important piece of theoretical writing on Surrealism which came to Williams' attention'.[42] As well as examples of French Surrealism, Parkes offered an explanation of the obstacles standing in the way of the movement's successful transplantation to the United States. At stake was a disposition that seemed to allow only one kind of rapport between writers and leftist politics:

> The American novelist's predilection for naturalism, reinforced by the application of the Marxist idea of the evolution of the masses,

had led to the proletarian novel with its ultimately idealistic basis.[43]

Parkes proposes Superrealism as a counter to this hegemony. With nominalism as his philosophical starting point, Parkes assumes a gap between the 'external world' and our ordering of it, considering 'our ideas and universals to be merely convenient ways of arranging phenomena, lacking objective validity'. To expose the illusory character of objectivity, Parkes advocates a destructive act, one that will 'smash all the accepted categories and rearrange phenomena in wholly new combinations'.[44] Clearly visible here are the contours of a critique in which language, as naming, might disrupt reality-as-it.[45] From the point of Parkes's article, then, Superrealism is certainly conditioned by its American context but it is also defined in terms that coincide in some respects with an attack on referentiality and a poetics of negation.

Blues

To broaden still further the Surrealist nexus within American literary modernism at this time, I want now to consider the small magazine *Blues*. Based in Columbus, Mississippi, *Blues* was initially edited by Charles Henri Ford but also came to involve Parker Tyler and Eugene Jolas as key players. In this respect, it reflects the concerns and stages the practices of writers who are usually described as 'orthodox' followers of Breton. Like many of its kind, the magazine was short-lived, running from February 1929 to December 1930. It nonetheless qualifies in Perloff's article as one example of the 'homegrown product' of Superrealism.[46] Subtitled *A Magazine of New Rhythms*, *Blues* wore its indigenous credentials on its sleeve. But critics have suggested that this self-positioning is somewhat disingenuous. In Dickran Tashjian's view, Tyler and Ford had their sights more on the high life of the Parisian avant-garde than on their own regional base.[47] Focusing on the political dimension of the magazine's self-proclaimed cultural territory, Steven C. Tracy draws attention to the tendency amongst some 'white modernists' to appropriate African-American musical traditions, transforming them into 'a potent analogue for the revolution in contemporary literature, but not as a catalyst for a revolution in contemporary race relations'.[48] Key to my reading of *Blues* are the critical pronouncements made in its pages by Williams in which he articulates his concern for the future of innovative writing in the United States, and the practical contributions of writers such as Parker Tyler, William Closson Emory and Charles Henri Ford. To examine the rubric under which Williams sponsors *Blues* is to acknowledge his hopes that it would perform the same restorative function *for writing* as Surrealism itself. To examine the prose and poetry published in the magazine is to see that hope partially realized.

Williams published only one poem in *Blues*, suggesting that his continued support was motivated not only by his wish to see his works in print but also by a desire to act as a mediator between first- and second-wave modernist writers.[49] So, his opening encomium, 'For a New Magazine', begins with the blast that 'Blues' was a good name for a publication trying to make its way through the literary sterility of contemporary America.[50] Here the implication is not that the first modernists failed in their own right but that they did so because their limited access to an audience that might support them meant that their innovations were too easily rationalized in 'the common mind' as 'post-war hysteria'.[51] It is in this context that Williams offers his services as a conduit between a younger and an older generation:

> the young writers today must not be allowed to lose what those of 1914 and thereabouts won – even to be held as weakly as it is – with difficulty. That would be the part I'd like to play now – and to keep on playing, to drive that home.[52]

One factor in Williams's continued support for the magazine may have been its preference for European over English *confrères*. For several contributors to *Blues*, England could not be divorced from the miring of the modern movement consequent upon the literary ascendancy of T. S. Eliot. After all, this was the period of Eliot's official Anglicization: he became a British subject in 1927 and published *For Lancelot Andrewes* in 1928. In his own contributions to *Blues*, Williams returns repeatedly to the negative influence of both Eliot and England. In 'A Note on the Art of Poetry', he recognizes the 'common disgust' shown by Eliot's 'former fellows' for his transformation into 'the academic thing'.[53] Later on in the piece we read that 'Ridicule. Retirement. The English. Morality. None of these things mean anything to writing.'[54] In an introduction written for the autumn edition of 1929, Williams can be found venting (while only thinly veiling) his spleen against Eliot's multiple capitulation to the forces of reaction. Brushing off the strident tone of the manifesto form, Williams tells the reader that he 'MUST come over', or else 'retreat' –

> swallowing whole, as complete as it is the SUMMA THEOLOGIA, the philosophy dependent therefrom and the poetry pinned thereto and go to rest with John Donne in that tight little island of dreams where all past wealth is garnered.[55]

Eliot is pilloried here as a traitor to the cause of writing proper, as a turncoat who has joined the ranks of the 'academicians' so disdained in *A Novelette* (p. 281). And just as Williams celebrates in that text Surrealism's 'living defense of literature, that will supplant science', so does he use the same vocabulary to energize *Blues*:

> Poetry especially is just at the brink of its modern development when it will with absolute certainty supplant a great part of the effectiveness now absorbed by science and to a lesser extent by philosophy.[56]

The editors of *Blues* were hardly academicians. Ford had left high school to begin publishing the magazine and Tyler was well known in Greenwich Village for his bohemian profile. Prising these two away from their status in criticism as 'orthodox' followers of Breton is easier if we consider their contributions to *Blues* in the specific context of that periodical. As scholars have increasingly recognized in recent years, small magazines often present contingent and ephemeral orders of literature that are overlooked by subsequent, 'grander' narratives of literary history. A comprehensive study of *Blues* is not possible or appropriate here but in order to give a slightly deeper impression of its local environment, I will begin my close readings with a prose passage that demonstrates nicely the 'equivocation between surrealism and naturalism' identified by Perloff. As the following extract from the beginning of the piece shows, 'Miner Away', by William Closson Emory, is unquestionably situated in the deprivation and social division of economic strife:

> On the hillside rusting and rotting and the house. Anton and Tina and Lena. Singing with the pinkcrunch and a soupsong. The night smile and the day smile not but enough. While deep in the dark pick flickers and the washing in the sun white glint day and day and day.
>
> There is no co-ordination. Fluctuations arose and were discounted vapidly. Figures appeared upon and were lost red and the mine suffered. Failures were and are the cause. STRIKE MINERS. A porter rode in a special car. A huge fatness was carried. Velvet and filet mignons. And Tina streaked her words while she sorrowfully. The boiled potatoes dismissal and the boiled cabbage. His whiskers were lean and his gauntface. He walked down and they walked down and all around. Burly were the clubs and the men burly. They all walked to jail. Eat less and nothing so the lined face and thoughts. The furcoat crumpled and the knife clattered. There was plenty to eat. But the burly clubs smashed pylons of night on his mind sky. The dawn swirled and night.[57]

The referential hooks of this piece are clearly foregrounded. That we are in the presence of a labour strike is signalled literally to us. With the introduction of the past tense in the second paragraph, we begin to become aware of a kind of narrative reconstruction. But any tendency towards cumulative meaning is seriously curtailed, by both the simplified and toneless constructions and the unorthodox word order. So, for example, the second sentence of the second paragraph fails to elaborate on whether the 'fluctuations' are concrete or abstract. The passive construction – 'were discounted' – leaves out the identification of the agent(s). A subsequent omission is suggested by the unconventional word order of the sentence that runs 'His whiskers were lean and his gauntface'. Grammatically, the period is complete but the copula is brought forward in such a way as to imply a further verb. Emory is clearly influenced by Stein in his efforts to invest a naturalistic scene with the 'landscape' of grammar but his method is much more directly interventionist in political terms. The statement that 'There is no co-ordination' acknowledges both the paratactic formation of the writing and the absence of a social or moral order by which capitalism might be controlled. Once it has been realized that the next three sentences are built around the language of the balance sheet, the tonelessness which results from their odd construction becomes unexpectedly mimetic. At this point the writing appears to be working with as little concern for its social implications and reception as the financial markets themselves. Except, of course, that the looseness of context allows words to travel their multi-referential vectors, such that the pun on 'figures' discloses the 'workings' of reification. It was not the miners that 'suffered' but the 'mine'.

Emory's piece seems to operate rather successfully as writing that achieves reference but does not capitulate to referentiality.[58] We can both recognize a world that is already given and participate in its recasting in language. 'The Room', by Charles Henri Ford, treads a similar path, although the referential hooks are less overtly political. 'The Room' is a short prose piece reproduced below in full:

> The room was disordered. We talked. I asked about her because. He told me she had a swan's movements.
>
> 'She has the movements of a swan,' he said.
>
> 'Did you used to be in the navy?' I asked.
>
> 'No. Why?'
>
> 'I don't know. You just look like a sailor.'
>
> 'Do I?'
>
> 'Yes. I don't know why . . You just do.'
>
> The sun threw a golden slab across the floor, slanting to the carpet. Tiny particles of somethings were visible. They may have been the dust of a body.
>
> 'Who knows?' I said. 'Those things in the sun may be a heart – or a lung, maybe.'
>
> 'What things?' he said.
>
> I went over to where he was sitting.
>
> 'Listen,' I said. While the clock in the cityhall denoted the hour. Inexorably the minutes. He laughed then and his teeth were white stabs. One can't always be lonely. That is what madness is. Loneliness intensely. I do not know how long after a falling back on the bed and a hand being burned by a cigarette. Mockery in the corridor and someone speaking who could not be understood.
>
> He said she had kissed him only once but then it had burned into his mouth right down into his guts – 'God,' he said.[59]

The initial sparseness of the writing, together with the anonymity of the location and the violence done there, give the piece a 'noirish' quality. The disorder of the room implies some kind of transgression, most likely an amatory one. The context of the 'love triangle' – so generalizable in life and literature – presents itself quite readily. But not conventionally. The third sentence is grammatically incomplete, holding back exactly the data we need both to flesh out the identity of the speaker and to understand what makes *this* love triangle specific and plausible. The metaphorical cast of the interlocutor's reply is very much at odds with the prosaic character of the opening three periods. The dialogue that follows is similarly unsettling. The first statement is redundant, since it only repeats in direct speech what has been communicated immediately previously in indirect speech. Williams's contemporary praise of Stein applies here; at this point in the 'narrative' it is writing itself that is 'envisioned as the first concern of the moment', not only in the logically redundant shift from indirect to direct speech but also in the associative drift of the 'conversation'.[60] The narrator does not respond to the characterization of the woman – even though he has asked about her – but asks whether the other man 'used to be in the navy'. Metaphor is in the driving seat now: *she* is to be identified by her resemblance to a swan; the other man is to be identified by his resemblance to a sailor; and sailors resemble swans in that they both float.

As with the lack of 'co-ordination' in Emory's piece, the 'disorder' of 'The Room' is to be found not only in the represented scene – such as it is – but also in the formal constituents of the representation. Negation is not all that is at stake here, however, for the 'Tiny particles of somethings' that subsequently become 'visible' seem both to suggest a kind of surreal 'profane illumination' and to demonstrate Williams's claim – made in his 1930 essay on Stein – that 'writing, like everything else, is much a question of refreshed interest'.[61] The interlocutor is initially made the rube for an attempt on the part of the narrator to re-animate the social space of the room. This he tries in a kind of alchemy that begins with the most insignificant material motes. But, of course, the 'particles' that are the usually invisible dust of social space are also the conventionally unacknowledged tillers of discursive space. The 'skeleton', as Williams calls the 'formal' parts of language in his essay on Stein,[62] is elevated in this transformation into the 'body' of the writing. The formal 'bones' of language no longer support the represented scene; they have become part of the scene itself.

So far, I have looked at two prose examples from *Blues*. Parker Tyler published a number of poems in the magazine and, in turning to these now, I have two aims in mind. The first is to demonstrate in some detail how the Surrealist nexus I am proposing was articulated in relation to Imagism. The second is to highlight a kind of writing in which 'dream' figures prominently but which cannot be read simply in terms of a poetics of the inner life. It should be noted at this point that my reading of this phase of Tyler's writing is not entirely in accord with Perloff's estimation of his work. For Perloff, Tyler's assimilation of Surrealism was 'skewed', a description that she also applies to Williams.[63] Although her evaluation is based primarily on a piece written by Tyler in 1940, Perloff's remarks are clearly provocative for a discussion of his earlier work. For Perloff, the oddity of Tyler's reading of Surrealism consists in his construction of it as involving a dialectical interplay between 'the representational value of the image (imagism) and the symbolic value of the image (symbolism)'.[64]

While she is correct to note the mismatch between this formula and Breton's 'originary definition of Surrealism as "pure psychic automatism"', Tyler's construction does appear to touch unwittingly on the paradox that lurked within automatism, namely that its 'purity' of expression relied on the same system of signs as representational modes of discourse. Perhaps, in this respect, Tyler was closer to the practice of Surrealist writing than he was to the aspiration of its poetics.

Closer in 1929, moreover, than he was in 1940. To track this proximity, and its implications for the career of Imagism into the 1930s, I will look closely at a 'suite' of poems published in the March 1929 issue of *Blues*, under the heading 'NEVER SAY YES TO THE SPROUTING (THREE POEMS)'.[65] The title of the first poem in the suite, 'This Dreaming Image', seems to announce almost programmatically an encounter between Surrealism and Imagism. And in several respects 'This Dreaming Image' can be defined against *that* modernist icon Ezra Pound's 'In a Station of the Metro':

THIS DREAMING IMAGE

Clean come to me
From both poles of the earth
This dreaming image, in
Or out the subway to be hung
Upon a strap, and five p.m.
To draw into itself...
This waking eyelash
To be sobbed into the sunshine
Muttered in the death of knowing
The ways of circulating dust
Are limited to one.

Fair over earth shall hang
This postulate, trapped in the air
Where sunlit stars
Are racing to approve
Of buds. Fair shall this be hung
To fall with goodbyes,
Blowing down the street with one, bound
To a China lost from sight
With sun of will upcoming in four hours
But peeling its own limbo from the minute
To hide among the lampposts.

Never to shape the budding hour of it
Or wishing it to shape
Is to turn crook to get a number
Chase upstairs to open a treacherous door
Inviting in a simile of lust
To tongue into the concrete.

> With the eye upon the postulate
> Fair shall it hang;
> Slaughterer of tears and distances;
> Keeper of the hothouse heart;
> So never shall the moment
> Be a heartbeat finished for the stop
> Or lingering, for between the poles
> There is a magnetism to ensure
> The head bent down, the legs sent up.[66]

Whereas Pound's image is securely located in the Parisian underground, Tyler's can be either 'in/Or out the [American] subway'. Where Pound's image ultimately achieves the secure separation of subject and object, Tyler's appears to blur the two in its status as a *dreaming* image. Whereas Pound's image secures separation by absorbing the embodiment of other subjectivities into the blank objectivity of 'Petals', Tyler's seems incapable or uninterested in such mastery – 'To draw into itself...' What? Indeed, this ellipsis points to one final antagonism between the two images. As a normal sentence, Pound's poem is incomplete but the omissions are in the interest of clarity and immediacy. In Tyler's poem, the gaps are harder to fill. The line following the ellipsis – 'This waking eyelash' – could easily complete the expression, were it not the case that the juxtaposition of evening ('five p.m.') and morning ('waking') takes us all the way back to the first verb in the poem. At first reading, 'come' can be read as a singular imperative, part of a surreal apostrophe in which oppositions ('both poles of the earth') are conjoined in a single 'dreaming image'. Indeed, the last three lines seem to confirm this reading, in their assertion that 'between the poles/There is a magnetism to ensure/The head bent down, the legs sent up'.[67] But by the seventh line of the poem, 'come' could also be a plural verb, the second subject of which is 'This waking eyelash'.

To read the poem in this way is to recognize how overwrought its syntax is, how its sense appears to be articulated both backwards and forwards. Hence, perhaps, the dominant motif of hanging, which appears, on the one hand, to hold the poem together but, on the other, to prevent it from taking a clearly defined shape. At the same time, the redefinition of the image that Tyler undertakes in this poem seems consistent with his later advocacy of the dialectical interplay between representational and symbolic values. Except that the dialectic itself hangs back from a synthesis. The image hovers between the representation of the subway scene and the potential for symbolic association (which is one way of reading 'To draw into itself...'). This poised incompletion, together with the ambiguous syntax of the poem, does not allow for the 'explanation and interpretation' that Perloff describes as *'de rigeur'* for Tyler's later construction of Surrealism.[68] Indeed, it seems much closer to Benjamin's understanding of 'ambiguity' as 'the imagistic appearance of dialectics, the law of dialectics at a standstill'.[69] From this point of view the suspense of the poem is 'utopian' and representative of the 'dialectical image' as a 'dream image'.[70]

It also points to an unwillingness to draw an absolute distinction between 'inner' life and 'outer' life. 'This postulate' is significant in this respect, not least because it stands in apposition to 'This dreaming image' and 'This waking eyelash'. Technically, a postulate is a beginning, a foundation from which one might develop a rational chain of thought. It conventionally belongs, then, to the intellectual interior, to the life of the mind. But this postulate is apparently 'trapped' in the external world, unable to develop its logical sequence or reach its conclusion. The demonstrative pronoun plays out an ironic function here. Up to the caesura in line 2 of the second stanza, the postulate seems to be behaving normally. We can read the first line of the stanza as a metaphor for the transcendence of abstract thought. The pronoun that follows appears then to be signalling the statement of the postulate's content – 'this postulate, namely that ...' – but at the very moment when thinking might reach out from an origin to master the 'earth', we discover that the postulate is not only already 'out there' but also unable to get back in. The pronoun is thus transformed retrospectively into a simple deictic. As in Pound's famous haiku, it works to insist on the presentness of the image but, unlike Pound's deictic, Tyler's does not 'fix' the subject in relation to the object so much as suspend them in a bizarre and incomplete juxtaposition. We may keep our 'eye upon the postulate' but it resists becoming a part of our thinking, even though that is where it ought to have originated.

Tyler pushes the mode of double articulation even further in the second poem of the trilogy, 'Sonnet'.[71] This piece parodies the conventional sonnet in its *dis*arrangement; there is a discernible formal design but one that works at the expense of sense:

SONNET

I smell an oriental luxury
from him
     his suit is brown
        I smell an or-
riental lux
     I love his nose
             ury
from him
     's slender hook
        I smell an or-
ien
     and he is strong as rope
        tal lux-
ury from
     excellently built
        him
          I
I dream of
     smell an oriental lux-

ur
          him at night that
                    y from him
                                   he
                                           I
makes love to me yes
                              smell an orien-
tal luxury from
              strenuous love
                                     him
sweet marvellous
                           I smell an orien-
tal
         he's in busi
                  luxury from him
ness
        I
                 A Jew and O his sex ap
                       smell
an
      peal
          rien
                 him
                       from
                              ury
                                    lux
                                            smell

Throughout the poem two compositional units clash like tectonic plates, resulting in not only the disruption of syntax but also the fragmentation of individual words. On the one hand is the repetition of a single declarative, 'I smell an oriental luxury from him'. On the other hand is an unpunctuated but linear confession of desire that combines everyday information – 'he's in busi/…/ness' – with erotically charged description and a short dream narrative. Described in this way the poem is a good demonstration of the way in which the personalities of our everyday lives might have another life in our fantasies. If we were to construct a realistic version of this poem, we could say that a physical encounter with the smell of the beloved acts as the trigger for an internal reverie and wish fulfilment. But this would be to subordinate unfairly the experience of reading the poem; the so-called trigger repeats (traumatically?) to break up the expression of the reverie at its most fundamental level. In so doing, it negates the world of commerce to suggest what in Parkes's terms might be described as 'wholly new combinations' of phenomena. This retranscription, as it also is, is most noticeable in the final 'deflating' section. Here even the formal design breaks down. The order of 'smell … from him' is reversed; the syllables 'or' and 'tal' are lost from oriental, and the first syllable of 'luxury' appears immediately after the last two. In the process, the abstract quality 'appeal' is transformed into an auditory phenomenon that complements both 'smell' and the Latin 'light' that seeps out of luxury's inversion. The paring down of 'oriental' to the French negative may suggest that there is really 'nothing' to the attraction of the orient after all and, consequently, nothing to 'him' either. Of course, nor can the possibility be precluded that the beloved's final demotion is the result of his involvement with us-ury, in the 'light' of which any glamour can only be skin deep.

Dream, then, plays a key role in these two poems, but in neither case is Tyler proposing a naïve transcription of 'inner life'. In the first poem, 'dreaming' is introduced as a critique, or reassessment of the Poundian image. At stake is precisely the secure division between internal and external, subject and object, upon which Pound's Imagism depends. Tyler's image does not mimic its modernist precursor in a crusade of mastery but nor does it withdraw from the world into the subjective interior. Rather, it proposes a new dispensation, in which psychic and expressive space cannot be definitively disentangled from physical space. The poem is over-egged with prepositions of place, a saturation that prevents satisfactory delineation. Perhaps the most graphic example occurs in the third section. Here, an action (expressed in terms of the infinitive rather than a specified subject) leads to a brief depiction of a recognizable space – 'Chase upstairs to open a treacherous door' – only for the direction of that action to be apparently reversed,[72] as would be permissible in a dream narrative, say, but the entry of 'a simile' reminds us once again of the 'formal parts of language'. We are not allowed to suspend criteria of plausibility and settle into the high jinks of a hallucinated journey but are encouraged to re-examine the 'skeleton' of the stanza. There are no similes in evidence, although there are three potential metaphors for lust: 'to turn crook to get a number' suggests a desire to make connection so strong that it will break the law; 'a treacherous door' implies the moral duplicity that may accompany lust; 'To tongue into the concrete' connotes a lust so intense and over-riding that it will launch itself at even the most resistant of surfaces. Crucially, this last expression might also be read as a figure for both the foregrounding of 'the formal parts of language' and the convocation of expressive and physical space. Indeed, perhaps language itself represents the synthesis of these two tropes. Language is the 'ground' upon which interior and exterior space converge. Maybe so, but it is a hesitant kind of synthesis that commits so readily to suspension and entrapment, that achieves such an ambiguous resolution. Hesitancy, however, is what we might expect in this transitional and turbulent phase of modernist poetics.

CHAPTER FOUR

The Surreal-O-bjectivist Nexus

I have tried to align my reading of *Blues* in the previous chapter with the slender but significant section that Marjorie Perloff has cut through first- and second-wave literary modernism. But to keep the coordinates as clear as possible I have deliberately delayed addressing one of her major claims, namely that what is at stake in her new mapping is 'the nature of the Objectivist experiment'.[1] Perloff specifically has her sights on Louis Zukofsky. She situates Zukofsky's early '"Objectivist" poetry' alongside the kind of Superrealist prose written by Erskine Caldwell and Edward Dahlberg.[2] In challenging preconceptions with this very localized analysis, Perloff is in tune with a recent trend to re-evaluate Objectivism in terms that assume as little about their 'object' as possible. In a recent collection of essays, for example, Rachel Blau DuPlessis and Peter Quartermain exhort readers to think about *The Objectivist Nexus*, where 'nexus' is preferred as 'a term useful for resisting definitive fixity while encouraging a continuing discussion of cohorts and groups'.[3]

The current work is offered as a contribution to this discussion. Notwithstanding the distinctions that Perloff draws between European Surrealism and American Superrealism, her analysis has the unnecessary and unfortunate effect of muting Williams's engagement with Surrealism and Superrealism. Given that the relationship between Zukofsky and Williams is part of the narrative of Objectivism – and I think this is hard to dispute – her mapping of the transition from first- to second-wave modernism also limits the account of what I would like to describe as the 'Surreal-O-bjectivist' nexus, a nexus in which the two tendencies meet in the field of desire. Indeed, in the traffic between 'real' and 'fantastic' that Perloff identifies in the lost aesthetic of the late 1920s, I discern a problematics of desire that both shapes the Objectivist relationship of Williams and Zukofsky and deforms it with Surrealist inclinations. This dynamic manifests itself in some unexpected material locations; my drawing of it will include Zukofsky's contribution of poems to *Blues* – the Surrealist pro-file of which is already in play – but will attend to these texts as tentative responses to what Richard Frye describes as the 'objectivist premonitions' of *Spring and All*.[4] Frye's expression has a special resonance in my reading of Willliams's *Spring and All*, where it signals both the protean charac-ter of his Objectivism and the phantom of Surrealism which lay in its future path. When he publishes poems in *Blues*, Zukofsky is responding to *Spring and All* from within a context that includes Surrealism. Surrealism also ghosts the foundational moment of Objectivism, in the shape of 'a symposium' between Zukofsky, Parker Tyler and Charles Henri Ford (on which, see below).

In exploring this network of encounters, I want specifically to resist the 'definitive fixity' that would divide Surrealism and Objectivism in the crucial phase of transition from first- to second-wave modernism. The boundary between these two modernist movements has already received scrutiny in the context of scholarship on the writing of Lorine Niedecker. Jenny Penberthy's work on the correspondence between Niedecker and Zukofsky draws attention to Niedecker's dual 'affiliation' to Surrealism and Objectivism.[5] Elsewhere, Peter Nicholls has pursued the Surrealist inflection of Niedecker's writing, finding it in both her early and her later work.[6] In subjecting this boundary to further interrogation, I am also call-ing into question the idea of an 'orthodox' Surrealism, crisply defined in terms of a commitment to dream imagery and a poetics of the inner life. In a movement given to commanding statements of position and led by forceful personalities, orthodoxy recurs again and again as an issue. But, as Perloff illustrates in her study of Superrealism, the international scope of Surrealism allows for many mediations. Much – often too much – is assumed when an American writer is labelled as a 'follower' of André Breton. I don't dispute the emergence of 'orthodox' Surrealism as an influence on twentieth-century American poetry – one that is construed sometimes positively, sometimes negatively – but I do think that the history of its emergence has been, at times, abbreviated. Concerned with the nuances of American modernism, critics have sometimes latched on to this orthodoxy as a secure point of contrast for their analyses.

The significance of the Surreal-O-bjectivist nexus for my broader dis-cussion of Language writing is twofold. On the one hand, it advances the case for the imbrication – if not influence – of Language writing with Surrealism. On the other hand, it helps to explain why this relationship has been subterranean and unsubstantiated, since it charts the increas-ing visibility of orthodox Surrealism as the *only* kind of Surrealism with which American poets might compare their work.[7] Objectivist writers have been acceptable antecedents for Language writing for some time. The materialist cast of their poetics and their exile from the canon of American literature – until recent years at least – chimes with the leftist and dissident stance that writers like Charles Bernstein, Ron Silliman and Barrett Watten took in the early phases of Language writing. In the context of this lineage,

Surrealism is too easily reduced to the subjectivist and bourgeois antithesis of a tradition grounded in the personal experience of strife and obscurity.[8] To show, as I hope to do, that the border between subjective and objective is not a secure one for either movement is to identify a crux that persists in the poetics and practice of Language writers. In this sense their declared bonds with Objectivism are ghosted by invisible ties to Surrealism.

The Surreal-O-bjectivist nexus is also punctuated by questions of political intervention. The transitions between first- and second-wave literary modernism at the end of the 1920s were by no means co-terminous with the political commitment generated as a response to the Depression but they were, nonetheless, part of the same historical process. At a practical level, the conditions in which poetry was produced and disseminated changed.[9] In theoretical terms, the pressures on the relationship between objectivity and subjectivity in writing intensified, as writers were called upon to justify their practice in materialist terms. This situation anticipates the questions that many Language writers put to themselves later in the century. The situations are not, however, smoothly analogous. For Zukofsky and Breton, the political picture was one where the left had a strong profile; by contrast, debates on referentiality staged in the pages of $L=A=N=G=U=A=G=E$ and elsewhere grew out of a keen sense that the commodification of writing was a well established norm. Nonetheless, it is not a misrepresentation to suggest that, in the late 1920s and early 1930s, both Zukofsky and Breton were engaged with 'the politics of the referent', Zukofsky through his commitment to historic and contemporary particulars, Breton through a stand against the emergence of 'neo-naturalism'.[10] Both resist the pressures to backtrack on the gains of first-wave modernism; both attempt to clarify the passage between consciousness and the material world. Emblematic of this struggle is Benjamin's idea of the 'long-sought image sphere', that state in which 'political materialism and physical nature share the inner man, the psyche, the individual'.[11] Benjamin's utopian concept inaugurates my travels through the Surreal-O-bjectivist nexus and will reappear in subsequent chapters.

Surrealism and Objectivism: points of contact

I want to begin with Zukofsky's essay 'American Poetry 1920–1930', published in 1931 (quotations here taken from the collection *Prepositions*).[12] Williams plays a prominent and celebrated role in this essay. Zukofsky considers the earlier improvisatory pieces, as well as *Spring and All*. The scope of his discussion is, in this respect, significant, since it makes visible the grooming of Williams for his role in an aesthetic according to which the unpremeditated character of improvisation must be schooled to greater responsibility. Initially, then, Zukofsky acknowledges the animated openness of the improvisations, describing 'the aesthetics of this material' as 'a living one, a continual beginning' (p. 140). Subsequently, however, he implicitly rejects the spontaneity of the improvisational method when he suggests that the reader needs to subject these texts to the same kind of revision as Williams himself has learnt to apply since their composition. Zukofsky expresses such revision in terms implying moral as well as aesthetic values, describing it as 'the process of rehabilitating the good to its rightful structure' (p. 140). Williams's work is here being shaped for its Objectivist future. In this respect, it is not surprising that *Spring and All* is praised without reservation, as Zukofsky applauds Williams's 'exclusion of sentimentalisms, extraneous comparisons, similes, overweening autobiographies of the heart, all of which permits factitious "reflection about," of sequence, of all but the full sight of the immediate' (p. 141).

Clearly, part of the attraction of Williams's writing for the younger poet lies in its challenge to conventional modes of literary representation. Political intervention is also at stake. 'The pure products of America go crazy' – which remains one of the best-known poems from *Spring and All* – is said to have realized both 'aesthetic, living values' and the 'social determinism of American suburbs in the first thirty years of the century' (p. 142). Zukofsky implicitly recognizes the negational function of Williams's poetry, in setting it against a social norm defined by 'the routine senseless repetition of events'. At the same time, he takes pains to stress that Williams's commitment is primarily artistic rather than political, as 'No outside program has influenced his social awareness' (p. 143).

Blues is a good place to explore the relationship between Zukofsky's own poetry of the period and Williams's 'objectivist premonitions'. Both writers contributed to the magazine, although it is worth noting that the younger poet offered far more poems than did the older – seventeen in total. This is not surprising, given the role that Williams takes as sponsor of the next wave of modernist innovation. By the same token, the context of transition allows for reference *backwards* as well as forwards: unlike his immediate poetic forebears, Zukofsky has an immediate past to which he can fruitfully relate. To extend this discussion of Zukofsky's response to *Spring and All*, and to bring Surrealism back into the frame, I want to invoke the work of two important critics: Charles Altieri and Rosalind Krauss, in particular their respective analyses 'The Objectivist Tradition' and *The Originality of the Avante-Garde*.[13] A comparison of their views on Objectivism and Surrealism makes sense, I think, in both literary historical and political terms. The points of congruence, as well as the divergences, testify to both the desirability and the difficulty of achieving 'the long-sought image sphere' identified by Benjamin, that utopian realm where 'political materialism and physical nature share the inner man, the psyche, the individual'. Benjamin, of course, looked for a Surrealist revolution to disclose this harmonious space but the contradictions he thought it would resolve were lived and reflected upon by many writers in the 1920s and 1930s. Zukofsky's dialogue with *Spring and All*, expressed in the poems he published in *Blues*, was part of this life and this reflection, as was the 'symposium' with Tyler and Ford.

To begin with a point of contact: according to Altieri and Krauss, the aesthetics of both Objectivism and Surrealism aspire to some kind of presence. Surrealists seek presence in automatic writing, which, Krauss states, unlike 'the rest of the written signs of Western culture', is not 'representation' but 'a kind of presence, the direct presence of the artist's inner self' (p. 96). In Objectivism, Altieri argues, 'the mind's act brought to objective form is as present to itself as are the objects it brings into relationship' (p. 32). Here, the contact between the two poetics seems to end. Whereas automatism remains expressive, the Objectivist seeks to objectify even his or her own subjective states. In Benjamin's terms, 'the inner man' takes on the character of 'physical nature'. What starts as an intersection between Surrealism and Objectivism now looks like a schism, with the 'image sphere' being tugged in opposite directions. But we should not forget the objective side of Surrealism. Automatic writing can be described as a kind of presence because it manifests the inner life in a form that *was never known before*. In this respect, its content can appear as exterior to the subject. In this context, it is important to distinguish between the different phases of automatic writing. As Tim Armstrong emphasizes in his account of Surrealist automatism, Breton took pains to deny the exteriority of both the 'voice' and the instrument of automatic writing.[14] This position was necessary to clarify the difference between Surrealist automatism and that practised by mediums. For mediums, the exteriority of the voice was required to validate the supernatural realm to which their practice gave access, but in automatism Breton sought to integrate the self, not to transcend it. That said, the 'mechanical' writing that results has an objective cast that complicates the expressive goal of Surrealist automatism. It discloses the inner life but in a form that, like improvisation, is not premeditated, is 'unforeseen'.[15]

From this perspective, Surrealism shares with Objectivism the shift from 'the inner man' to 'physical nature'. But this disclosure is not quite the terminus of automatism, since the point of objectifying the inner life is to make it available for interpretation. This interpretation may occur almost immediately, and with the minimum of conscious intervention, as when an automatic expression picks up on the one that precedes it, or it may take place some time afterwards, and involve conscious reflection, as when Breton retranscribes his automatic poem 'Sunflower' in *L'Amour Fou*.[16] By contrast, when Zukofsky writes of objectification in 1931, he famously speaks of it in terms of a 'rested totality'.[17] Altieri's account of Objectivism helps us to understand this difference in terms of desire:

> So long as language remains essentially denotative and the energies of mind can be maintained within the lines of compositional force that the field establishes among the layered references in the poem, there need be *no residue of unnameable desire* or shaping will behind the poem, and no need of universals beyond it. There is nothing that can return in self-consciousness *to haunt one with the fear* that his or her fictions evade to transcend

empirical conditions. The mind's act brought to objective form is as present to itself as are the objects it brings into relationship. (p. 32, my emphasis)

Here, desire is at stake in the rested totality but not in play. Objectification does not arouse desire but fulfils it in the 'perfection' of the aesthetic object. Zukofsky's definition continues, 'the apprehension *satisfied* completely as to the appearance of the art form as an object'.[18] Altieri's account of 'the Objectivist tradition' does not touch on Surrealism explicitly but it is the unacknowledged antagonist in his claim that 'Objectification is a property of writing committed to composition rather than to interpretation' (p. 33). That said, Zukofsky's appreciation of Williams's early writing discloses a time when the battle lines between Objectivism and Surrealism were not so clearly drawn. The 'continual beginning' that he identifies as the method of Williams's *The Great American Novel* has more in common with the restlessness of automatic writing than it does with the rested totality of Objectivism. Nonetheless, although he acknowledges the swift transitions in attention that the 'shifting' American scene demands, Zukofsky discerns in Williams's writing a mind strained in its ability to compose rather than one distracted to the point of unconscious revelation:

America, the shifting, as one hurriedly thinks of it or sees it perhaps as one changes from street car to street car, resulted in this book in the swift hold of art on things seen, in the sudden completeness of the words envisioning them.... Such things are seen and recorded not as notes, but as finished, swiftly trained deliberations of the mind between leaps to other work or the multiplicity of living scenes.[19]

In her reading of Surrealism, Krauss comes to 'generalize the aesthetic of surrealism' around the concept of 'Convulsive Beauty', her discussion of which has a place, I think, in the Surreal-O-bjectivist nexus. Indeed, her pithy summary of 'surreality' as 'nature convulsed into a kind of writing' (p. 13) is especially provocative in the context of Zukofsky's dialogue with *Spring and All*. Her account of Convulsive Beauty (p. 112) focuses on an instance in *L'Amour Fou* where Breton laments that he his not able to reproduce in his text a photograph of 'a very handsome locomotive after it had been abandoned for many years to the delirium of a virgin forest'.[20] This photograph is an example of one of the three types of convulsiveness identified by Breton, 'the expiration of movement' (p. 112). The personification of one of modernity's celebrated objects recalls Williams's ironic characterization of the car in *The Great American Novel* but Krauss's account of convulsiveness appears to have little in common with the controlled sensibility that Zukofsky discerns in that text. Krauss writes:

The convulsiveness, then, the arousal in front of the object, is to a perception of it detached from the continuum of its natural existence, a detachment which deprives the locomotive of some part of its physical self and turns it into a sign of the reality it no longer possesses. The still photograph of this stilled train would thus be a representation of an object already constituted as a representation. (p. 112)

Here, the relationship between subject and object is governed by desire rather than the rational mind. Convulsiveness is an 'arousal' of the subject because the detachment of the object from 'the continuum of its natural existence' makes it available for libidinal investment. In Krauss's analysis, this detachment occurs in the objective world; once the locomotive has become derailed, it has lost some of its identity *as* a locomotive. Hence its transformation into a sign. Bearing in mind, however, Benjamin's aspirations for the image sphere – his wish to see the commonality of political materialism, the physical world and the inner man – we might say that the wrench of the object from its natural existence takes place both objectively and subjectively. Breton did not cause the derailment of the locomotive but it was he who perceived it *as* 'detached from the continuum of its natural existence'. Perception here attains an agency that might be compared to that ascribed by Zukofsky to the rational mind. Both are active; both intervene in the world. For Convulsive Beauty to be convulsive, however, perception must be unconsciously motivated rather than consciously directed. Moreover, desire does not depart and arrive but circulates. In helping to transform the object into a representation, the convulsing perception also makes it *legible*, a site where desire might be read. In Benjamin's terms, the 'arousal' of the subject is political as well as personal. Breton 'wakes up' not just to himself but also to the spectre of obsolescence that haunts modernity's objects. Indeed, in its denial of 'the reality it no longer possesses', the derailed locomotive can be thought of as an 'objective negation'.

The objects of modernity are not the only ones that qualify for Convulsive Beauty. As Krauss notes, the other two types fall under the headings of 'mimicry' and 'the found-object or found verbal fragment' (p. 112). Mimicry focuses on 'those instances in nature when one thing imitates another – the most familiar, perhaps, being those markings on the wings of moths that imitate eyes' (p. 112). Imitation entails convulsiveness: 'Mimicry is ... an instance of the natural production of signs, of one thing in nature contorting itself into a representation of another' (p. 112). Mimicry bears comparison with Objectivist poetics in terms of the homologies that the Objectivist seeks between objects. Once again, however, it is desire that divides them. Whereas the concept of homology proposes a strictly objective relationship, mimicry includes the convulsive power of desire, a power expressed in the subject's perception *of* nature, not just in natural objects themselves.

The third kind of Convulsive Beauty also bears a relation with Zukofsky's early writing. Krauss summarizes this species as 'the found-object or found verbal fragment'. She makes explicit the interplay of subjective and objective states engendered by this kind of Convulsive Beauty. Both the found-object and the found verbal fragment are 'instances of objective chance – where an emissary from the external world carries a message informing the recipient of his own desire' (p. 112). As with 'expiration of movement', the object consequently becomes a sign. It is tempting to compare the found-object with Zukofsky's aspiration to 'writing ... which is the detail, not mirage, of seeing, of thinking with the things as they exist, and of directing them along a line of melody'.[21] To the extent that words and their combinations also qualify as things, the comparison does not exclude the Surrealist found verbal fragment. One of the things at issue in this comparison is 'sincerity'. For Zukofsky, intellectual and sensory openness to the givenness of the world is an important aspect of sincerity, one that, as we shall see, has positive connotations for Language writers. Michael Palmer, for example, understands Objectivism as entailing an 'unrelenting exposure' of the self, while Barrett Watten's 'Constructivist' Zukofsky respects his given materials as he works with them. Convulsive Beauty articulates a different kind of sincerity, in which the force of desire is acknowledged, not negatively, as a hindrance – a 'mirage' – to the 'detail of seeing' but as constitutive of sight itself. The sincerity of *L'Amour Fou* lies in the willingness to see the world as desire's sacred text. Linking sight with interpretation, Breton writes, 'what attracts me in such a manner of seeing is that, as far as the eye can see, it recreates desire'.[22]

Zukofsky's contributions to *Blues*

How well do the poems that Zukofsky contributed to *Blues* fare in the context of the comparison that I have been making? My reading will focus on four poems included in the February issue of 1929. Published in *Blues* under the heading 'Group from Ten Poems (1924–26)', their arrangement in the magazine implies a break with the order of their previous composition, since the first three are numbered 'I', 'III' and 'VI', while the fourth – to the Hungarian violist 'Tibor Serly' – is signalled as '(from *Two Dedications*)'.[23] Written between 1924 and 1926, their moment of composition is, therefore, closer in time to *Spring and All* than their appearance in the magazine. Looking forward in time, two of the four poems reappear in *Complete Short Poetry*.[24] Aesthetic rationales for the arrangement of poems have to compete with a range of other priorities in the production of a periodical, a situation which presents another version of 'thinking with the things as they exist'. In this case, the things in question are themselves poems and it is a moot question to ask whether the four of them, as they appear in *Blues*, resolve into a 'rested totality' or not. From another perspective, of course, any apparent resolution could only ever be provisional, subject to future interpretations of the poems and their 'place' in Zukofsky's *oeuvre*.[25]

My own method for reading this group of poems is to begin by following what I take to be the grain of Zukofsky's poetics in the late 1920s and early

1930s. I want then to present the poems as part of the Surreal-O-bjectivist nexus. To articulate this nexus, I need a voice that can go across the grains of the cultural artefacts that are now Surrealism and Objectivism. One of the issues at stake here is the fact that critical analysis tends to assume the 'definitive fixity' that the concept of a nexus seeks to avoid. One can only take something apart if there is a something there in the first place. My critical comparison of Objectivist poetics with Convulsive Beauty is to some extent misplaced in the original context of these poems, since the definitions it assumes lie in their future. Which is not to deny the possibility that such definitions are prefigured in them. When Nicholls writes of the 'objectivist premonitions' of *Spring and All*, I think this is the kind of idea he has in mind. It is impossible for the critic to avoid reading backwards to the primary material from his or her own historical and cultural moment, but I am aiming at a voice that will be self-reflexive enough to register and communicate the necessary fabrication that this journey involves. The reader may experience a sense of disjunction between the two phases of my discussion; if so, I hope it is a fruitful one.

As I have already implied, disjunction seems to be at stake in the arrangement of this 'group' of poems. The most jarring break occurs between the three numbered poems and 'Tibor Serly'. Working with the grain of Zukofsky's statements about his poetry, however, this fracture can be recuperated by recognizing 'Tibor Serly' as a contemporary particular, in this case presenting the detail of a specific musical performance. Thematically, this poem is set in relation to the ones that precede it by its references to nature, specifically, to sun, sea and sand. In hinting at the onset of night in 'Blue – / Withdraws sunset –', Zukofsky allows the possibility that the group of poems represents the natural cycle of one day. The scene of the first poem is a riverside at evening, a summer evening:

I

Not much more than being
thoughts of isolate, beautiful
being at evening, to expect
    at a river front:

a shaft dims
with a turning wheel;

men work on a jetty
by a broken wagon;

leopard, glowing-spotted
    the summer river
under; the Dragon:

Both historically and seasonally, the next poem moves backwards in time but appears to begin with a periphrastic reference to morning. The inclusion of the word 'diurnal' bolsters the view that, as a group, the four poems trace the course of a single day:

> III
>
> Always the May-day sun
> sought out night's bed when love
> coursing thru Athens' trees
> the diurnal odysseys
>
> love came and by the night was led
> Marathon ran on to wed:
>
>   Hymenee!
>
> against the temple torch
> hymned the boyish head –
>
>   Hymenee!
>
> to its mouth the double-pipe,
> cheek blown, apple ripe
> eyes bright from out the dark!
>
>   *   *   *
>
>   'Hey! – hey!'
>
> still lighted after Athens,
> still May, still reveller's each gaze,
> night's constant – not his choice,
> Love firing his voice –
>
> 'It's great to be a Mormon,
> they've so many wives! – '
> the corner boys serve Aphrodite,
> sub aeternitas specie

In its references to sunburn, the subsequent poem may well represent the time around mid-day, when the sun is at its height and hottest:

> VI
>
>   The sun—
> Sign on the wave
> On the shoulder: dun
>
> Flesh grows darker even
> Before the eye.
> Sand: the foot
> Sinks in it.

Cannot be hurt:

Each bone single
When, if ever,
Did it crush to mingle,

Tortured? Stand
Naked by the wave, in the sun,
Burn,
Burn dun.

Treating these three poems as a group, for a moment, desire seems to be at the heart of them. The second poem invokes the traditions of fertility associated with May Day, extending them from the Classical period into the poetic and historical present that surrounds them. The continuity between past and present is partly realized in the word combinations that Zukofsky deploys. Exemplary in this respect is the coordinating preposition 'thru'. Semantically, it expresses continuity, just as its contemporary American spelling continues the sound of its 'proper' grammatical parent. Indeed, this pared-down preposition fits well with its antique neighbours, streamlined as it is for love's hectic 'coursing' through 'the diurnal odysseys'.[26] Measure also coordinates the relationship between past and present. The crucial transformation here is of the ancient praise word 'Hymenee!' to the modern exclamation 'Hey! – hey!' The quotation marks around the contemporary expression signal that Zukofsky is thinking with things as they exist, finding a relationship between two found verbal fragments from historically different contexts. But it is measure that brings this relationship into 'completed sound or structure, melody of form'.[27] The dash between the repeated 'hey' is constitutive here, since it takes the place of the middle syllable of 'Hymenee!'

The juxtaposition of these two words is also crucial as a test of the limits of Zukofky's poetics. As almost pure exclamations, they do not signify in the way that most other words do. Their content is almost entirely exhausted by their expressive function. The risk to objectification is surely extreme here, as successive subjective outbursts threaten to overwhelm representation altogether. And yet, Zukofsky seems to manage the risk. In 'An Objective' he recognizes that the symbolic function of words extends beyond objects to 'states, acts, interrelations, thoughts about them'.[28] In its management of a desire that threatens to get out of hand, Zukofsky's poem both honours its classical sources and, to paraphrase section III of 'An Objective', extends their context from their own time 'into the present'.[29] Hymen, or Hymenaeus, was the Greek and Roman god of marriage. He figures more than once in Ovid's *Metamorphoses* (characteristically marking the end of Book IX and the beginning of Book X, by flying from one to the other), and is the subject of Catullus' sixty-first 'hymn', a text that Zukofsky and his wife translated much later.[30] 'Always the May-day sun' is in tune with both of these historical particulars. Like Catullus' nuptial hymn, the poem manages desire at a critical moment. The light of the sun draws the heat of clandestine desire into the clarity of social responsibility, through marriage: 'love came and by the night was led, / Marathon ran on to wed: / Hymenee!'

At the same time, true to the logic of the *Metamorphoses*, the poem charts the changing social forms of desire, as it is ritualized into religious structures. Echoing within the juxtaposition between past and present is the metamorphosis of Classical myth into Christian myth. In this respect, the 'double-pipe' plays a double tune. The 'apple ripe' clearly signals the sinful potential of desire within a Christian mythology. But the 'boyish head' has come from Athens, reminding us that Eve's apple once belonged to the Hesperides, the fair maidens of Paradise, until Hercules stole it and gave it to Athene. The Hesperides were followers of Aphrodite, who appears at the end of Zukofsky's poem, as a presiding deity. In a move that Pound would surely have approved of, Zukofsky thus seems to see the details of the universal reality of desire through the mirage of contemporary fabrications.[31] The 'corner boys' may appear to be motivated by Christian salvation – 'sub aeternitas specie' – but in reality it is Aphrodite they 'serve'.[32] At the same time, just as the final Latin phrase returns the poem to its first English word – 'Always' – , so does the return to the Greek goddess parallel the 'course' of the Greek myth, in which Athene puts an end to the Olympian rumpus that follows Hercules' theft by giving the apples back to Aphrodite.

The end of the Greek myth is of some significance for my reading of this group of poems. Desire puts both cosmic and social order at stake. As at the end of *The Oresteia*, it is Athene, goddess of wisdom and justice, who restores order. Given the way Zukofsky's poem ends, it is important to remember that Athene's justice entails the recognition of Aphrodite's power. The final stanza of Zukofsky's poem registers a fissure in the social and religious order of modern America. In 1890, the Church of Jesus Christ of Latter Day Saints officially abandoned the practice of polygamy, after conflict with the US government. Like the myth, Zukofsky's poem attempts to heal the rift in America's social fabric by binding desire back into a balanced structure.[33] This structure reaches out to two other particulars from recent history, both of which begin with the letter 'm'. May Day was designated international Labour Day by the International Socialist congress of 1889. Originally a battle in which the Athenians defeated the Persians, in 490 BC, Marathon gave its name to a long-distance running race in 1896. Language and history provide the medium in which Aphrodite can make *m*etamorphosis; poetic structure is the means by which Athene can bring them into harmonious disposition.

This binding operation extends throughout the group of four poems. Poem VI follows the course of desire through the figure of wave motion, a figure that itself coordinates sight, sound and heat. This motion is brought ostensibly to rest in the final word, in which the closure of 'done' signifies through the same sound as that which depicts the colour of sunburnt flesh. Waves recur in 'Tibor Serly', in the context of music being played. Musical structure is expressed metaphorically in the interaction between the fluidity of the sea and the solidity of sand:

> The sea –
> Go chase
>
> It – a
> Salt pact
>
> Ranged over
> Bars – white
>
> Ribs pervade
> In constant
>
> Measures the
> Rounds – Its
>
> Wet frosting,
> A kiss

The 'salt pact' is the fruit of this union, since it belongs with both elements. The slide across 'Bars' to 'Ribs', and thence to 'kiss' figures forth the desiring thread linking this poem to the ones that precede it. Once again, it ends with an image of resolution pitched perilously close to chaos:

> A kiss
>
> Opens nothing,
> Bend head
>
> No! lips
> Not this
>
> An assumed
> Poise among
>
> Crowds! Blue –
> Withdraws sunset –
>
> Tones sound –
> Pluck – dissonant –
>
> Stops sing
> The welter.

As in 'Always the May-day sun', the poem can work as an aesthetic object only if it includes and transforms the elements that would disperse it. Separately, silence ('Stops') and confusion ('welter') would undermine and overwhelm the objectification of the poem; in combination, they perform it.

My reading has become closely bound up with Zukofsky's poetics as I read them and I want now to begin to cross threads by considering a little further the implications of this group of poems as political intervention. To the extent that it records and resolves tensions between 'historic and contemporary particulars', the rested totality of Zukofsky's poem both represents and contributes to a structure that continues outside the work itself. Benjamin's terms might be invoked here. The objectification of the poem is the outcome of the poet's thinking mind, including the thoughts themselves. From this point of view, objectification unifies the inner man with both the physical and the political world. Zukofsky's thoughts find their place in relation to river fronts, deep mythological structures, contemporary musical performances, cultural rifts. But what prevents the rested totality from becoming totalitarian? Zukofsky's early writings imply an awareness of this risk. The shift from totality to totalitarianism equates with a lapse from objectification into subjectification, since it is only in a realm of subjects that issues of power arise.[34] Sincerity is surely meant to guard against such a fall, keeping the subject close to 'things as they exist'. Hence, his warnings against 'predatory intent'.[35] Zukofsky's is not a poetics of mastery so much as of temperance:

> No predatory manifestation – Yet a manifestation making the mind more temperate because the poem exists and has perhaps recorded both state and individual.[36]

Sincerity in these terms takes responsibility with regard both to mental energies and to desire. But to locate sincerity in the poem itself is also to risk a reification, one that Altieri comes perilously close to when he offers the following account of the way in which Objectivism manages desire:

> Objectivism, then, is not merely attention to objects: it entails the construction of aesthetic objects in such a way that the conditions of desire are themselves dramatized and forced to take responsibility for their productions.[37]

The passive voice is telling here, marking the ostracism of the inner man from Benjamin's image sphere. Altieri's comments on the dramatization of desire are provocative when applied to Zukofsky's hymn to Hymen, which is offered, I suggest, under the aegis of Athene. But responsibility is surely a subjective quality and not an objective one. *Un*forced by writer or reader, the relational structure of language will produce, does produce, ad infinitum. This is the eternity that Aphrodite has to offer and the condition with which Zukofsky's poem flirts.

The Surreal-O-bjectivist nexus: a sketch

A flirtation that I want to pursue and, in pursuit, sketch the Surreal-O-bjectivist nexus as it appears to me. Imagine a pot, a Grecian urn. Always a 'still unravished bride of quietness' it nonetheless expresses the 'wild ecstasy' of an image akin to Man Ray's *Fixed-Explosive*. As ever, the face of the figure is not visible but the outline implies a 'Fair youth', possibly Attic in shape, possibly a Mormon. In a certain light, the figure has a double that looks like writing – 'Hey! – hey!' In its repetition, the double excites and affrights in equal measure, threatening and promising to distort the well wrought urn.[38] The provocation of these words is to the ears as well as to the eyes. They echo within each other and overlap with a cry that exults and invokes the god of marriage – 'Hymenee!'

As words and pictures circulate around and through the pot, they summon up texts from the near and the distant past: Catullus' sixty-first 'hymn'; Ovid's *Metamorphoses*; Keats's 'Ode on a Grecian Urn'; Walt Whitman's apostrophe to the marriage god, published in *Children of Adam* in 1860:

> O HYMEN! O hymenee!
> Why do you tantalize me thus?
> O why sting me for a swift moment only?
> Why can you not continue? O why do you now cease?
> Is it because, if you continued beyond the swift moment, you
>   would soon certainly kill me?

These texts are not just facets of the aesthetic structure of the pot, fragments shored against the ruins. They speak also to the conditions in which the pot rotates. For the very space in which it appears is contested. Its would-be champions and curators are subject to allegations of crimes against literature, the state, nature itself. They are variously labelled as 'communists' and perverters of the natural distinction between the sexes.[39] The pot's literary provenance cannot be disentangled from the efforts to regulate desire going on around it and through it. The points of contact are mobile and subject always to interpretation. To invoke Whitman is, perhaps, to call up a figure whose literary authority outweighs his 'unorthodox' sexuality. That said, *Children of Adam* challenges the negative image of human sexuality implied in the Christian myth of the Fall. Ovid is a parallel figure in this respect. His *Metamorphoses* have been seminal in the development of Western literature but let's not forget that his love manual, the *Ars Amatoria*, was too much for the Emperor Augustus and was part of the reason for the poet's banishment. When one reviewer of contributions to *Blues* describes Gertrude Stein as a 'literary jellybean of a she-man with a feminine name', the critical voice is that of the regulator.[40] But the poetic voice is maybe more sympathetic. The monstrosity of the she-man is mitigated by the confectionary promise of the jellybean. What a tender button that might be! How well did the reviewer know his Ovid? At the end of Book IX of the *Metamorphoses*, Hymen presides, together with Venus and Juno, over the marriage of Iphis to Ianthe. The marriage has been postponed – deferred – for a while, due to the complication that both bride (Ianthe) and groom (Iphis) are female. Iphis and 'his' mother, Telethusa, are the only humans aware of the difficulty, which is not resolved until Telethusa appeals to Isis to transform her daughter into a boy. Hymen and the two Roman goddesses have no problem sanctioning this transsexual union. At the same time, they appear to overlook the role in it of a deity outside the Roman pantheon. Indeed, the transformation from female to male is publicly inscribed in the votive tablet offered by the newly weds at the nuptial altar:

DONA · PUER · SOLVIT · QUAE · FEMINA · VOVERAT · IPHIS

These gifts as a man did Iphis pay which as a maiden he had vowed.[41]

From the perspective of a new nation with pretensions to power and a huge immigrant population, Ovid's little tale presents an apt lesson in inclusion, 'solving', as it seems to do, issues of national, social and individual identity. His own metamorphosis from imperial poet to exile testifies to the risks taken by anyone who advocates inclusion, particularly of desire itself. To use a simile, it is as if the faster the pot spins, the more scenes it can net, but the greater the risk of it flying apart. This image is at odds with the 'rested totality' that Zukofsky offered as the outcome of objectification but we are still passing through the Surreal-O-bjectivist nexus, where such definitive fixity does not apply. In this respect, Whitman's plea for bodily transcendence in *Children of Adam* gives a further spin to Zukosky's hymn. As does Williams's *Spring and All* (quotations taken from *Imaginations*). Particularly forceful is a passage that runs from the prose analysis of the imagination through to poem XXII. Objectivist premonitions abound in the prose section. Williams distinguishes between prose and poetry by the ability of the latter to make emotion dynamic, transforming it 'into a separate form' (p. 133). Emotion as point of origin for the work of art might indicate a romantic residue in Williams's thinking at this point but he is concerned to assert that the poem has a reality that matches that of the world around it. Indeed, there is even a hint of the 'rested totality' that lies in Objectivism's future:

Time does not move. Only ignorance and stupidity move. Intelligence (force, power) stands still with time and forces change about itself – sifting the world for permanence, in the drift of nonentity. (p. 134)

On the other hand, the intelligence – objectified in the scientific terms that were alluring for many modernists – does not withdraw from the world, having only the mind's temperance as its object. Rather, it intervenes in the world by virtue of its separation from it. Negation is surely at stake here, as well as the future of Objectivism. Williams's discussion of the Spanish writer Pío Baroja extends the analysis of the imagination into the social realm. Williams himself points to 'a sharp division – the energizing force of imagination on one side – and the acquisitive – PROGRESSIVE force of the lump on the other' (p. 135).

Desire is nowhere mentioned in this prose section; Williams prefers to intervene with a vocabulary that fuses political and scientific discourses. By the end of the section, he is talking about 'the imaginative reality' in terms of 'crescence and ebb'. Zukofsy's group of four poems is fast approaching, arriving, for this reader, on 'the wave rhythm of Shakespeare watching clowns and kings sliding into nothing' (p. 135). In poem XIX, Williams feels more at liberty to express the creative power of the imagination in terms of desire. In contrast to Zukofsky's nuptial hymn, the scene of this poem is of a desire that exceeds regulation. Interestingly, Williams signals this excess (which also crosses the colour line) through the mythological figure of the satyr, which blurs the boundary between human and animal and runs riot through the structures of responsible sexuality. At the same time, the disorder represented in the poem is contained by both its natural occurrence and the ritualized transformation (convulsion) of nature into signs:

XIX

This is the time of year
when boys fifteen and seventeen
wear two horned lilac blossoms
in their caps – or over one ear

What is it that does this?

It is a certain sort –
drivers for grocers or taxidrivers
white and coloured –

fellows that let their hair grow long
in a curve over one eye –

Horned purple

Dirty satyrs, it is
vulgarity raised to the last power

They have stolen them
broken the bushes apart
with a curse for the owner –

Lilacs –

They stand in the doorways
on the business streets with a sneer
on their faces

adorned with blossoms

Out of their sweet heads
dark kisses – rough faces
(pp. 135–36)

This poem points towards Objectivism with 'vulgarity raised', an expression that clearly picks up on Williams's claim in the preceding section that 'Work which bridges the gap between the rigidities of vulgar experience and the imagination is rare' (p. 134). But anyone who has seen visual representations of satyrs on Grecian urns will be aware that aesthetic elevation is not the only kind. Nor should we forget that the natural disorder of this poem is articulated *against* the unnatural world of property and commerce.

The wave rhythm of desire flows on into poem XX (pp. 136–37). The scene of this poem is a natural one. In the context of sea, sand and sun, desire is allowed to find its inherent fluency. The satyrs are no longer required to mark the threshold of 'the acquisitive – PROGRESSIVE force of the lump' but give way to an environment where the dynamic force of the imagination holds sway. In this environment, language itself takes a break from its symbolic function. Freed from the obligation to acquire and to progress, words may be offered for the libidinal pleasures of a rhythm almost purged of signification. As in the first stanza:

> The sea that encloses her young body
> ula lu la lu
> is the sea of many arms—

Such liberation remains a possibility throughout the poem but it is routinely quarantined by the symbolic realm. In the stanza just quoted, the play of sound is 'enclosed' by two lines that express a period, almost reducing the love song to the status of a parenthesis. Almost but not quite, as the extended dash refuses to close the statement – at least until the subsequent sentence announces its arrival:

> The blazing secrecy of noon is undone
> and and and
> the broken sand is the sound of love—

To shift into a surreal register, this poem presents a somewhat obscure object of desire. Like the mysterious young girl who drifts through city streets unnoticed before, it offers a glimpse of pleasure without bounds. But a glimpse cannot be sustained, is but a brief hiatus in the normal order of vision:

> a wink over the shoulder
> large as the ocean—
> with wave following wave to the edge
> coom barroom—

Except that this poem does not so much close as drift off, taking with it clarity of vision and clear meaning:

> la lu la lu
> but lips too few
> assume the new—marrruu

> Underneath the sea where it is dark
> there is no edge
> so two—

Perhaps the finish of the poem lies in the resolution of its final rhyming line. But, again, the extended dash exceeds this limit, just as the homophones, 'too' and 'two' signal a break from unification. A break that Zukofsky's poem VI seems altogether aware of. His poem begins by answering to the teasing invitation of Williams's 'wink over the shoulder':

> The sun—
> Sign on the wave
> On the shoulder: dun

But this poem is also schooled in the Classics; like Odysseus, when he gets tied up to enjoy the torture of the song of the Sirens, the speaker knows that to follow one's desire, as it is expressed in the pleasing voices of others, is to risk getting burnt. At the mast here is a surrender to the semiotic that will dissolve the boundaries of personal identity, even as it liberates language from the obligation to differentiate between one thing and another. Or, as Zukofsky puts it in a related poem of the same period:

> Siren and signal
> Siren to signal.[42]

In the poem under discussion (VI), Zukofsky evades the risk/temptation of this surrender by keeping his 'foot' dry. To be sure, it 'sinks' in the sand but total dissolution is harder to imagine in this element, where waves have a granular tangibility. Shakespeare's famous Sonnet 130 also helps to keep this poem's feet on the ground, reminding us that, in the wrong hands, nature becomes embroiled in the representation not of 'things as they exist' but as they are desired to be, particularly by poets and courtiers of 'predatory intent'. In this respect, a gesture that uses the body to signify – 'over the shoulder' – is transformed into a mark that registers the potential risk of taking that gesture seriously – 'on the shoulder'.[43] Shakespeare mediates the dialogue between Zukofsky and Williams in another telling way. As we have seen, Williams invokes Shakespeare at the threshold between his prose commentary on the imagination and poem XIX – 'rhythm: the wave rhythm of Shakespeare watching clowns and kings sliding into nothing'. In the context of poetry, moreover, something can come from nothing: the subsequent satyrs oe'r leap the gap 'between fact and the imaginative reality'. At the same time, they look forward to Williams's enthusiastic reception of Surrealism in *A Novelette*, since they preside over 'a fantastic reality which is false'.[44] In the context of negation, another something comes out of nothing, as the energizing force of the imagination shapes the grotesque – and shady – double of reality-as-it-is:

> Out of their sweet heads
> dark kisses—rough faces[45]

Double, double. In this fantastical realm, even what's undone can be dun, as if Zukofsky's attention to the relations that exist within and between words is part of a colossal effort to bind the desire upon which words, we and the world float. As if a pun objectified is a pun purged. 'Siren to signal' coordinates the required transformation about as efficiently as words can manage. And yet, how close in this effort Zukofsky comes to achieving the opposite of what he intends. Krauss's analysis of Convulsive Beauty is once again relevant here. It seems uncannily apt, in fact, given the way in which the first two lines of poem VI 'convulse nature into writing'. Neither the speaker nor Zukofsky is looking for nature's inherent mimicry, however, so maybe Altieri's reading of Objectivism is more appropriate. From his point of view, the conditions of desire are 'dramatized' by the transformation of nature into representation but, again, this is in the interests of a kind of purgation, whereby desire is steered into the structuring grooves of poetic cadence. I am reminded here that when Zukofsky discusses Williams's early work in 'American Poetry 1920–1930', he encourages 'the process of rehabilitating the good to its rightful structure'.[46] It is not too far-fetched to claim, in this respect, that 'The sun—' rehabilitates 'The sea'. Core to the sea's undoing was the simple repetition of 'and' that occurs in the second stanza. 'And' is a paradoxical conjunction, since it also separates the things that it brings together.[47] Its contradictory nature makes it a good candidate for the verbal equivalent of the double that, for Krauss, defines Surrealist photography. The double engenders 'an experience of fission' within the order of signification:

> [it] elicits the notion that to an original has been added its copy. The double is the simulacrum, the second, the representative of the original. It comes after the first, and in this following, it can only exist as figure, or image. But in being seen in conjunction with the original, the double destroys the pure singularity of the first. Through duplication, it opens the original to the effect of difference, of deferral, of one-thing-after-another, or within another: of multiples burgeoning within the same.[48]

To admit such duplication would be to flatten the emerging Objectivist structure along a restless and generative axis akin to that of automatic writing, or improvisation. Zufosky's poem avoids 'and', except to rehabilitate it incrementally, through the substance of 'sand' and the rest of 'stand'.

But how secure is this rehabilitation? The collapse of differentiation is described as 'torture', but what if rest turns out to be stasis? At the end of the poem, standing results in exposure to a withering repetition that is only half-heartedly relieved by the final word. The end of the poem registers the anxiety that the 'rested totality', if ever *fully* realized, would entail some kind of annihilation. To bind desire completely within the structure of the poem would be to wipe out the subject. Whitman's unorthodox nuptial hymn explores similar territory and is, I think, crucial for my understanding of the Surreal-O-bjectivist nexus. To remind the reader of this brief poem:

O HYMEN! O hymenee!
Why do you tantalize me thus?
O why sting me for a swift moment only?
Why can you not continue? O why do you now cease?
Is it because, if you continued beyond the swift moment, you
    would soon certainly kill me?

In its transgression of the classical conventions of the nuptial hymn, the poem paradoxically reminds us that Hymen's is a border that exists to be crossed. In a heterosexual world, this legitimate transgression admits the subject into an adult life of authorized desire. In symbolic terms, to suspend the moment of transgression would be to halt the social integration of the subject. In psychic terms, this suspense represents the termination of desire, which is death for the subject. And yet, there is a bizarre similarity between a stalled Hymen and Man Ray's *Fixed-Explosive*. Both represent a moment that persists artificially by removing it, in Krauss's terms, 'from the continuum of its natural existence'. Desire is not at risk, however, because such representations are not the end of the line but are themselves available to be read and interpreted.

Hymen, then, is the benevolent deity who keeps the pot spinning in the Surreal-O-bjectivist nexus, who reminds us that the rested totality of each poem is only provisional and should not be translated into a world vision. Here, the omens are good for Surrealism too. What a coo-coup for Convulsive Beauty it would be to capture Hymen in the moment of crossing. Hymen rupturing as the fixed explosive *par excellence*, the purest convulsion, the ultimate sign of desire.

'Symposium'

I want to extend this nexus further into the historical space of Objectivism, by considering the status of the 'symposium' that appeared at the end of the special, 'Objectivist', issue of *Poetry* in 1931. Hymen hovers over this 'event', both formally and thematically. 'Symposium' appears close to the end of the issue, after Zukofsky's piece 'Sincerity and Objectification'.[49] Situated here, it occupies a liminal space, creating uncertainty as to whether the two poems by Ford and Tyler share in the special status of the Objectivist issue. The classical provenance of the 'symposium' also suggests a thematic link with the god of marriage, since both inaugurate legitimate forms of desire. In his text of the same name, Plato does not distinguish between recreation and intellectual debate. Perhaps Zukofsky wants to signal a dialogic frame for the development of American poetics, rather than an antagonistic one. It is also worth noting that a good part of Plato's dialogue focuses on the relationship between the sexes.

Aristophanes' reported belief that humans have suffered a split in their original hermaphroditic state can be read as a psychoanalytical premonition, since this split begins an endless search for the missing part of the self. The sexual politics of *Blues* may well be one of the things at issue here and there is some reason to speculate whether the poems of Ford and Tyler are themselves in dialogue with Zukofsky's contributions to that magazine.[50]

Burton Hatlen describes the 'symposium' as

> a watershed moment … between two ways of reading Pound and between two poetic methods, one turning inward to explore possibilities of alternative modes of perception, and the other directed outward toward the physical world; and the 'Objectivists' followed the second of these paths.[51]

Hatlen's focus is the history of American poetry, a history in which the significance of Pound is already inscribed. For him, 'definitive fixity' is of more use at this point than 'nexity'; indeed, the antagonistic scene he sets demands it. Rather than exploring the 'symposium' as a zone where both Objectivism and Surrealism are in formation, he allows that complexity only to the former movement. Tyler and Ford are labelled as 'American Surrealists', as if the orthodoxy of this cohort had already been established.[52] Hatlen goes so far as to designate specifically the dialogue between Zukofsky, Tyler and Ford as a '"symposium" on surrealism', even though that word is not used by any of the participants.[53] It is not even accurate, strictly speaking, to say, as Hatlen does, that Zukofsky 'objects to a strain of "hallucination" in their writing'.[54] From a perspective in which Surrealism has already been recognized and vilified as 'turning inward to explore the possibilities of alternative modes of perception', the 'dictation' of images by 'intuitive judgement' advocated as one method of composition by Ford and Tyler understandably looks suspect. But if intellective states can count as particulars, why not intuitive ones?[55] In his response to their explanatory 'Note', Zukofsky does distinguish between 'two types of symbolism: the word as symbol for the object, and – hallucination', but not to dismiss the latter altogether, since 'objectivity and even merit may be claimed for the last'.[56] Zukofsky is more concerned to excise the role of the 'arbitrary' from the poetics of his interlocutors. Hallucinations can be objectified, perhaps, just as thoughts, events and things can but only if the unconscious mind is not in charge of this phase of the operation. Structure, it would seem, cannot emerge out of arbitrary combination; there is no place for Objective Chance in Zukofsky's poetics.

To the extent that they accept the priority of conscious manipulation of images, Tyler and Ford are hardly orthodox Surrealists:

> The poem is a gratuitous and arbitrary organism designed to contravene the hypothesis of continuous experience through time and space. It must *consciously* eliminate the assumption of a continuous

or historical type of experience by the projection of a system of correlated images having an inevitable dramatic pause.[57]

Their statement of position also points to an acceptance of the rested totality, in its insistence on 'an inevitable dramatic pause'. Taking into account both sides of the dialogue, the 'symposium' testifies to an absence of definitive fixity rather than a watershed moment. At this party, Imagism, Objectivism and Surrealism are in play. Thus far, I have emphasized the degree to which Tyler and Ford bend towards poetic commitments that will come to belong to Objectivism. From another perspective, we need to take note of their claim that the poem 'contravenes' the assumption of continuous experience. This statement is issued to support the case for the poem as a separate reality but it also implies hostility to rather than acceptance of 'things as they are'. In this respect, any distance between poem and world signals the potential for a critique of reality-as-it-is. The suggestion of discontinuous experience also prompts a comparison with Convulsive Beauty. Tyler's 'Hymn' celebrates 'one proud moment' for a grotesque jack-in-the-box that combines organic and mechanical elements. In Surrealist terms, the representation is a complex one. Caught in an instant of 'release', it closely resembles Man Ray's *Fixed-Explosive*, not to mention the 'Hymen rupturing' I mused on earlier. At the same time, it expresses a sensibility akin to European Surrealism's fascination with what Hal Foster describes as 'the uncanny confusion between life and death' that characterized 'the strange (non)human character of the mannequin, the automaton, the wax figure, the doll'.[58] Here is the poem in full:

HYMN

for one proud moment
is the lid rolled back and fran-
tically the birth of springs releases
hood of the humble hour, in which
growth of the sensual face
creeps from the creamy white stalk
like wrinkles of a spring wound
in a faultless conformity up to
the head

no where, when men decide
lust is a moment for shock will this
momentless jack-in-the-box fail
of its head and its speech
or the wordless twinge of its
wire-filled arm, for
one curved moment is

the ruff supreme: the
nose provoked: the
mouth articulate with

```
        rhetoric, and is the strained
        mechanical form ousted for
        the easied air the softer earth, suffusing
        all the grave childwristed brain—

        so, till the thing shall rust of
        using too many times the fatal
        button, dust or the remote will
        will not detain
        laugh of the opened lid, the strained
        cheeks or the crested cap from
        being shock of the moment:
        faultlessly the well-known
        secret fast on the click
```

Lacking in full stops and capital letters, this poem is as wound up as the spring itself. It defies geometric coordination; its spiralling syntax makes it all of a piece, such that contradictions in sense ('momentless'/'moment') are somehow allowed. The word 'shock' occurs twice, raising the possibility that this convulsion has a critical function. Hal Foster notes that the Surrealists were part of the Baudelairean project to 'redeem the outmoded and to mock the mechanical-commodified'.[59] Targeted in Tyler's poem is the investment of desire in the artificial excitements of modernity. Indeed, shock itself – figured by the 'well-known secret' of the machine's repeating logic – has been partially commodified. Partially, because the uncanny status of the 'ejackulabox' makes it available as a vehicle to release the human relations reified beneath the lid of the mechanical toy. This redemptive shock tells most when space and time combine to present – in the 'curved moment' – the grotesque double of the human subject, outlandish to both eye and ear. In a move that prefigures the oppositional method of Language writers, Tyler exposes the reification of language into 'rhetoric' by meeting one distortion of human expression with another. The image of the mechanical form is stretched to its limits until it admits its opposite; mechanical strain is suddenly punctured by a mellifluous image of natural relaxation.

Pound is also bound up in this Surreal-O-bjectivist nexus, although not in the way that Hatlen suggests. Zukofsky prints 'Hymn' and 'Left Instantly Designs' partly by virtue of 'their objectivity of cadence'.[60] In 'Hymn' the repeated use of the colon as a prosodic device is reminiscent of 'The sun—' but in the context of 'the strained mechanical form' it also indicates syntax wrought to breaking point. At issue here is Pound's injunction 'to compose in the sequence of the musical phrase, not in sequence of a metronome'.[61] Is it too fanciful to propose that Tyler's poem represents an attempt to redeem the opposition between these two modes, to resolve musical with mechanical measure? If so, the resulting synthesis is a radical reworking both of Pound's 'instant' and of mechanical time. The subjectivity of Pound's instant is retained but charged with a shock that precludes 'sudden *liberation*; that sense of *freedom* from time limits and space limits'.[62] This has to be so, since the instant occurs as a revelation of the coincidence between subject and object. The objectivity of mechanical time is punctured by the same coincidence. Tyler's poem implies that modernity must be measured in jolts that shake both humans and machines.

This chapter began by articulating the possibility of a Surreal-O-bjectivist nexus in relation to debates around the transition from first- to second-wave American literary modernism. In its revision of the Poundian image, Tyler's poem brings the discussion full circle. The grotesque spectacle of the 'ejackulabox' presents a different kind of 'grimace' demanded by a different kind of age.[63] Perloff argues that after 1929 the 'utopian work of the early modernists' could not be invoked without qualification.[64] The transition is a complex one; indeed, the crossing places are multiple and not always complementary. This sojourn through the Surreal-O-bjectivist nexus warns against the temptation to over-simplify the history of Surrealism in America in this crucial phase. Even as late as 1931, it is inaccurate to talk in terms of an 'orthodox' and an 'unorthodox' American Surrealism.[65] It is difficult to write the criticism of a protean moment and, to some extent, I have traced conjunctions between Surrealism and Objectivism that occurred in passing and were never formally acknowledged. Another way of putting this is to suggest that a 'marriage' between the poetics of the two movements has always had potential. My reading of the problematics of desire that shapes the Surreal-O-bjectivist nexus suggests that this promise lies in the effort to integrate subjective and objective worlds. Benjamin's image sphere still beckons. As we move into the territory and time of Language writing, we will find Michael Palmer expanding the subjective envelope within Objectivism. His writing also pushes for a poetic image appropriate to its times, one that acknowledges the prevalence of its informational counterpart but does not give way to it. Benjamin's critique of modernity is not only relevant to this effort, it is an explicit touchstone for it.

CHAPTER FIVE

Michael Palmer's Poetics of Witness

The complex temporality of influence

To shift from one of the foundational moments of Objectivism to the scene of Language writing is a leap that requires justification. Louis Zukofsky's 'symposium' with Parker Tyler and Charles Henri Ford, discussed at the end of the last chapter, may have raised significant tensions in the development of American literary modernism but it certainly did not resolve them. The accommodation of Surrealism continued to be awkward and contested. The advance of the Nazis across Europe made transatlantic passage a personal event for several Surrealists, including André Breton. Not that the presence of the 'magus' of the movement necessarily improved its standing in the United States. New initiatives did emerge: Breton began publishing *VVV* in New York in June 1942, while Ford took advantage of the flight from Paris to launch a longer-lived successor magazine to *Blues*, called *View*.[1] Despite these developments, geographical proximity did not necessarily lead to cultural exchange. William Carlos Williams met Breton in 1941 at a party to welcome the French exile to the United States. According to his own recollections, his attempts at dialogue were haughtily dismissed.[2]

In passing over this period, I am responding to the complex temporality which mediates the contact between Language writers and their 'antecedents'. As we have seen (Chapter 2), when Ron Silliman scouts around for a work that will (almost) serve as a precedent for the 'new sentence', it is to *Kora in Hell* that he turns. Charles Bernstein celebrates Williams's 100th birthday mainly through an appeal to *The Embodiment of Knowledge* and *Imaginations*, collections which included no material written after 1932.[3] The significance of Williams's early texts for Silliman, Bernstein and others depends partly on the fact that they became aware of them after their exposure to his official image as the national icon of democratic plain speaking. *Imaginations* was published in 1970, *The Embodiment of Knowledge* in 1974. The delayed accessibility of his earlier hybrid texts might then serve as evidence for the ideological imperatives behind canon formation, while the texts themselves had the rare virtue of offering a 'contemporary tradition'. More than the influence of Williams is at stake here, as the following remarks by Bob Perelman suggest:

> a clear distinction between the categories of modernism and post-modernism, from a poetocentric point of view, is pretty dicey. For instance, it's not really a distortion to say that the objectivists were coeval with the language writers. It's not perfectly accurate. But it's definitely not the case that the objectivists simply began in 1931 with the publication of the 'objectivists'' issue of *Poetry* magazine. Some of their careers hit brick walls and resurfaced or restarted in the 1950s and 1960s. The work was really beginning to circulate a bit more widely in the 1960s and 1970s. So that, when I was a young poet, George Oppen had books coming out. Now he was obviously an older poet; it's not like we were fully contemporary. But his work was coming out as I was starting to write. For me, the complete version of Williams' *Spring and All*, with the fractured Dada-like prose, came out in 1970, not in 1922. And for most people it came out that way.[4]

In Perelman's experience, then, the gap between modernist and post-modernist poetry is narrowed. To say that the Objectivists were 'coeval with the language writers', however, is not to say that their poetics are co-terminous. More than one writer associated with the Language school has noted the problematic role of vision in Zukofsky's poetics. In his lengthy essay 'Words and Pictures', for example, Bernstein notes that 'Zukofsky's *Bottom* is filled with a nostalgia for a primal world of instant, unmediated perception, severing eyes from erring mind and memory'.[5] On the other hand, this aspiration is not borne out in the poetry that Zukofsky actually wrote:

> If one didn't know Zukofsky's poetry, and had read only *Bottom*, it might seem that he would be involved with the direct treatment of the objects of perception.... Yet nothing could be further from the case. Despite his tenaciously 'objectivist' poetics, his works present some of the most realized alternatives to the poetry of sight in modern American writing.[6]

Realization in this context demands the 'the disassociation of language and sight'; what results is a recognition that words are not transparent but 'become solid, solace for the loss of sight of the world'.[7] Perelman, too, notes Zukofsky's 'essentializing premise concerning sight', the tendency to treat the visual sense as 'immediate and unquestionable'.[8] If this model of vision is meant to enable clear differentiation between subject and object, it has the virtue of failing, from Perelman's point of view. His focus is on the definition of objectification given in the introduction to the special edition of *Poetry* (discussed at the end of the last chapter) but derived from 'A'-6:

> My one voice. My other: is
> An objective—rays of the object brought to a focus,
> An objective—nature as creator—desire
>   for what is objectively perfect
> Inextricably the direction of historic and
>   Contemporary particulars.[9]

In its original context, Perelman argues, the definition is 'far from being either "rested" or a "totality" and courts the risk of remaining thoroughly subjective writing'.[10] As in my readings of Zukofsky's poems (Chapter 4), this 'deformation' relies on the play of signification, be it of 'opposed connotations', typography or syntax. Perelman's reading of the passage above makes the case strongly that subjectivity is part of the definition of the objective and, moreover, that otherness is part of the definition of subjectivity:

> 'My one voice' and 'My other' seem opposed, but the spacing and the colon after 'other' tend to unite rather than separate them. If subjectivity is being eliminated, nevertheless the objective is still personal: '*My* other.' In the next lines, 'An objective' is used cannily, under the guise of being repeated: the first time it is a noun signifying a lens and connoting impersonal science; the second time it is – or can be read as – an adjective modifying 'desire,' thus forming a phrase that is finally an oxymoron, since desire has to be felt by a subject. This tension is hard to notice because in both lines the word is interrupted by a dash. In the second line, however, the dash is not the sign of a copula but signals the interruption of the phrase 'nature as creator.'[11]

Ron Silliman links otherness with objectification too. His touchstone in this respect is not sight but sound. Reminding us that Zukofsky's parents spoke Yiddish, Silliman suggests that the poet's 'English always carries some trace of Other (hence *Catullus*), tending toward objectification'.[12] If one's experience is expressed in two tongues, neither one can be assumed to be an invisible envelope for subjective expression.

Palmer and Objectivism

This chapter will concentrate on the writing of Michael Palmer. Like Clark Coolidge – with whom he edited *Joglars* in the mid-1960s – Palmer is slightly *avant* Language writing in chronological terms. His tenacious interrogation of reference, however, occupies a similar field of critique and enquiry. He also shares with many Language writers a strong 'sense of interplay or exchange with the international avant-gardist movements of the century, an exchange which has been formative for so many of our more profound and innovative poets from the twenties through the eighties'.[13] I hope to show that both Objectivism and Surrealism feature in Palmer's own exchange with the literary past, although the 'past' barely covers their significance for his writing. Otherness is a nodal point for this discussion. On the one hand – and recalling Tim Woods's account of Objectivism (Chapter 1) – Palmer's search for an ethical method of representation means that he deserves to be considered amongst those writers who extend 'the discourse of responsibility in American modernist poetry'. Woods draws on the ideas of Theodor Adorno and Emmanuel Lévinas to construe otherness not as predatory or threatening but as an aspect of subjectivity that can be met with 'fidelity'.[14] Palmer's writing takes the desire to be faithful to others to its own demanding limit. In this respect, his work can be validly described, I think, in terms of a poetics of witness. Witness which is not passive, however, but active. Active witness engages a different kind of otherness, according to which alterity can be mobilized for critical purposes. What links his poetics of witness with Surrealism, then, is the stake it has in negation, its urge to disrupt and 'say no' to conventional representation.

The image sphere persists as a fraught but sought prize in the effort to resist reality-as-it-is. One of the reasons why it is hard for contemporary poets to accept the promise of Zukofsky's visual paradigm is the fact that they have grown up in and inhabit a social reality in which the image has been simultaneously evacuated and hijacked from the point of view of any critique not amenable to capital. In their ubiquity and their apparent equivalence, broadcast images seem unrelated to physical nature, irrelevant to political debates, so lacking in depth that they float through the psyche without conscious registration. And yet, as Palmer's writing testifies, the images of the mass media are, by definition, the ones we share and witness. In no instance, perhaps, does this paradox cry out more urgently for an ethical representation than in the case of US military involvement in other countries. For this reason, much of this chapter will focus on 'Seven Poems Within a Matrix for War'. To enter Palmer's texts at any point is to set off resonances in multiple directions. In this respect, a criticism faithful to its 'primary' material is a tall order but a worthy injunction. The first Gulf War was the immediate instance of war to which Palmer's matrix responds. In relation to that conflict, he expressed 'the desperate need' to reassert 'the critical and epistemological authority of poetry'.[15] My witness to Palmer's poetry has an ethical dimension, to the extent that it recognizes a similar need for criticism.

In interview with Peter Gizzi, published in *Exact Change Yearbook 1* (1995),[16] Palmer has talked about his early life in terms suggesting that the oppositional stance of his writing was provoked by the failings of American social and political structures. Born into an Italian-American household, he has described his youth in New York as shaped by the 'reality' of a 'characteristically repressive, repressed fifties middle-class environment – not without love, by any means, but constricted' (p. 168). The scene seemed set for some kind of Beat rebellion. Palmer's growth as a writer was certainly influenced by the New American Poetry but his recollections in interview (p. 168) assert that the wilful disaffiliation of the Beats was not ethically convincing for a generation witnessing the start of full-scale US intervention in South-East Asia:

> I think a lot of us of the Vietnam generation, in late '63 and '64 – as the horrifying reality of what we were facing dawned on us – we realized that we not only couldn't make do with urban displace-ment, we couldn't make do with existential alienation either, that that in itself was criminal, that it was a complicity in this thing.

Palmer was studying at Harvard at this time, where he arranged for Zukofsky to contribute to a reading series. The younger poet recalls the event as an iconoclastic one: Zukofsky stood out against the 'academic formalists' usually 'served up' at Harvard, and drew an audience from 'Cambridge's then counterculture-in-formation'.[17] Poetry and politics were closely intertwined at this point in Palmer's life; indeed, the stakes were upped further when he proposed Charles Olson as one of the con-tributors to the series. The Harvard authorities took fright at Olson's reputation for unruliness and pulled the funding. For Palmer, the con-troversy around the reading series provided 'an interesting lesson in the politics of culture' (p. 173).

His critical writings demonstrate that Objectivism was part of the solution to the ethical dilemma of writers belonging to the Vietnam generation. What Objectivism offers here is a poetics in which the subject neither retreats from the world nor seeks to master it. Palmer finds in the work of Zukofsky 'an ethics of representation', which emerged as Imagism began to lose its radical novelty and to degenerate 'into a passive and decorative form'.[18] Invoking the work of Christa Wolf, he elaborates this ethics in terms of 'subjective authenticity', which calls upon the subject to be 'prepared to undergo unrelenting exposure'.[19] To produce ethical representations is an ordeal for the subject, then. Palmer's assessment of the work of George Oppen sets both poets squarely within the 'discourse of responsibility' identified by Woods:

> He [Oppen] argues as well for a gaze turned outward, a responsibil-ity of the self to find its realization, its form as a thinking subject, its relation to the visible and invisible things of the world.[20]

Crucial for my argument is the way in which Palmer re-evaluates form as immanent to 'the act of (or in an active objectification)'.[21] As he moves away from the early Objectivist aspiration to the 'rested totality' he moves closer to the Surrealist commitment to the 'incessant work of interpreta-tion', in theoretical terms at least. Rest is always a transitional experience when reading Palmer's work; almost programmatically, he deflects or unpicks moments of resolution, and closure usually beckons only as a limit never reached. As will be recalled (Chapter 2), the 'incessant work of interpretation' is Peter Nicholls's phrase; the terms in which he elaborates its significance for Surrealism prompt further comparison both with Objectivism and with Palmer's critique of it. Because interpretation takes place in the realm of signification – where there is always a gap between sign and referent – a 'residual opacity clings to the object, preventing its complete assimilation to discourse'.[22] Interpretation entails, then, an element of 'fidelity to otherness'; whatever the aspiration of the Surrealist subject, she or he is unable ultimately to impose meaning on the world around her or him. Nicholls also makes clear that the work of interpretation is, for Surrealism, 'the very medium of the self's engagement with the world'.[23] For Palmer, *active* objectification performs a similar function, since it provides the means by which the self 'finds its realization, its form as thinking subject, its relation to the visible and the invisible things of the world'.[24] Palmer suggests that Oppen's goal is 'at best problematic', perhaps for reasons that the Surrealists might recognize.[25] As far as the thinking subject relies on writing, or any system of representation, he or she runs the risk of being *de*-realized, dispersed in a proliferation of meaning that cannot be controlled by a single consciousness. One of the abiding features of Palmer's writing has been his willingness to explore territory where the horizons of identity lie open:

> Poetry often seems a talking to self as well as other as well as self as other, a simultaneity that recognizes the elusive multiplicity of what is called 'identity.' It is heuristic, that is, a procedure of discovery within which identity may appear as negative or in negative.[26]

As we have seen, the temporality of Objectivism is a complex one. In this respect, it presents what Andrew Crozier describes as 'an enduring embarrassment to criticism and poetry alike'.[27] The problem is caused by the ability of the Objectivists 'to occupy two positions at the same time in our cognitive map of poetry in the twentieth century'.[28] Crozier has in mind the 1930s and the 1960s but, reading Palmer's comments in interview on his own work in the mid-1990s, it seems that Objectivism was continuing to animate the present of poetry at that time. Arguably, Objectivism lies in the future of poetry, too:

> And you take any of those terms that are currently being (not in a bad sense necessarily) looked at, 'authenticity' and so on; well possibly it's an interesting time to rearticulate an idea of authenticity. Not in a mystifying way, but in some urgent relation to work, beyond the postmodern queries which drove so many people into endless ironization, endless play, endless 'screen' so to speak, which becomes a sort or protection against that deconstructive critique. (p. 163)

Gizzi's interview offers a range of interesting perspectives on Palmer's life and work. The context is a discussion of contemporary poetics but is linked to another potential embarrassment to criticism, namely the temptation in literature faculties to 'fetishize' continental theory in the interests of their 'academic certification' (p. 164).[29] Here, the usual representation of Language writing as invigorated by theory is turned on its head with the suggestion that post-structuralism's potential for 'critique' was all too easily evacuated in an *un*ethical shift; in a textual world where irony is a given, not an option, the question of authenticity – be it for poets, theorists or academics – neatly becomes redundant.[30] Valid post-structuralist critiques of the subject have, perhaps, narrowed the space in which authenticity can be re-articulated but, in this respect, the belatedness of Objectivism is a virtue. Indeed, it is tempting to describe the critical situation of the grouping as 'traumatic', the Objectivist nexus as an unexpected eruption in a narrative that wants to secure both the history of modernism and postmodernism, and the terms of their elucidation. Despite its entanglement with disjunctive temporalities, Surrealism does not retain such virtuous volatility. Peter Bürger's influential account of the historical avant-garde made Surrealism crucial to the theoretical understanding of aesthetic production in the twentieth century.[31] From other perspectives, the Surrealist aspiration to integrate the self has stood out as a prime target for anyone stalking naïve models of subjectivity.

Clearly, for Palmer, the question of authenticity is far from redundant but is bound up with a poetics of witness. Particularly urgent is what Gizzi identifies as Palmer's 'preoccupation with the need to somehow reconfigure or think through or write the reality of war' (p. 167). Palmer agrees, explaining that he 'was also looking for a means of representation that I could feel honest with'. He goes on to analyse the tendency of 'an overtly political poetry' to align itself with 'newspaper reports', at the expense of 'witness' (p. 167). Also under scrutiny, albeit implied, is the recent tradition of anti-war poetry in the United States. For Palmer, the 'American tendency' is a *dis*honest one, since its main concern is to validate the politics and the poetry of the poet rather than to give witness to events. The logic of mastery holds sway in this mode: 'distant events' become legible as the signs of political commitment, enabling poetic texts in which the self celebrates its 'oppositional work'. In Palmer's terms, an honest means of representation must acknowledge two things: firstly, that poetry may at times be inadequate to represent 'horrible' events external to it; secondly, that witness involves a greater or lesser degree of mediation.[32] As far as most non-combatants were concerned, witnessing the first Gulf War was a highly mediated experience. In this respect, the critical 'encounter' for the poet is not with the events themselves but with the experience of mediation:

> And so what I tried to face (speaking of the 'Seven Poems within
> a Matrix for War' now) was, what we did experience of that

thing – which was the overwhelming flood of images, the controlled imagery that was poured over us, whether that be the exploding suns over Baghdad on the CNN nightly news, or.... (pp. 166–67)

If Objectivist poetics have a part to play in securing the authenticity of this encounter, they will need some qualification. Zukofsky's praise of *The Great American Novel* resonates with Palmer's understanding of authenticity as the 'unrelenting exposure' of the subject. Zukofsky says that Williams's aesthetic is open to 'the multiplicity of living scenes'; his 'expression' does not baulk at 'the numb terror around him'; history itself cannot be divorced from the 'becoming conscious' of the human subject.[33] But what kind of 'vision amid pressure' is available to Palmer at a time when the scopic regime is so thoroughly hostile, when the image has been wrenched from the poets and only a fool or a cynical manipulator of words would suggest that we might find therein 'the full sight of the immediate'?[34]

The critical force of negation is also under scrutiny in Palmer's search for an honest means of representation. Intervention of this kind is difficult when the state has co-opted its terms. As Palmer puts it, the 'reality' of the war 'was done with an extraordinarily skillful contempt for anything that might say no to it' (p. 167). Political and military leaders, it seems, have become adept at the fabrication of reality. Their contempt manifests their confidence that the majority of citizens will not 'become conscious'. If they were to, they would surely recognize the 'contradictions' of US foreign policy, would realize their 'agreement'

> to slaughter, with our experimental weapons, 100000 or more members of the Iraqi underclass ... and leave Saddam alone, so that Iraq itself would be crushed but not totally destabilized, so that the reality of those artificial Gulf states would not be terminally altered. (p. 167)

In Palmer's reasoned account of an unreasonable political disposition, there are uncanny echoes of the 'symposium' between Zukofsky, Tyler and Ford. He describes the contradiction to which the American people signed up as a 'hallucinatory conclusion'. At stake here, of course, is a mass hallucination which had – and goes on to have – fatal consequences for thousands of human beings. Now, poetry has to manage a social reality that is erringly fictive rather than protect reality from the irresponsible fantasies of errant poets. And what does it have to work with? Contrasted with the uncanny provocation of Tyler's jack-in-the-box, the images that 'flood' from the TV screen are, in Fredric Jameson's terms, 'utterly without depth' and will not serve as 'a conductor of psychic energy'.[35] From this perspective, it seems that Benjamin's long-sought image sphere is already occupied and subject to martial law. Palmer's ability to identify the hypocrisy of US foreign policy testifies, however, to the residual possibility of critical intervention in the public sphere. Being active rather than passive is what distinguishes the witness from the consumer and Palmer accounts for 'Seven Poems Within a Matrix for War' in terms of his effort 'to look into the contradictions that were *directly before my eyes*, the only reality that was, in effect, being allowed' (p. 167, my emphasis). In Jean Baudrillard's terms, the poems attempt to wrench both the writing and the reading subject from the 'spectacle of his own powerlessness'.[36] Full sight may not be possible but Palmer keeps faith with Williams and Zukofsky by beginning with his 'immediate' environment. At the same time, while experience is 'mediated by power', it is not necessarily saturated by it. In this respect, as Palmer states in the interview, poetry retains the potential to expose the weaknesses of rational discourse, through negation:

> what poetry knows is a certain not-knowing. And that's not just a Romantic negativity, a turning away. It's a specific area that challenges the discourse of reason in its authoritative rationales for things and its authoritative claim to knowledge. And poetry – even, let's say, a lyric poetry (using that term in quite a broad sense as a poetry that's personal, again in quite a broad sense, not the lyric poetry of the 'little me' that is churned out in America) – poetry has a force of resistance and critique. At least I would hope it does. Again, it's not something that ends up changing the world, but it ends up bringing something possibly to the attention of the world, and bringing something into the world so that it's not quite as it was before. (p. 169)

The resulting sequence of poems is modestly and almost hesitantly described as a 'construction which is not essentially a political one. I don't know. An experience' (p. 167). Unqualified as it stands, Palmer's description of the sequence can apply to the reader as well as to the writer of the poems; it may extend even to the reader of *this* critical work, who may not yet have read 'Seven Poems Within a Matrix for War'. Authenticity, I would suggest, is at stake for all of us. At the verge of interpretation, I am reminded of the way in which Zukofsky casts the critic's role in responsible and loving terms; 'no criticism,' he writes in 'An Objective', 'can take care of all the differences which each new composition in words is'.[37] In which case, the onus is on each critic to take responsibility for the differences he or she chooses to cherish.

'Seven Poems Within a Matrix for War'

To some extent, the dictionary has already taken care of my reading of this sequence of poems. Zukofsky would surely relish the word 'matrix'. Both semantically and historically, it exemplifies his claim that 'each word is in itself an arrangement'.[38] Its root lies in the Latin for 'breeding female' and gives that language the letters for 'mother' (*mater*). In late Latin, the word comes to signify 'womb'. In its origins, then, 'matrix' is a maternal place, a place of nurture and regeneration. I would like to think that the dictionary is taking care of the poems too. But this word is not immaculate – further along the chain of its significations, it fosters creations that seem at odds with the natural order of reproduction. In the middle of the twentieth century, it comes to signify both the mechanism of image construction in computing and a circuit for transforming different inputs into linear outputs in television and broadcasting. In Benjamin's terms, 'matrix' has converted to the era of mechanical reproduction. In Baudrillard's terms, the 'informational image' threatens to issue as its slick progeny. But a host of meanings have clustered around the word during the time between its classical inception and its capitalist reification. Its root definition branches out to signify more broadly a place or medium in which something is bred, produced or developed. In this sense, 'matrix' has anatomical, zoological and botanical applications: it is formative tissue, as well as a substrate on which fungus or lichen may grow. At this point in the edition of *The New Shorter Oxford Dictionary* that I am using, nature converts into the technology of representation.[39] In the late sixteenth century, you could read 'mould' for 'matrix', recognizing thereby the manufacture of type, or coins or medals. A commemorative function accrues to the word in the middle of the nineteenth century, when it points to the 'hollow place' in a slab wherein a monumental plaque might be affixed. It gains a little in glamour when it turns photographic in the middle of the next century, throwing itself into relief to receive and transfer dye in the formation of a final colour print.

In borrowing the history of this word from the dictionary I particularly want to register the difference between its natural and its mechanical instances, and to identify the persistence with which it brings something out of nothing, or shapes substance in a form that differs from the final product. In this respect, I would like to offer 'matrix' as a figure for 'a certain not-knowing' that poetry knows. The natural functions and technological applications of all the examples above support Palmer's aspiration to write poetry that does not simply withdraw from the world but can intervene in our habits of attention or add to the stock of available reality. Another way to think 'matrix' in poetic terms is as a hypothetical realm, a world in waiting. Logic puts this point of view well when it uses the term to describe 'an expression that would become a statement if its variables were replaced by constants (i.e. by names of individuals, classes or statements)'.[40] To the extent that poetry makes no claims to objective truth, it deals in variables, not constants. Palmer's writing often skirts round, veils or unstitches statements, offering expressions that seem to have arrived by chance rather than intention. Poetry that veers too far in this direction risks 'turning away'. But 'matrix' has a stake in the discourse of responsibility, too, since it can signify 'an organisational structure in which two or more lines of command, responsibility or communication may run through the same individual'.[41] In the context of oppositional poetry, the linkage of power, ethics and communication is a provocative one, as is the analogy between an organizational structure and Objectivist form. As a metaphor for Objectivist poetics, this kind of matrix appears benign, with the poet as the steady point of intersection. As part of a social or political reality, however, the individual stands out as a potential site of conflict. 'Relentlessly exposed', perhaps, to contradictory instructions, obligations or representations, we can only hope that he or she is able to make choices.[42]

To choose, for one, in what sense Palmer's seven poems will be 'within' the 'matrix', and in what sense the 'matrix' will be 'for War'. Like Zukofsky, Palmer articulates major issues around apparently innocuous prepositions. The title of the collection in which this sequence of poems appears is one such instance. *At Passages* introduces a collection of poems that can barely find a place, in which reference is a pressing but fraught affair.[43] In one respect, the seven poems are 'within' the formative tissue of language. Two of the poems are titled 'H'. Although the first comes at the beginning of the sequence, the second does not come at the end, suggesting that the 'at' of this passage is not simply a formal affair. If these two are 'twins', the start of the first poem hints that they might be the fruit of the historical union between US foreign policy and nuclear physics:

> H
>
> We sat on the cliff-head
> before twin suns.
>
> For all I know we were singing
> 'Dancing on the Ceiling.'
>
> Descending I became lost
> but this is nothing new.
> (p. 15)

'Within' signifies both a linguistic and a historical matrix, then. But the matrix of 'letters' within which Palmer's poems are composed does not shape history in the conventional sense of presenting a record of past events external to the text. For the fall-out of nuclear explosion is present in the passage of the poem, as an expression if not a statement:

> Unvoiced as breath
> voiced as ash.

Poetic expressions of this kind may be the most honest means to represent both the lost voices of the past and the continuing influence of past events. The dead victims of Hiroshima and Nagasaki can no longer speak 'for' themselves – their expressions, statements, pleas and accusations are 'Unvoiced as breath'.[44] But Palmer avoids the 'American tendency' to assume the voice the dead have lost; he offers no strident persona, gulping the air of outrage that the dead can no longer breathe. Witness remains possible, however, and once again it is the matrix of language where past and present subjects come to pass. In this respect, 'ash' is a good example of 'active objectification'. On the one hand, it signifies the almost total destruction of human beings in their material state. On the other hand, it represents and performs a kind (of) material persistence – when voiced, 'ash' coincides with the 'out' breath. This is not to say that witness is simply a question of disclosing the coincidences that language allows in different contexts. Active objectification entails the unrelenting exposure of the self, which is a matter of sensibility as well as intellect. Two stanzas on from the one just quoted, Palmer subtly registers that the conjunction of past and present breathes through a voice that grieves and is bitter:

> Echo and wormwood
> conspire at the base of the throat.[45]
> (p. 16)

Such a voice is unlikely to be 'for war' in the sense of speaking 'on its behalf' or 'in favour of' it. Adjacent stanzas suggest that this conspiracy is born of the not-knowing of poetry and, as such, speaks 'instead of' war:

> The difficulties with burying the dead
> she may then have said.
>
> But this letter is something like a door
> even if a false door.
>
> Unvoiced as breath
> voiced as ash.
>
> To that I would add
> there is a song opposite itself.
>
> To that I would add, we have drawn
> necessary figures from the sack of runes and tunes.
>
> Echo and wormwood
> conspire at the base of the throat.
>
> Snail climbing acanthus
> measures our pace.
> (pp. 16–17)

That a door might be 'false', or a song 'opposite itself', is an indication, I would add, that 'this letter' – which was never sent but always arrives – 'challenges the discourse of reason in its authoritative rationales for things and its authoritative claim to knowledge'. The means of representation 'necessary' for this letter, then, must derive from discourses beyond the imperious scope of reason, be they realms of occult insight or popular entertainment – 'runes and tunes'. But to book passage too far in this direction runs the obvious risk of erasing the voice from any matrix of power and, thereby, denying its potential for 'resistance and critique'. The poem – and the sequence – begins with an expression of community that most of us can share. Although not on a literal cliff-head, most members of Western society are at some point in their lives brought to 'face' the risks associated with a nuclear age. When the voice shifts from the collective to the individual, however, it signals how easily marginal discourses are reduced to distractions which displace engagement and responsibility:

> We sat on the cliff-head
> before twin suns.
>
> For all I know we were singing
> 'Dancing on the Ceiling.'
> (p. 15)

To be critical, then, 'this letter' must also cross paths and swords with the discourse of reason if it is to escape indictment as the hallucination of a crazed mystic or the disposable diversion of pop culture. In this respect, the 'figures' 'drawn' in the poem – elusive as they are – are 'necessary' to register the alliance of reason with force. Again, language is the site of the encounter, as 'sack' indicates both the critical resource of marginal discourses and their destruction by 'reasonable force'. I should have said above that language is the textual site of this encounter. The alliance of reason with force takes place outside the text as well. Language also participates in this encounter, more often as victim than as witness. In this respect, 'ash' points forward to the 'burnt pages' and 'the disappearing pages' that feature in the final poem of the sequence, 'or anything resembling it' (p. 25). Nor is this a generalized scene of the sword's mastery over the pen but a reference that shares in the particular relevance of the matrix to the Gulf War. In a 'brief coda' to a talk that Palmer gave to the Keats–Shelley Society in December 1991, he reminds his audience of a cruel irony that attended Operation Desert Storm, which had ended only a few months previously:

> Certainly it did not escape poets and concerned intellectuals that, whatever the causes and motives, a nation which designated itself as current defender of Western Civilization had been moved to assert its righteousness by massively bombing the birthplace of written language.[46]

This talk is germane to the current discussion in a number of respects, not least of which is its invocation of Benjamin. Palmer begins his talk by recounting how Benjamin's interpretation of Paul Klee's painting *Angelus Novus* had led him to discern a similarity between this image and 'so many crucial verbal figures in Shelley'.[47] What they share, in Palmer's view, is their 'polysemous' character. Benjamin interprets the figure as 'the angel of history', whose 'face is turned to the past. Where a chain of events appears to *us, he* sees one single catastrophe which relentlessly piles wreckage upon wreckage, and hurls them before his feet.'[48] Benjamin's subsequent description of the catastrophe as 'the storm [from Paradise]' sets the scene for Palmer's later comments on the Gulf War.[49] He draws on the polysemy of the *Angelus Novus* to 'refigure him as the Angel of Poetry', and emphasizes 'its uncertainty or ambiguity, its backward-forwardness'.[50] The prospects for Benjamin's image sphere are not good from the contemporary perspective that Palmer adopts. Against a backdrop of 'ten years of Reaganbush' in which have flourished 'a shamelessly exploitative materialism and a know-nothingism worn with a kind of violent pride', he points to utopias and revolutions undermined from within and to the evaporation of 'various malioristic futures'.[51] As already noted, the informational image has been active in this collapse – where it 'floods' on an apocalyptic scale in the interview with Gizzi, it 'swarms' in Palmer's talk on Shelley.[52] The contemporary 'marginalization' of poetry echoes the 'censorship' and 'suppression' of much of Shelley's work while he was alive, and Palmer takes this coincidence as an opportunity to state the 'desperate need' to reassert 'the critical and epistemological authority of poetry'.[53]

In such a hostile climate, negation itself requires some revision. For it might be argued that the informational image hijacks the inbuilt negativity of sign systems, away from critique. This is to say that the symbolic death of the referent in words and pictures has come to mask the actual deaths of beings, human and otherwise. In this matrix, the image stifles affect. To return to the first 'H' poem:

> From the screen poured
> images toward me.
>
> The images effected a hole
> in the approximate center of my body.
>
> I experienced no discomfort
> To my somewhat surprise.
> (p. 15)

But the poem is within 'this' matrix, not that one, so that the subject is at least able to register with shock the loss of affect. At the same time, when Palmer offers the absurd picture of representations capable of passing through the body, he gestures towards the redemptive potential of the image. On the one hand, the 'embodied' image reminds us that simulation only pretends that the referent is not there, a reminder which prompts a return to an ethics of representation. On the other hand, and in Benjamin's terms, he hints that the poetic image retains some power of revelation, out of which we might turn back the 'pacification of the means of representation'.[54]

In the formative environment of Palmer's matrix, the image sphere is replenished if not renewed. At several points in the sequence, representation conspires with physical nature. Often, it is the body that provides the physical element, as in this brief passage towards the middle of the first 'H' poem:

> The body has altered
> many times since.
>
> Has bent a little over on its stem
> and shed a layer of film.
> (p. 15)

I will let my attention rest a little longer on the second poem within the matrix, 'Construction of the Museum'. A dialogue with automatic writing demands my attention at this point. I quote the poem in full:

> 'Construction of the Museum'
>
> In the hole we found beside the road
> something would eventually go
>
> Names we saw spelled backward there
>
> In the sand we found a tablet
>
> In the hole caused by bombs
> which are smart we might find a hand
>
> It is the writing hand
> hand which dreams a hole
>
> to the left and the right of each hand
>
> The hand I called day-inside-night
> because of the colored fragments which it holds
>
> We never say the word desert
> nor does the sand pass through the fingers
>
> of this hand we forget
> is ours
>
> We might say, Memory has made its selection,
> and think of the body now as an altered body
>
> framed by flaming wells or walls
>
> What a noise the words make
> writing themselves.
> (p. 18)

This construction shares with Surrealism a strong interest in the physical aspect of writing.[55] To 'forget' that the writing hand is not simply a mechanism but part of our subjectivity is to cede responsibility for the representations we produce, to reduce writing to mechanical reproduction without agency – 'What a noise the words make / writing themselves'. By contrast, to 'remember' that the writing hand is 'ours' is not only to take responsibility for our representations but also to re-integrate physical nature and 'the inner man'. It is in this sense, I think, that the writing hand 'dreams'. Why 'dreams' and not 'thinks', we might ask. From the point of view of negation, unconscious memory might have more to contribute to the construction of *this* museum than conscious memory might have. Conscious memory tends to represent the past only as if it *were* past. Unconscious memory allows one to pass through the other, in a 'backward-forwardness' that the Angel of Poetry might gaze on with good grace. Unconscious memory speaks with what Palmer elsewhere describes as 'the other voice'; in 'the site of the poem' it speaks the past in the 'now-here' of composition and of reading – 'to the left and the right of each hand'.[56]

It will not, however, give witness in the form of public images arranged in the official matrix of a museum. This museum constructs our attention differently – imagine a severed hand, not unlike the one that appears in the middle of the street in the Surrealist film *Un Chien Andalou*. A crowd of citizens gather in the thorough-fare around it, anxious and curious to understand its provenance and its import. The frame shifts to an identical hand in a glass case, next to which a handwritten citation states: 'The hand is called day-inside-night because of the colored fragments which it holds'. The designation is cryptic, to be sure, but the hand may be a metonym for the kind of museum poetry might build, a museum which gives no rational account of an official past but in which time's breakages are tenderly tended and tenderly tendered.[57]

I want to think a little further about time and the image. The speaker in the first 'H' poem is unsure how to represent the passage of time and senses a conflict between his means and those of history:

This was many weeks ago
many times of days ago.

Yet as far as history goes
It was no time at all.

Many kinds of days ago
I should have said above.
(p. 15)

The second 'H' is also passing through troubled time, attempting to represent it in an adverse environment. The poem begins by re-opening the nuclear scene and bringing it all back home:

'H'

Yet the after is still a storm
as witness bent shadbush[58]
and cord grass in stillness

sand littered with the smallest of fragments
whether shell or bone
That city we are far from

is still frozen, still in ruins
(except its symmetries be renewed
by sleep, its slant colors redeemed)
(p. 21)

The image in the first stanza – be it poetic or photographic – is 'witness' to the after-effects of a nuclear storm. The scene of destruction unfolds in an image that also constructs a museum of delicate attention to 'the smallest of fragments'. Attentive observation is supplemented by the redemptive possibilities of dream. The scene is becoming increasingly surreal and the connotations of the 'still frozen' make it tempting to re-view the image as a tellingly literal version of the 'fixed-explosive' (discussed in Chapter 4). As both adjective and adverb, 'still' suspends the moment at which nature reels in the storm, wrenches it from 'the continuum of its natural existence'. In common with the derailed locomotive that gave Breton pause (see Chapter 4), the 'bent' attitude of bush and grass testifies to a loss of identity: nature is no longer nature when the bomb drops, but is convulsed into representation.[59]

Like Breton's image of the locomotive, Palmer's 'after still' depends on a subjective perception that is at odds with convention. In general, people who look at photographs accept them as records of the past, not the present. They are also unlikely, I think, to consider the objects depicted as already transformed into signs. In Palmer's poetics, however, the defiance of conventional perceptions of time is crucially bound up both with the authenticity of witness and with negation. To return to the first poem 'H', its unfamiliar expressions of the passage of time make sense in relation to his past thinking on periodicity. In a talk given in 1982, he describes a moment of composition that resembles the scene of Surrealist inspiration: 'A few weeks ago the sentence came into my head, "A week lasts as long as three lines of light"'.[60] As in automatism, the significance of this cryptic statement lay dormant for a while but in his talk Palmer conjectures:

> It is as if I were trying to project the measure of duration into some other area of perception, distance it to prove its foreignness, or my distance from it; and at the same time, as always, control it, manufacture an image.[61]

Such a projection is a negation of reality-as-it-is, since it departs from conventional measures of duration. These are constructed through 'recurrence' and 'periodicity' and work through representation:

> So it is that recurrence and periodicity allow us to project images
> of time onto the variousness of events, to make our particular
> measures in a sense, and to distract ourselves for the moment from
> time, to choose a moment from time.[62]

Images habitually produced in this way are suspect from the point of view
of authenticity because they distract us from 'the sense of specific duration'.[63] Although Palmer does not say it, we could argue that a sense of
specific duration is an important element of experience, as distinct from
habit. How is my experience to be specific if it is mediated through customary images? Images are necessary, however, to protect against what
George Kubler describes as 'a duration without measure of any sort, without
entities, without properties, without events – a void duration, a timeless
chaos'.[64] The *Angelus Novus* as Benjamin interprets him is at risk from this
'void duration' – the Angel of History needs images to differentiate events
from within the 'one single catastrophe'.[65] What the Angel of Poetry offers,
however, is something closer to 'an ahistorical periodicity … a moment
in which to dwell'.[66] This periodicity remains critical to the extent that
it exposes and questions the tendency of historical images to reduce and
homogenize individual experience. This periodicity also realigns time with
a responsible subjectivity, makes 'kinds of days' into 'kind time'.

In what I hope has been a responsible reading of 'Seven Poems Within a
Matrix for War', I have sought to sketch continuities between Objectivism,
Surrealism and Palmer's poetics of witness. As I suggested earlier, otherness
is a nodal point for these cords of 'influence'. Palmer's ethical representation of his experience of the first Gulf War entails both fidelity to others
and a commitment to alterity. His witness resists the temptation to speak
'for' others, be they combatants, casualties or other witnesses.[67] The matrix
generates neither a special sensibility to carry the burden of response nor
a public voice of official commemoration. Such records are not desirable
and not possible: not desirable because they are not ethical; not possible
because they distort experience – experience of the present, of the past,
of informational images and of the poetic sign. In the final poem of the
sequence, war still lacks definitive frames of representation:

> From the view of what is in any case long gone and never was
> A war might be playing itself out beyond the horizon
>
> An argument over the future-past enacted in the present
> Which is an invisible present
> (p. 25)

The need to address others, however, is pronounced. The lines just quoted
are themselves framed by a sketchy scene of an amatory encounter:

> Our bodies twisted into unnatural shapes
> To exact maximum pleasure

> From the view of what is in any case long gone and never was
> A war might be playing itself out beyond the horizon
>
> An argument over the future-past enacted in the present
> Which is an invisible present
>
> Neva streaming by outside the casement
> Piazza resculpted with bricolage
>
> Which way will the tanks turn their guns
> You ask a woman with whom you hope to make love
>
> In this very apartment
> Should time allow
>
> What I would describe as a dark blue dress with silver threads
> And an overturned lamp in the form of a swan
>
> A cluster of birches represents negativity
> Flakes of ash continue to descend
>
> We offer a city with its name crossed out
> To those who say we are burning the pages.
> (pp. 25–26)

On 'view' here is a collective of two whose carnal gymnastics appear to defy the world of destruction and death outside the amatory refuge – theirs is a matrix generating 'pleasure'. But the frame will not hold: the division between private and public, pleasure and pain cannot be guaranteed in this representation. This uncertainty is an aspect of experience, honestly expressed as a question to another: 'Which way will the tanks turn their guns'. As readers, we are part of this experience, implied in the use of the second-person pronoun. Another frame is dissolving here, in the reminder that our authenticity is also at stake, active in the experience of reading.

The demand made of others in this passage is balanced, perhaps, by the gift that comes at the end of poem. The change in pronoun extends the address to subjects who may not be reading the poem. At the same time, the alterity of otherness seems to be very much to the fore in the final four lines of the poem. In this respect, the amatory scene is even more suspect. There is something grotesque about their private union: their movements are 'unnatural' and express predatory intent. Notwithstanding the capitalization, the run-on into the next line implies that their (and our) pleasure is generated not by physical relations but through voyeuristic engagement with images. These images may be of war, or they may be of their own experience. The 'unnatural shapes' signal, perhaps, the transformation of a natural matrix into a technological one. In Rosalind Krauss's terms, this is 'nature convulsed into' a kind of writing (Chapter 4), as is 'A cluster of birches represents negativity'. But the liberatory potential of Convulsive

Beauty as the Surrealists saw it seems now outmoded. The image sphere does not present itself as a communal space where subjects and objects can meet in a beneficial encounter but as a plane, or screen in which they are both flattened into mere signs and where the logic is one of mutual predation, not reciprocity. To borrow one of the shortest passages from Palmer's *The Danish Notebook*: '"Flesh-Eating Virus Takes Another Life"'.[68]

In which case(ment), we'd all better look 'out'. This is a zero-sum game, in which the image virus draws sustenance at our expense. And yet, the fact that *this* reading, of *this* poem remains possible is an encouraging reminder that the predatory image sphere, fostered by material networks of power, is not yet total. The subject retains some agency to represent his or her experience in alternative forms that articulate resistance and opposition. To read Palmer's work is to experience how difficult this passage will be, fraught as it is with risks of complicity and bound as it is by the alluring law of its own counter-logic. If the poem ends optimistically, the 'we' of the penultimate line might be poets, whose offering is a place that cannot be officially designated and may, thereby, remain accessible to all who wish to go there. From this point of view, the community of poets is to be distinguished from the 'we' of the second line, which signifies a national identity: the American people who gave their assent to the bombing of 'birthplace of written language'. But the critic's witness is also at stake here, implied as he is in a community of aggressors that extends well beyond the borders of the United States.

Attending to Echo

In the light of this interpretation, it is no coincidence that the next section of *At Passages* – 'Six Hermetic Songs' – is declared as 'for Robert Duncan'. Duncan features heavily in the interview with Peter Gizzi, in which Palmer articulates the importance to him of the idea of a community of poets. Significant for my discussion is the way in which this community is defined both in terms of a relation to other writers and in terms of negation. Crucial for Palmer is

> that idea of imaginary community in which poets tend to dwell
> with others. Not to say that it's outside the real, but it's constructed
> through the imagination and sometimes in opposition to the prin-
> ciples of reality that are laid on us, all of which say 'you should not
> be doing this.' (p. 162)

Palmer dwells with Duncan in 'passages' that express a commitment 'to re-negotiate polis and the political' (p. 166). Another constituent is Williams. As we have seen, Williams also discussed the power of the imagination to displace reality-as-it-is. Palmer dwells tellingly with Williams in 'Alogon', a sequence eventually incorporated into *Notes for Echo Lake*. There is a direct reference to Williams in the fourth section, which seems to position him specifically in time and space:

> This is as good a place as any. A curious thing happened to me. A curious thing happened one day. I stopped and turned around with my mouth gaping open. What else could I do. Old Doc Williams from Rutherford will understand what I mean. So I find myself watching. I sit beside myself on a park bench.[69]

'Alogon' means 'without words' and, as Alan Soldofsky has pointed out, there is possibly a reference here to the difficulties Williams had in speaking after his first stroke.[70] So, in one respect, this difficult and 'unproductive' phase of Williams's career bears fruit much later in the form of a figure for the counter-logic of poetry. This is an 'ahistorical moment in which to dwell' – the historical Williams is dead and gone but the Williams who surfaces is *Echo Lake* retains the power to 'understand'. At the same time, Palmer bears witness to an aspect of *another* poet's life which conventionally goes unnoticed. Those who champion Williams as the representative poet of 'the unmarked voice' will not turn to this episode for their shining examples. Williams has already broken water near the beginning of the collection. He appears in 'Notes for Echo Lake 1', in good, albeit mediated company:

> Such as words are. A tape for example a friend had assembled containing readings by H.D., Stein, Williams, others. Then crossing the bridge to visit Zukofsky, snow lightly falling.[71]

The bridge may be literal, conveying a reference to Zukofsky's contribution to the reading series at Harvard, but it also represents the affiliation between poets from different generations. The musical connotations of the word further express how significant Zukofsky is for the collection and one of the ways to read *Notes for Echo Lake* is as a kind of fugal structure, interweaving the pasts and the presents of poetry. I would add, however, that echoes require careful attention, attention that cuts across the grain of our usual habits and eludes expectations of enlightenment. Once again, these notes float in 'kind time': 'Memory is kind, a kindness, a kind of unlistening, a grey wall even to which you move'.[72]

Echo, such an important figure for Palmer, performs for poetry the doubling that Krauss finds crucial to Surrealist representation. Shaping a voice that is both present and absent, Echo sounds the fissure in representation.[73] She will be the guide 'for' the final passage through my discussion of Palmer's work. What motivates this final sally is the suggestion that Palmer's concern to construct alternative forms of periodicity intersects with the disjunctive temporality of Surrealism. I have already implied something of this conjunction in my reading of 'Seven Poems Within a Matrix for War' but it merits more explicit description, as an aspect of method that has proved resilient in Palmer's writing. In this matrix of enquiry, the call to re-articulate authenticity might be reformulated – re-membered, perhaps – as a statement to the effect that authenticity entails re-articulation. To begin, another section through the interview with Gizzi. Here, Palmer recounts how *Notes for Echo Lake* came to have that title:

> I was looking through my notebook the other day and found a quotation I noted when I was reading Michael Ondaatje's *The English Patient* – ... with this figure who is no one, who is without a name, who is a crashed pilot for whatever side, it's uncertain who he was even fighting for and it's beside the point – and one of the quotes that Ondaatje uses at the beginning of the book is, 'For echo is the soul of the voice exciting itself in hollow places,' which he took from Christopher Smart. And I thought well, if *Notes for Echo Lake* were meant in some way to reconfigure a model of communication having to do with the figure of Narcissus and the figure of Echo, that was just a perfect, beautiful thing. But the recognition of it came later to me, I mean years later. Which makes it no less true to that figure one is after, it's just a gift – in this case from Christopher Smart via Michael Ondaatje – to the work that one does. (pp. 161–62)

On one level, this account serves as a practical guide to subjective authenticity. The self exposes itself to the influence of the work of others, relinquishing authorial control over its own material. To the extent that the significance of the literary work is not completely premeditated, automatism echoes in this process. Crucially important for a comparison with Surrealism is the way in which the import of the quotation becomes apparent *through the articulation of a delay*. In this respect, Echo is both the substance and the form of Palmer's recognition, a recognition in which both past (quotation) and present (*Notes for Echo Lake*) are altered. Gizzi suggests that this process of 'reading oneself back' into the figure of Echo is ongoing. Not the total illumination of epiphany, then, but something more akin to 'the incessant work of interpretation'.

As far as Echo unsettles notions of the unitary work of art, she also authorizes both the disclosure of work-in-progress – since there is no other kind – and a departure from the strictures of genre. Hence, perhaps, Palmer's keenness to publish material from his notebooks. Caution is needed here, as a false distinction beckons. What is *Notes for Echo Lake*, if not a 'note' book? And what of 'Some Notes on Shelley, Poetics and the Present'? This is a talk to a learned society, in which Palmer begins by reminding his audience that 'the Romantics themselves have taught our century the epistemological weight of the fragment, whether the sundered Orphic body and scattered limbs of Osiris or, less exaltedly, the quick thought on a scrap of paper'.[74] *The Danish Notebook* is a small book; it runs to fifty-one pages and was published with 'generous grants' from the California Arts Council and the Fund for Poetry, aided by a contribution from Marjorie Perloff. Thus are some fragments kindly gathered. Criticism might be easily tempted to treat *The Danish Notebook* as supporting evidence for the architecture of explication but the notes in this book resonate, both amongst themselves and with other notes in other books. The book might be described in Palmer's own words as 'symbiotic', simultaneously poetic, critical and autobiographical. Like *L'Amour Fou*, or works by Walter Benjamin, they present writing as part of a lived commitment to the world, as a kind of witness that pays no heed to genre, has no need to be 'written up' later.[75] In the preamble to notebook excerpts published in the magazine *Ironwood*, Palmer tells us that he has made 'a few minor changes for the sake of referential clarity' but has not tried to make the writing better. The text that results appears improvisational, continuous with the world of experience. In Palmer's words, it is 'often nothing more than rapid notation or recording of thoughts'. Further, the publication of the excerpts is not intended to be 'narcissistic' but is offered 'as an aspect of my continuing dialogue with poetics'.[76] Not, then, a privileged insight into the workings of the poet's mind but a feature of practice that highlights both the continuity of writing with life and the importance of opening the self to others. Echo presides over this text, not Narcissus.

In *The Danish Notebook*, witness is often configured in terms that suggest, sometimes explicitly, links with Surrealist constructions of recollection, recognition and coincidence. A salient example comes early in the book. Over the course of several 'entries', Palmer sets up a constellation of 'events' involving a walk through Paris, a brief love affair terminated by political necessity, and two other writers, Norma Cole and André Breton. To flatten this constellation into a linear narrative, Palmer records how an 'obscure emotion' came upon him while crossing the Place Dauphine with Norma Cole.[77] The sensation was not unknown to him, and he recognized it as one which 'often precedes the recollection of a vanished thought or experience'. Repairing to the Hotel Henri VI, Palmer tells Cole of the 'incident' in question, an affair with a young dancer, a Hungarian émigrée who had fled to France with her family after the failed uprising of 1956. The affair comes to an end after 'two men with thick Hungarian accents' appear at a party to inform him that the dancer is in danger and must leave France. At some unspecified time after his walk with Cole, Palmer leaves Paris himself to return to the United States, there to grapple further with 'the story':

> Returning to the United States, I wrote a tortuous version of it as a piece called 'Autobiography 11.' On December 2 of that same year, 1994, after completing the latest draft of 'Autobiography 11,' I came upon this passage in Mark Polizzotti's biography of André Breton:
>
> > 'A kiss is soon forgotten,' Breton had said elsewhere in 'Soluble Fish,' speaking of an amorous encounter in Place Dauphine – a square that always caused him an indefinable malaise. On the evening of October 6, it was the same Place Dauphine that Nadja led Breton to in a taxi. On the way she had offered her lips for the first time....
> >
> > A footnote reads in part, 'Breton later attributed this malaise to the realization that, for him, Place Dauphine was "unmistakeably the sex of Paris."' (pp. 18–19)

Coincidences tumble from this constellation of events. Witness the fact that Palmer recollects his affair with the dancer while in the company of another artist; that both he and Breton have an 'amorous encounter' in the Place Dauphine; that both Nadja and the dancer combine naïvety with a sense of danger.[78] But how surreal is Palmer being here, and what is the relationship to witness? We might start by noting that the reference to Polizzotti's biography ends with a footnote that recounts how Breton resolved the coincidence to which he was subject. The resolution occurs very much at the level of Surrealist aspiration, since it entails a moment of self-realization, in which Breton becomes aware of his own psychic investment in the physical topography of Paris. The autobiographical aspect of the notebook form makes it hard to argue that the series of coincidences which befall Palmer do not have some personal meaning 'for him'. That said, in the immediate context of his encounter with the dancer, Breton, Nadja and the Place Dauphine, resolution is posed as a conjunction between form and experience. Two entries on from 'Breton' comes the following:

> I am leaving in a few weeks for Paris, and I have promised to tell this story to Claude, if he will agree to meet me at the Place Dauphine on May 23rd, Nadja's birthday. Then this little notebook will be done.
> (A call from my French publisher. It seems that Emmanuel Hocquard's translation of my book, *Sun*, will appear in Paris during that same week.) (p. 19)

Since this encounter is *planned*, it does not participate in the oneiric quality of Surrealist coincidence. That said, it remains hypothetical, conditional upon the rendezvous actually taking place. Only then will the notebook form be realized. The word 'done' is ambiguous in this context. It could mean 'finished' or it could mean 'carried out; effected'. The latter interpretation, in pointing to the continuity between writing and life, helps to explain why the non-linear temporality of Surrealist memory is useful for Palmer as a formal procedure entailing and enabling witness. The delay through which Surrealist recollection and recognition are articulated is, it seems, more faithful to experience, one's self and those one loves. So, it takes Palmer two goes to get 'the story' under way. Anxiety is at stake here but, just as a *conscious* attitude to form shapes the story's resolution, so does it structure the 'trauma' of its inception:

> I broke off the above some weeks ago, unable to continue, fearing that I would fall into novelistic language in telling what, after all, is a fairly simple story, but one that I had repressed from my memory for many years. Now the heat today once again brings me back to it. I'll start again. (p. 15)

In an odd way, then, Surrealism inhabits both the past and the future of the postmodern. As an antecedent, it represents a 'defense of the self' (as Barrett Watten would put it) that was necessary at the time but which had to be superseded. As an aspect of the future, it contributes to a 're-articulation of authenticity', in part by proposing authenticity *as* re-articulation. As Palmer tells to Norma Cole the story of his love affair – 'as she ate ice cream and I drank beer' – he feels it 'turning into fiction', which he immediately construes as a 'betrayal' (p. 18). In this single, linear telling, the story is 'done' for. But the story told to Cole is only one – albeit the most 'novelistic' – articulation. It will not stand alone, monolithic and inauthentic, when the notebook itself is 'done'.

A second fragment in *The Danish Notebook* is a letter to another which begins 'You ask me to connect the dots' (p. 9). Have I entered a delirium of interpretation, or is there in this encounter with Surrealism an echo of Zukofsky's 'Sign on the wave' (Chapter 4)? If so, the 'done sun' would seem to support the view that, unlike Breton, Palmer does not read his Parisian experience solely in terms of desire. As with the two 'lovers' at the end of 'or anything resembling it', the affair he relates suffers direct intervention from the political realities of turbulent times. *At Passages* echoes more than once in *The Danish Notebook*, as here in a direct entreaty from 'another woman':

> A woman approaches me after last night's dance performance, holding a copy of *At Passages*. 'Your poems are all so sad! Couldn't you write some happy poems? I'm too old for sad poems. When I was young, I read Edna St. Vincent Millay (she recites a few well-known lines). And Ogden Nash – I always liked Ogden Nash.' (p. 36)

Perhaps this woman is not keen to read herself back into the sadness that she feels in Palmer's writing. Perhaps she expresses a timely warning to avoid the customary nostalgia of old age. Hers is a kind of witness to her experience of the work, however we choose to interpret her responses. This chapter has been listening for echoes of Objectivism and Surrealism in Palmer's poetics of witness. As echoes, these findings exhibit a dual temporality, shaping the past and the present of American poetry. Both are unstable; both remain invisible to some extent, to criticism as well as to poetry. My soundings will have accentuated the positive of the negative in Palmer's poetics of witness, have sought to take shapes amenable to his critical expressions, amid the pressures of a social reality that has little space for poetry. But I also wish to have registered the difference between this enabling experience and those in which the poetic sign is overwhelmed by events so horrific that they defy, as well as destroy, representation.

Witness: a short passage through *The Danish Notebook*, where Palmer contemplates the limits of Lévinas's ethics. The fragment in question comes soon after the encounter with the fan of Ogden Nash:

> The place where Levinas's ethics invariably founders: where 'the Other' cannot be equated with 'someone else'; where 'the Face' is faceless. (p. 36)

Witness: the photograph of himself, 'by Michael Palmer', that appears on the final printed page of the *Notebook*, above nine lines of 'official' biography. In Palmer's photograph of himself, there is nothing represented in the space where the face should be, only a flash of light that would have momentarily blinded the author, as its twin waved back from the mirror's surface.

'Nothing' is represented, I might have said.

CHAPTER SIX

Scorch and Scan:
The Writing of Susan Howe

At first sight of her biography, there is little to connect Susan Howe with the themes of this study. Born in 1937, hers is not the 'Vietnam generation' to which many Language writers belong. As a writer, her influences derive predominantly from the textual history of America, not from the experiments of the European avant-garde. She is fascinated with the Puritan testimonies of seventeenth-century New England and with their persistence in the American literary tradition. Emily Dickinson is a key figure in this respect, as are Herman Melville and Henry David Thoreau.[1] Not that the textual history of America includes only texts written *in* America. Howe's Emily Dickinson corresponds with Emily Brontë, Elizabeth Barrett Browning, Robert Browning and Charles Dickens. Shakespeare is also a recurrent point of reference for her.[2] Her maternal roots in Ireland have helped to shape her interest in the history and literature of that island.[3] Language writing is sometimes described in terms of its resistance to, or exile from, the academy. This description fits Howe in a singular way. In a literal sense, she was very close to the institution of scholarship. Her father taught constitutional law and legal history at Harvard, where both F. O. Matthiessen and Perry Miller were friends of the family.[4] His legal work included writing the biography of the distinguished lawyer Oliver Wendell Holmes Jr. While such proximity to the elite of Harvard left her with a strong perceptual memory of the skin on Perry Miller's ankles, it did not lead naturally into an academic career of her own.[5] Despite her 'genteel' Boston background, she did not go to college but went to Ireland, to become an apprentice at the Gate Theatre in Dublin.[6] It is also the case that Howe's writing and broadcasting have developed at more of a tangent to the academy than has been the case for other writers with whom she might be compared. Her interest in the irregular form of Emily Dickinson's writing, for example, put her at odds with Dickinson's 'official' editor, the Harvard professor R. W. Franklin.[7] Howe has, nonetheless, taken up academic appointments. In 1987, she was a visiting foreign artist-in-residence at the New Poetics Colloquium in Vancouver, and she became a professor of English at the State University of New York at Buffalo in 1989.

The tender recuperation of history

First sight is not necessarily best sight; one of the primary motivations of the current study is to qualify and extend the history of Language writing. This is not, as I hope I have already demonstrated, a question of *more* detailed, *more* extensive mapping of an objective field of enquiry. A responsible criticism, I believe, should tend towards a perspective offered rather than a gaze imposed. Notwithstanding the traps that language sometimes sets. In this respect, critics and poets alike work in a compromised medium; to speak or write the 'history' of anything is, potentially, to collude with a discourse of mastery that may be malevolent to some of the subjects concerned. I will have more to say about the 'prefatory' statements that Howe has written for recent anthologies of her work but for now I simply want to draw attention to two brief sections of 'THERE ARE NOT LEAVES ENOUGH TO CROWN TO COVER TO CROWN TO COVER', which appears at the start of her 1990 collection *The Europe of Trusts*.[8] The first section I receive as a *caveat scriptor* to anyone who would write any kind of history:

> Malice dominates the history of Power and Progress. History is the record of winners. Documents were written by the Masters. But fright is formed by what we see not by what they say. (p. 11)

The second section concludes 'THERE ARE NOT LEAVES ENOUGH' and points the way for the perspective I will offer on Howe's writing:

> I write to break out into perfect primeval Consent. I wish I could tenderly lift from the dark side of history, voices that are anonymous, slighted – inarticulate. (p. 14)

It is 'on' the dark side of history that this writing prompts tussles with the vexed question of reference. It is not necessarily the case that *all* of the voices here summoned emanate from actual people, but some of them assuredly do. Howe raises a mixed congregation of voices, including canonical writers, enthusiastic antiquarians, zealous ministers and family members. In this respect, she is engaged in a project of recuperation such that her writing cannot be considered as non-referential. The forms of her work routinely unsettle the representation of past and present but, in so doing, they open unexpected channels towards historical referents.

On the dark side of history, however, recuperation will not have been successful if it has simply returned those disadvantaged voices to the light. For the light of history is partial, partial to positive images granting full sight. Such exposure may both blind into silence those who are not used to it and obscure the nuances of their particular character in its indiscriminate glare. '*Revealing traces*' risks, in this respect, '*Regulating traces*'.[9] The mission is also compromised by the fact that in the archive of the 'Documents ... written by the Masters', when one figure is drawn into the positive, another is generally relegated to the negative.[10] Tender recuperation requires great care, then, and it is in this context that Howe's method bears some comparison with the disjunctive temporality of Surrealism. In exploring the connections, I will return to the discussion Freud's notion of deferred action. If the occluded voices that claim Howe's attention are on the dark side of history, it is because they have suffered a failure of translation. In this condition, they are without representation. In the image of writing 'to break out', Howe expresses a wish to address the traumatic suppression of dissenting voices within American history. Such a liberation requires a readjustment of the subject's relationship with time, an accommodation that will 'break apart the present to make the future once again an open question'.[11] 'Whose future?' might be a fair question to ask at this point. The women who gave testaments of their faith to Puritan ministers and the men who risked their sovereign masculinity in the chaos of the wilderness are all dead. If their trauma was partly a question of finding the words to represent their experience, are they released as subjects when and if those words are found? By the same token, if their trauma has been bestowed upon their descendants, in the blanks and the gags of the nation's self-narration, then it is all American subjects – including Howe – who wait to gain from a re-articulation.

Such resolution figures as one possibility in Howe's writing. When she declares her motivation 'to break out into perfect primeval Consent', the spatial metaphor binds her poetics, equivocally, to an abiding American theme of mapping and settlement, while 'Consent' points to social unity as a desired outcome. But the aspiration sounds naïve, or ironic when it pins its hopes on a return to origins. Howe's historical consciousness is far too nuanced for her to be proposing such a return at face value and it may be that here she is deploying a kind of hyperbolic naïvety to signal the nigh impossibility of a goal that is nonetheless devoutly to be wished. On the other hand, just as the gap between language and reality was turned to critical ends by the Surrealists, so is the failure of translation deployed by Howe to 'break down/break open the fixtures of historical representation and literary space'.[12] Without wishing to describe Howe's writing as itself driven by a compulsion to repeat – although certain scenes and situations do recur in her work – I would like to suggest that, as an American writer, she is necessarily implicated in the stories that the nation has both told and not told itself. Peter Quartermain puts the case nicely when he argues that the 'great energy' of Howe's writing 'arises from a series of tensions', one of which is between her

> enchanted fascination with and desperate possession by history and with language, and her intense desire to be free of them;

between her desire for the secure, the stable, and the defined, and her apprehension of them as essentially false; between her impassioned attraction to, and sheer terror of, the wilderness.[13]

A good place to explore this tension in terms of the equivocal force of deferred action is in one of Howe's distinctive forms. With what have been variously described as 'airy grids' and 'word boxes', Howe has peppered her more poetic work with pages on which writing has been dissolved to the point where words manifest singly, across intervals of white ranged both up and down.[14] I approach these pages as border zones between the tenacious grip of the Victors' records, extended in discourse, and the revelation of a verbal landscape untainted by the past.

As I have already suggested, trauma is, for Howe, part of the American experience, whether it manifests as the condition of the first emigrants, of the settlers gauging identity from the Unknown, or of mothers and daughters left behind when their menfolk disappeared to participate in global conflict.[15] To assert the importance of her entanglement with the nation's trauma is also to continue qualifying the relationship between Surrealist poetics and American poetry. As we have seen (Chapter 4), Peter Nicholls has paved the way for a critical division between the 'orthodox' and the 'unorthodox' followers of André Breton, between those who accept wholeheartedly the lure of Surrealism as 'a poetics of the inner life' and those more discerning writers, like William Carlos Williams, who receive it as 'a praxis of writing'. The implication in Nicholls's work on Howe (discussed below) is that she is affiliated with the second camp. While I do not dispute that Surrealism appeals to Language writers primarily for its innovations and interventions in literary representation, I hope that my reading of Howe's 'tensed' writing will remain open to the possibility that the partition between a writer's inner life and her praxis need not be absolute. An awareness that this dividing line might be permeable is salutary, given Howe's recent practice of opening anthologies of her work with prefatory texts that include explicit autobiographical material.[16] It would be a mistake, however, to imply that there is a secure generic distinction between the 'prefaces' and the 'poetry' they precede. The former do not elucidate or introduce the latter in any consistent or clear fashion. They are structured around the same motifs that drive the poetry and are routinely punctuated by dense, cryptic expressions as compelling in their beauty as they are renegade in their grammar. In my view, these texts are 'primary' material and I will try to meet them as such in my discussion.

Howe's close engagement with the dark side of history, her determination to seek out and identify with smothered voices, also aligns her writing with the 'discourse of responsibility' that Tim Woods has identified as one legacy of Objectivism (see Chapter 1). Indeed, her writing's bold reception of texts in which violence, confusion or fear routinely threatens to overwhelm intelligible communication merits comparison with Michael Palmer's interpretation of 'subjective authenticity' as the 'unrelenting exposure of the self' (Chapter 5). This exposure shares with Objectivism a commitment to particularities over generalities. At the same time, this preference manifests Howe's inheritance as an American writer working within a tradition of witness. In common with illustrious precursors such as Cotton Mather and Mary Rowlandson, Howe habitually sacrifices formal unity and narrative continuity, so that the writing can embrace the broadest range of 'singularities' possible. The following is a description by Howe of Mather's *Magnalia Christi Americana* but it suggests strong parallels between his roaming text and her own:

> The general style is oddly fixed and declamatory; yet the provincial nonconformist author constantly disrupts the forward trajectory of his written 'service ... for the Church of God, not only here but abroad in Europe,' with blizzards of anecdotes, anagrams, prefatory poems, dedications, epigrams, memories, lists of ministers and magistrates, puns, paradoxes, 'antiquities,' remarks, laments, furious opinions, recollections, exaggerations, fabrications, 'Examples,' wonders, spontaneous other versions.[17]

Howe's writing also allows for an alignment between Objectivism and Puritanism in the realm of the senses. In this alliance, hearing rivals seeing for sensory supremacy. When Howe writes that 'fright is formed by what we see not by what they say', she perhaps expresses a debt to Puritan aesthetics by associating vision with a disturbed sensibility rather than with a masterful intellect. The eye was not the sovereign organ for Puritans that it was for subsequent 'enlightened' generations, particularly in the context of a sacred text that was beginning to sound familiar when translated into vernacular English.[18] Howe has acknowledged the importance of sound both for the colonialists in New England and for her own writing.[19] She has also claimed that 'Poetry is a kind of music', prompting the speculation that her poetics might bring about a bizarre conjunction between Objectivism and the Puritan sensorium.[20] If so, however, it is not a seamless union. Tim Woods suggests that for Louis Zukofsky music serves as 'a model for perfection'.[21] Sound is a vital element of Howe's poetics, so much so that the symbolic order often yields to it. But the pressure from the dark side of history agitates against the resolution of sound into music. Cooped between this impossible 'upper limit' and a degraded national idiom, silence is a possible option, one that Howe contemplates positively in relation to Dickinson. Also viable, perhaps, is the courting of an uncanny resonance within language, another border zone where sounds are simultaneously familiar and strange. In this respect, the overlap between the Puritan and the Objectivist sensorium broadens further, to become a nexus that includes at least an echo of Surrealism. I have noted the importance of the figure of Echo for Michael Palmer (Chapter 5); for Howe it is often historicized in relation to the persistence

of native linguistic forms within English designations. Thoreau's openness to this unsettling characteristic of American identity, his recognition
of the 'understory of anotherword', is partly what attracts Howe to his
idiosyncratic testimonials.[22] 'Thorow', her 1990 work, is named after a
play on Thoreau's name by Daniel Ricketson, and emphasizes in its prefatory citations the slipperiness of American names:

> *Henry David Thoreau to Daniel Ricketson.*
> – am glad to see that you have studied out the history of the
> ponds, got the Indian names straightened – which means made
> more crooked – &c., &c.[23]

For Palmer, Echo is an emblem not only of a relationship between
sound and meaning but also of a community of writers impossibly conceived in opposition to the principles of reality as it is usually rendered.
Howe shares the conviction that writers find the significance of their
works in the expressions of others, and the range of her correspondents
shows a preference for those who have been denied general recognition
or have been recognized in ways that make them conform to a prescribed
range of cultural expectations. Williams belongs in this community,
and I am concerned in this chapter to discover the reciprocity between
his understanding of Puritanism and Howe's. At stake initially is the
Williams who wrote *In the American Grain*. In this idiosyncratic work,
which coincides with the improvisational phase of his writing, Williams
offers his own renegade history of America, one in which the Puritan
authorities are repeatedly taken to task and their legacy blamed for the
narrowness of contemporary life. In this respect, Williams's attempt in
the 1920s to alert modern American readers to 'the unstudied character
of our beginnings' prefigures Howe's undertaking to register the persistence of Puritan controversies in 'our present American system and events,
history and structure'.[24] One way of expressing this relationship is to say
that both writers seek to negate national myths based on assumed Puritan
authorizations of 'Power and Progress'. Howe's reading of Puritanism,
however, implies that the account of negation should be qualified in this
context. She reminds us of the powerful negativist impetus mobilizing
Puritanism's early phases. Communities dissenting from the laws of the
English nonconformist churches and living a touch-and-go existence in
the New World did not inhabit a settled reality and often contemplated
the abolition of *this* world. In *My Emily Dickinson*, Howe returns more than
once to the significance of negation for the development of American writing within a Puritan matrix. Indeed, Dickinson's 'penchant for linguistic
decreation' (p. 13) is what qualifies her – along with Gertrude Stein – as
'among the most innovative precursors of modernist poetry and prose'
(p. 11). Equally provocative, perhaps, is the implication in this text that
Williams's radicalism retains a Puritan cast, even as he embraces the critical stance of the European avant-garde.

The kind of criticism

Overshadowed by the 'frame structure' that I have just raised for my discussion of Howe's work, it seems a bit late to speculate on the kind of criticism that her writing calls for. But a sally in this direction is justified, given the questions she takes up from Dickinson and Stein's 'skillful and ironic investigation of patriarchal authority over literary history'. I am not keen to play the part of critic-policeman over 'questions of grammar, parts of speech, connection, and connotation'.[25] Nor is this chapter a hunting trip.[26] In this respect, I share with Hank Lazer an awareness of the risks of preying on Howe's writing. For him, this is an ethical matter that arises from the indeterminacy of her work:

> This resistance to unification is also why it is dishonest criticism of her work to cite coherent pithy passages from the poems as if the experience of the poem crystallized with some finality in such remarks.[27]

The 'resistance to unification' is a tactic to fracture, to stymie re-appropriation by the scribes of the Masters, whose archives are always comprehensive but ever elastic. In a similar vein, Rachel Back suggests that 'the enigmatic nature of Howe's poetry invites the rejection of the supremacy of monolithic meaning'.[28]

To suggest or imply a single, dominant meaning is also to prey on the reader. Drawing on Howe's own statements, Back notes the writer's willingness to acknowledge the reader as 'a full citizen of the textual terrain, with equal rights and obligations in the making of meaning'.[29] Although we might question the notion of *equal* rights, part of the reader's obligation, it seems, is to take responsibility for the 'difficulty' of the writing. In an early interview, Howe's answer to the charge that her work is 'inaccessible' was to say that 'it's accessible to whoever really wants to access it'.[30] In what I take to be one of the most honest criticisms of Howe's poetry, Charles Bernstein elaborates on this stance:

> Howe reverses the dynamic of the 'difficult' text excluding the reader by shifting the burden of exclusion outward. For the words are shut out at your own risk. *Inarticulate true meaning.* – It is not the 'marginal' anti-articulate text that is doing the excluding but the one who closes eyes, refuses to listen.[31]

These remarks *for* Howe remind me of the beginning of Palmer's *Notes for Echo Lake*. In general, we tend not to listen to what is 'inarticulate' or, if we do attend to it, it is as a lapse from or precursor to articulate expression. Bernstein's distinction between an *in*articulate text and an *anti*-articulate text prompts, however, a recognition of the need to revise our habits of attention to include the border between what can be understood and what cannot. To visit this space, the critic must break with custom, foster what Palmer might call 'a kind of unlistening'. This gesture is, I would like to believe, an ethical gesture.

Bernstein breaks with custom by offering 'only' 'paragraphs for Susan Howe'. This structure both demonstrates his commitment to what he elsewhere describes as 'a modular essay form' and honours by imitation the kind of organization deployed by Howe in prose works such as *My Emily Dickinson* and *The Birth-mark*.[32] This resemblance is not surprising given his claim that 'there is no better model of scholarship, or research, than the works of Susan Howe'. These works are exemplary for their openness 'to unanswered – not always even unanswerable – questions. Questions that never finish or dispose or encapsulate or surmount, but continuously examine.'[33] Unlistening to these questions entails, perhaps, a gentle refusal to answer them in a definite way. The modular essay is valuable here because it does not depend on an 'argument' built in 'linear sequence'. Rather, its constituent paragraphs, which are 'semi-autonomous', not disjunctive, present something akin to a cubist image, in which the object can be seen 'from multiple points of view or different angles'.[34] Such elaborate attention is at odds with the singular purpose of the predator. The 'shift' or 'torquing of perspectives' that occurs in 'the jump between paragraphs' might also be understood as a refusal to take captive the object of enquiry. In this respect, Bernstein's 'paragraphs for Susan Howe' complement and exemplify her aspiration to follow the lead of Williams and others in writing a 'fusional' criticism. Citing Olson, D. H. Lawrence and Simone Weil as precursors, she envisages such a criticism in the following terms:

> It seems to me that as writers they were trying to understand the writers or people (in Williams's case writers and others), not to explain the work, not to translate it, but to meet the work with writing – you know, to meet in time, not just from place to place but from writer to writer, mind to mind, friend to friend, from words to words. That's what I wanted to do in *My Emily Dickinson*. I wanted to do that. Not just to write a tribute but to meet her in the tribute. And that's a kind of fusion.[35]

As far as this fusion is a question of the relationship between words, as well as attitude, the critic might also aspire to 'meet the work with writing'.

Bernstein's outline for the 'modular essay' returns us to the question of reference in Howe's work. This kind of writing is to be compared with the 'new sentence' in its formal tussle with the conventions of critical writing but Bernstein distinguishes the effect of shifts between paragraphs from 'the rupture of radical or extrinsic parataxis'.[36] Bernstein, it seems, hopes for more than partial local coherence from the modular essay. At stake here is the difference between a method that keeps attention at the level of the writing and one that is itself attentive to a referent, or referents, of some kind. As I have suggested, the modular essay is kin to the forms adopted by Howe in *My Emily Dickinson* and *The Birth-mark*. Bernstein's respect for Howe's method is co-terminous with his understanding of her particular approach to the question of reference:

> Here's the rub: the historically referential (exophoric) dimension of Howe's work is not used to ground the poem in an extra-linguistic truth any more than the literary allusions that permeate her work are there to send readers back to canonical sources (as if in replay of High Eliotic Modernism). Howe's collage poems use their source materials to break down/break open the fixtures of historical representation and literary space, so the *work* – the poetic *activity* – exists at the border of representation and presentation, allusion and enactment, surface and depth.[37]

Bernstein's reading makes the point that Howe's work *is* referential but not in standard ways. History does not provide an objective reference *point* for her poetry but is a medium for her opposition to the dominant modes – including literature – through which the past is represented. Elsewhere, Howe has herself agreed with the suggestion that history 'is an actuality'. Responding to Edward Foster, however, she qualified his further suggestion that the writer works 'against' history with the reply 'In and against'.[38] The qualification is an important one because it makes clear that the writer cannot get outside history, that she is also a medium for its representation.

I am nudging the discussion towards Surrealism here, and the suggestion that Howe's version of reference might be understood in terms of some kind of allowance for repressed material. In speaking 'for' Howe, Bernstein endorses both her suspicion of official history and her scrutiny of it when he writes that 'History is a lie, but we are no better than dupes or fools if we ignore it'.[39] He also draws attention to the 'internal textual dynamics of backward and frontward reverberation' in Howe's writing, an expression that invites comparison with the complex temporality of trauma.[40] Peter Nicholls reads Howe along these lines, invoking both Sigmund Freud and Jean-François Lyotard to frame his discussion.[41] Citing Howe's own use of the term 'counter-memory' to describe her poetry, Nicholls suggests that 'History is grasped ... as a force which invades the poet', prompting a tension between a kind of memory that is persistently painful and 'its belated inscription in a language somehow disfigured by it'.[42] Automatic writing faced a similar problem with regard to the unconscious in general, of course. Nicholls goes on to discuss Howe's intervention in historical representation in relation to her interest in the 'idea of hesitation', a word that Howe's scholarship has traced back to its Latin roots, and linked thereby to associations of 'sticking', 'stammering', 'difficulty in speaking'.[43] In relief, perhaps, is the traumatized cousin of Breton's 'murmuring' unconscious and it is useful to remember at this point Freud's gloss on deferred action as 'a failure of translation'. Hesitation might also be understood as the captivity of a subject ensnared in the 'articulation of two moments with a time of delay' (Chapter 2).

Frame Structures

Such captivity manifests in dissociated passages that pepper Howe's prose as well as her poetry. In her writing, dissociation erupts at the level of the sentence, the paragraph and the page. In this connection, I am drawn to her rendition, in *Frame Structures*, of 'the story of Fanny Appleton Longfellow's death by fire', which occurred on Independence Day 1861, when she was preparing locks of hair to be sealed in boxes as 'souvenirs' of her two younger daughters (p. 14). This story is one of the 'frame structures' set up by Howe to 'preface' the collection of four of her early works.[44] Her version of the story covers three paragraphs. The following passage comes from the second:

> A spark from a match maybe hot wax ignites her flowing muslin summer dress. Her husband, sleeping in his study nearby, his custom always, hears short phrases not words. Compare the phenomenon of sleeping with the phenomenon of burning. I suppose him a great distance off in pastures detached from memory. Enveloped in flame she runs into vision a succession of static images a single unbroken movement under her breath 'dead woman' she bats at wing strokes. Arcadia Accadia L'Acadie sea birds clang. Why can't he see that the loved object will perish? Well we don't see dark spaces between film frames, why, because of the persistence of vision. God's sun-clothed bride wades backward while petticoat tabernacle body as in dream I perceive distance a great way off. She grips him. Print your symptoms of melancholia on a sheet of paper in a singsong manner now get better. He tries. (pp. 14–15)

Howe knows this story by virtue of a chance encounter with a significant object; 'a little blue parasol' belonging to Fanny found its way into Susan Howe's grandfather's apartment in Boston. From there, it was passed to the National Park Service – 'faded and tattered' – in 1995 (p. 14). The parasol came into the possession of Howe's family when Fanny Longfellow visited them one summer. It was passed to the Park Service because that organization manages the Longfellow house as a 'museum'. Over time, then, the parasol shifts from 'memento' to memorial, from family history to national history (p. 14).

This information is delivered by Howe in the first paragraph; in the two that follow, she writes for Fanny a vivid present that itself 'runs into vision'. At stake in this passage is a meeting with Fanny, which itself entails a complex relationship both with time and with discourses on time. Fanny's use of 'sealing wax' to fix her love for her children appears to provoke a conjunction, or problem, although Howe's paratactical expression refuses to clarify the connection:

> She has cut small locks of hair from her two younger daughters is using sealing wax to close these souvenirs of love in boxes. Two doctrines materialism and spiritualism. The objects which surround

> my body those which are near to my body frame a simple idea of
> time. (p. 14)

The absence of a verb in the second period keeps its abstract content in the
vivid present of the narrative – as Fanny's thought, maybe – but also allows
for a shift into the intersecting present of the narrator's reflection. The
grounds for this shift are sustained in the third period, where the personal
adjective also might apply both to the narrator and the character of Fanny.
In this way, the writing allows for a dual temporality in which the speaker
meets with Fanny. To meet on anything like common ground, however,
entails an exposure to risk. Fanny's story involves a tragic reversal of the
power relations between subject and object. Three sentences later, the narrator steps back to occupy the distance of commentary, when suggesting that
'Envelopes and boxes are often metaphorically linked with motherly contrivance' (p. 14). In the subsequent paragraph, after the ignition of 'her flowing
muslin summer dress', we witness Fanny 'Enveloped in flame' (p. 15). Just as
her materials escape her control, so does language ever threaten to spark its
own 'contrivance'. What happens to my interpretation if the link between
the first and second periods of the above quotation is simply a question of
number – two daughters prompting two doctrines? On the one hand, my
interpretation takes off in an associated direction, as I am led to reflect how
often abstract qualities present as female figures. On the other hand, I notice
how both 'Envelopes' and 'Enveloped' are the first words in their respective
sentences. This thought, only possible after, or as I read the third paragraph,
re-articulates the two nouns of the first sentence – 'Envelopes and boxes' – as
verbs lurking to combust in a future already tolled.

Perhaps the story of Fanny would be less fraught if she only had *one*
daughter. But the double works for neither side exclusively. Howe's version
of a narrative that is part of the actuality of her personal history is itself
ghosted by one of the Masters' voices. The reflection on the relationship
between objects, the body and time is picked up in the third paragraph by
a direct reference to 'melancholia'. When the second paragraph ends with
the claim that 'The wax is here just so things *are*', it is tempting to shift
attention from the particular narrative scene to Freud's discussion of the
mystic writing pad.[45] 'Two' attitudes towards time, then, expressed in the
work of one Master. In the one, the past is grimly retained through objectification; in the other, the past persists as traces. At one level, the meeting
with Fanny is at risk from the analyst's regulation of female pathology –
'now get better' – but at another, it refuses to regard its dissociated states as
ill. Patriarchal judgement – 'get better. He tries' – flares metamorphically
into a bereft man's attempts to recover – 'get better. He tries'. At the same
time, Freud's ideas about time are themselves re-articulated within the
frame of a particular, rather than a general, narrative. As objects, words
persist through time but the ambiguity of Howe's writing suggests that
their recurrence does not simply repeat moments from the past but articulates 'two moments with a time of delay'. Subjectivity is clearly in play

in this re-articulation but Howe stresses elsewhere, I think, that language itself is the agent of 'deferred action'. Towards the end of 'THERE ARE NOT LEAVES ENOUGH', she writes 'Poetry brings similitude and representation to configurations waiting from forever to be spoken'.[46] Language, it seems, shelters an eternal present.

The configurations that await the poet have significance for national as well as personal history. The second paragraph of Fanny's story begins in the mythical time of national commemoration, before 'torquing' that time into the specific narrative of Fanny's own memorial gesture: 'Independence Day. She is sitting near an open window in the family library' (p. 14). If one act of memorial mimics the other, so do they share a violent moment of conflagration that unsettles the fixtures of their representation. As a container, Howe's second paragraph conveys a war 'report', echoing, perhaps, from the revolutionary era. So violent is it, so detrimental to the records of both sides that it sounds as if it is only just getting through. It seems to have been scrambled in transmission, riven by the repetition of a 'shot' that propels it forward but remains so hot it will not be held in the formation of the sentence:

> The objects that surround my body those which are near to my body frame a simple idea of time. As shadows wait on the sun so a shot soul falling shot leaves its body fathomless to draw it out. The armies are tired of their terrible mismanagement not counting the missing. Envelopes and boxes are often metaphorically linked with motherly contrivance. (p. 14)

This is, I think, a good example of the kind of textual 'disfigurement' that Nicholls has in mind. Its tactics to fracture 'memorial' history remind us that 'The failure to speak fluently' is not a question of personal pathology on Howe's part but an aspect of political intervention, a 'sort of strength' that 'sets up a resistance to conceptuality and dialectic'.[47]

'Thorow'

The same might be said for those instances of Howe's writing where dissociation takes place more on the plane of the page than within the order of the sentence.[48] Her awareness of the compositional potential of the page is in part a legacy of her training as an artist but it also reflects her recognition of the materiality of history. If words are to yield their hidden configurations, they must be preserved as material artefacts. Where the voices of the 'slighted' are at stake, of course, these artefacts may well be partial, mediatory, or fragmentary and incomplete. Take, for example, the exploded verbal views that appear at the start of section 3 of 'Thorow'. 'Thorow' is the second piece in *Singularities*, which appeared in 1990. It is a text bound to Howe's experience of a specific place. In early 1987, she was a writer-in-residence at the Lake George Arts Project.

The town was 'a travesty', of both settler aspirations and the indigenous culture it overlaid (p. 40). Howe avoids, Thoreau-like, this degraded environment, giving herself up to 'the weather's fluctuation' and a re-articulation of the 'pathfinding' narratives of the 'seventeenth century European Adventurer-traders' who 'burst through the forest to discover this particular long clear body of fresh water' (p. 40). As in her version of the story of Fanny Appleton Longfellow, Howe's re-articulation of these narratives goes against the grain of official accounts produced by the 'positivist efficiency' of 'paternal colonial systems'. In the place where such systems tame and appropriate 'primal indeterminacy', Howe thinks 'a history of the world where forms of wildness brought up by memory become desire and multiply' (p. 40).

Rachel Back interprets the exploded verbal views of section 3 of 'Thorow' as the enactment of 'language's liberation, its release from the bonds of syntax, word units, and normative use of page space'.[49] But this reading lets slip the collision of some units of text with others.[50] Further, the block of text in the top right-hand corner – beginning 'Parted with the Otterware' – manifests fairly standard syntax for the first four lines. These are not 'words in freedom', I would argue, so much as renegade citations, failures of translation that 'multiply' excessively – like 'a very deep Rabbit' – despite 'positivist efficiency'.[51] These beastly projectiles are 'shot' through the same disjunctive temporality as the 'report' that sounds in Fanny Appleton Longfellow's account but are expressed differently. The wrenched dispersal of words on the page reproduces the confused spatiality experienced by the early explorers. This is not simply a matter of simulation on Howe's part, however, since some of the phrases might be read as coordinates from her personal mapping of Lake George. If 'Places to walk out to' and 'Picked up arrowhead' are received as citations from a journal she may well have written, then it is time as well as space that has been 'disfigured'. These exploded verbal views begin to take on a kin-ship with Freud's mystic writing pad. Sensitive as I am to Lazer's warning against quotation as a search-and-rescue mission into the polysemy of Howe's writing, it seems to me that the poem that precedes these scattered pages has cut a clearing for them. Each might be aptly described as

> The expanse of unconcealment
> so different from all maps
> (p. 65)

Note that 'unconcealment' is preferred to 'discovery', a word that is itself broken on the pages that follow by other reckless signs evoking primal scenes – 'disc lily root swamp Fires/by night covery' (pp. 56–57). Howe's clearing is not clear in the enlightened sense; she will not drag the past into the light. As a guardian of the 'inarticulate truth' of the nation, she tracks trauma. The difference between the dark and the light side of history resonates in this respect in the ambiguity of a couplet from the previous poem (p. 54):

Maps gives us some idea
Apprehension as representation.

On the light side of history, 'apprehension' means the exercise of power
through capture and custody; on the dark side, it is always tinged with
fear. To return to the poem that immediately precedes 'The expanse of
unconcealment':

tent tree sere leaf spectre
Unconscious demarcations range

I pick my compass to pieces
(p. 55)

Conscious at-tent-ion only cloaks the scope of unconscious associations.
On the border between settled and wild, language catches on gunlock
and leaf and the violence of usurping sovereigns avails nothing against
ghosts.[52]

The poem as border zone

There are other, more promising sites to scout for the kind of linguistic
freedom Back has in mind. The following 'grid' comes from her 1978 work
Secret History of the Dividing Line (reprinted in *Frame Structures*, p. 116). It
appears as a neat rectangle in the middle of the page, has no instances of
textual overlap (in physical terms, at least) and defies syntactical order in
an extreme fashion:

green chaste gaiety purity sh inca

deity snare swift leaf defile   dispel

poppy sh snow flee falcon fathom sh

flame orison sh children lost fleece

sh jagged woof subdued foliage sh

spinet stain clair   sh char sh mirac

To consider this poem as a border zone is to reflect one of the key themes
of the work. The title of Howe's text derives from an uncanny pair of
reports written by the same author. William Byrd's 'History of the Dividing
Line' was the result of his participation in an official survey to establish
the border between the states of Virginia and North Carolina in 1728.
Although not published until 1841, this work immediately did the rounds
of metropolitan society in England, 'providing them with an entertaining
and highly informative report of the natural details and Indian lore of
the New World'.[53] As Back tells us, Byrd wrote another account of the
expedition. Called 'The Secret History of the Line', it was not intended
for publication, since it satirized the participants of the survey, drawing

attention to their 'squabbles'.[54] Perhaps it is this secret history that we can hear being hu-*sh*-ed back into the dark even as it crosses the line to 'defile' the sacred virtues of 'purity', and chase the 'chaste' into 'gaiety'. Repression is unstable, however; to 'subdue' may well make the forbidden more attractive and the acceptable more forbidden. If 'sh' chases 'purity', then how much more seductive is that quality when it is rendered clandestine and not 'clair'? Two pages before this 'green' grid (p. 114), Howe offers – at the centre of the page, again – a quotation from *A Midsummer Night's Dream*:

> Thisbe: I kiss the wall's hole
> not your lips at all.

Like the rest of the mechanicals, Flute has a lot to learn about language. The spaced words in the grid may have lost the support of syntax but they – and the intervals between them – do not become empty thereby. Released by an economy more liberal and illicit than the unidirectional plodding of the sentence, association enters cheekily the breach.

> My voice formed from my life belongs to no one else. What I put into words is no longer my possession. Possibility has opened. The future will forget, erase, or recollect and deconstruct every poem.[55]

This discussion is becoming part of the future of Howe's writing – what am I forgetting? What am I erasing? How continuous with the concerns of the 'poem', how deconstructive is my reading of it? If this 'green grid' is a matrix in the *generative* sense of that word, then one of the relations it breeds in this reader's mind is with Charles Baudelaire's famous poem 'Correspondances'.[56] How viable is it to consider Howe's cryptic verbal topography as a 'forest of symbols'? As an image, it might well fit both the general and the specific contexts of *The Secret History*. Along with deserts, forests have been the stuff of wilderness for centuries. Surviving primarily as symbols in the poetic discourses of nineteenth-century Europe, they presented material risks to explorers of America in the same period. From the perspective of Puritan ideology, the correspondence that Baudelaire establishes between nature and signs bears comparison with the idea of nature as God's creation and God's text. The suggestion that nature's text is sometimes hard to interpret, that its 'living pillars' utter 'confused words', seems apt both for the early Puritan settlers, whose first encounters with the New World were often at odds with the biblical landscape they had been encouraged to foresee, and for Byrd's surveying team looking for clear markers of the land's organization.[57] At the same time, there are some striking similarities between the verbal contours of the two texts. The first word in Howe's grid echoes, perhaps, the colour of Baudelaire's third stanza:

> Il est des parfums frais comme des chairs d'enfants,
> Doux comme les hautbois, *verts* comme les prairies,
> Et d'autres, corrumpus, riches et triomphants,

There are perfumes fresh and cool as the bodies of children, mellow
as oboes, green as fields – and others that are perverse, rich and
triumphant,[58]

From the last line of the grid, 'clair' can be read as the adjective from the
French noun 'la clarté', which appears in the second stanza of Baudelaire's
poem. Part of the significance of the poem for the Symbolists was its advocacy of synaesthesia, a characteristic that also seems to feature in Howe's
matrix. In addition to the reference to colour in the first line, 'jagged'
invokes the sense of touch, while 'spinet' (which, like 'green', occupies a
significant station at one corner of the rectangle) signals both sound and
the harmonious resolution of mixed sensations.

Such resolution is the horizon of Baudelaire's poem. In the second
stanza, he writes of 'prolonged echoes which merge far away in an
opaque, deep oneness'.[59] As Nicholls points out, however, the 'unity' of
correspondence is 'a fantasy', since 'such moments seem to take place only
in recollection'.[60] The absence of grammatical and syntactical connection
from Howe's matrix might allow for the kind of sensory connectedness for
which Baudelaire's poem yearns. In addition to the texture of sound that
emanates from the interplay of long and short vowel sounds, different
senses are combined, as in 'jagged woof', where the reference can be both
to weaving and to the jarring sound of a dog's bark. On the other hand,
the extended syntax and prosodic deftness of Baudelaire's poem contribute
to the effect of 'merging' sensations, while also coordinating a temporal
distance secure enough to frame it as recollection. By contrast, the spacing
of words in Howe's matrix establishes them as discrete, although not isolated 'singularities'. Bearing in mind her desire to 'break out into perfect
primeval Consent', it is tempting to *see* the matrix as 'the sounds of an
open landscape, virgin territory'.[61] Landscape is not quite the word, however, since it implies land already framed, already prepared for the gaze.
The true pioneer, the explorer who retains 'wonder' and 'curiosity' for the
New World, looks wide-eyed at aspects of terrain yet to be arrayed.[62]

Except that the virginity of this terrain has already been 'defiled' and
'snared'. The synaesthetic union of 'green and 'spinet' is pronounced by
the corresponding stations of the two words at the border between text
and margin. Their harmony is strengthened semantically by the spinet's
alternative designation, 'virginal', and its sylvan cousin, 'spinney'. Not to
mention the aural pun – 'spin it' – that neatly binds them all. Were it not
for the 'stain' that draws the first and last letters of the musical instrument
into its own defilement. Were it not for the repetition of the injunction to
silence the new land of sound just as it is coming into view. Baudelaire's
poem begins with an image that prefigures the Surrealist fascination with
Convulsive Beauty. In the first stanza, nature is transformed first into architecture and then into signs. Howe's matrix gives Baudelaire's 'confused
words' a particular context in the mapping of America. In the second
line, the collocation of 'deity' with 'snare' suggests, perhaps, alternative

interpretations of natural phenomena within the framework of incomplete knowledge of indigenous – 'inca' – culture. In the same locale, we might ask whether 'swift' qualifies the operation of the snare or the escape from it. Is it a bird (Byrd?) passing by, or does it describe 'leaf' from a discourse of native medicine or theology that the explorer's narrative has yet to master? This failure (of translation) does not come as a surprise if we think of the repeated 'sh' as the *mark* of a fissure in representation, the hole in the wall of the nation's self-narration, through which the violence of its past returns to stain the official record.

But what of Surrealism itself? Breton picks up on 'the forest of symbols' in his discussion of Convulsive Beauty in *L'Amour Fou*. He is not interested in a synaesthetic resolution, however, so much as the correspondence between inner and outer worlds. His description of interpretive delirium seems apt for the Puritan pilgrim, anxious and in fear of a landscape transcribed by a jealous God: 'Interpretive delirium begins only when man, ill-prepared, is taken by a sudden fear in the forest of symbols'.[63] By contrast, the man who wishes to apprehend the convergence of his inner life with external nature must expose himself in both directions. Sensitive to signs that reach him below the level of conscious perception, he must also be able to interpret them as the answers to personal blockages in desire:

> I am profoundly persuaded that any perception registered in the most involuntary way – for example, that of a series of words pronounced off-stage – bears in itself the solution, symbolic or other, of a problem you have with yourself.[64]

Notwithstanding the parallel between this 'ceaseless interpretation' of self and Puritan rituals of self-scrutiny, I wonder how far Breton's psychological problem solving will come out to meet my reading of Howe's matrix. When it hesitates between articulation and silence, between expression and repression, it presents, perhaps, 'a series of words pronounced off-stage'. And yet, not all the words are *complete* words. Given that 'clear meaning' is 'inarticulate', *un*listening is called for at this juncture. The 'problem' of the American narrative, at least as it is articulated across official channels, is that so many have been 'lost' from it, 'subdued' by it. Dragging the disappeared back into the glare of the flame that burnt them black to begin with is not to restore them to their rightful place. Set in the interval between 'sh' and 'mirac', one letter might return the female subject to the American continent. Such a mirac-ulous intervention on the part of language waits always patiently, perhaps, along the 'jagged woof', beneath the 'foliage', in the sh-elter of poetry. At the same time, just as each solution is routinely superseded by other psychological problems, drawing the subject into 'ceaseless interpretation', so is desire elusive quarry in Howe's writing:

> The track of Desire
> Must see and not see

Must not see nothing

Burrow and so burrow

Measuring mastering[65]

The opacity of personal experience

Howe's matrix sets up a correspondence: between the past and the present; between her writing and the texts of Byrd and Baudelaire; between what we can see and what we can hear. But the impersonality of the composition, its lack of tone makes it hard to read, in Breton's terms, as the vehicle of a solution to a personal problem. In this respect, Nicholls seems justified in implying that Howe is part of that community of American writers who have mined Surrealism as a 'praxis of writing' rather than 'a poetics of the inner life'. He is at pains to exclude the personal from her praxis when he compares the 'opacity' of her writing with Ezra Pound's. Arguing that the intractability of her work goes beyond 'the particular unreadabilities of *The Cantos*', he suggests that the difference has something to do with the way in which history is experienced by the writer, experienced as text, at least:

> If poetic language thus becomes cryptic, it is perhaps because 'history,' *if not felt as literally traumatic*, appears partly unreadable in the wake of modernism.[66]

The reluctance to read Howe's writing through the lens of biography is understandable, particularly when trauma grinds the glass. But what are we then to make of the fact that the first word of the first matrix to appear in *Secret History* is 'mark', which happens to be the name both of Howe's father and of her son?[67] Or of the fact that she appears to include a dedication to both of these family members *within* the text rather than before it?

Back also draws attention to this embedded dedication and I agree with her suggestion that '*Secret History* may *not* be read without acknowledgement of its individual and highly personal dimension'.[68] As she points out, the other source text for *Secret History* is Howe's father's edition of the letters and diary of the distinguished legal figure Oliver Wendell Holmes Jr.[69] Particularly provocative for my discussion is Back's claim that 'Holmes' letters to his father function as an opening for Howe to enter into a dialogue with her own father as she *belatedly* pays attention to his life's work'.[70] Belatedness need have nothing to do with trauma, of course, but it may do here and elsewhere in Howe's work. Telling in this respect is the repetition in the second section of *Secret History* – headed 'THE LAST FIRST PEOPLE' – of a line taken directly from Holmes's war letters home: 'When next I looked he was gone'.[71] The repetition of this brief factual report can be read as a marker of the subject's attempts and failure to experience the feeling that might attend such a loss, if it had not happened so suddenly and at a time when Holmes had his own duties to attend to.[72] It is important to note that in their written form, each instance of this line is 'marked' with a difference from the one that precedes it. Whereas the first is capitalized, the second is not. The third instance involves a typographical shift of a different order:

> I am another generation
> *when next I looked he was gone.*[73]

In temporal terms, the use of italics signals a lapse into the past; as one generation succeeds another, utterance becomes the echo of citation.[74] This 'repetition with a difference' also applies to the doubling of the personal pronoun, wherein the experience of one subject is marked by that of another. Howe's own experience is on/in the line here, I think. At least, to the extent that the prefatory texts appended to two relatively recent collections of her work – *The Europe of Trusts* and *Frame Structures* – re-articulate the relationship between her life and her writing. Both 'THERE ARE NOT LEAVES ENOUGH' (1990) and 'Frame Structures' (1996) begin with the field of international conflict into which Howe was born. Both refer to Howe's experience of her father's sudden departure for the Second World War. Indeed, both documents record, in different ways, the significance in this respect of one specific day. From the former:

> American fathers marched off into the hot Chronicle of global struggle but mothers were left. Our law-professor father, a man of pure principles, quickly included violence in his principles, put on a soldier suit and disappeared with the others into the thick of the threat to the east called west.
>   B u f f a l o
>   12. 7 . 41
>   (Late afternoon light.)
>   (Going to meet him in snow.)
>   HE
>   (Comes through the hall door.)
> The research of scholars, lawyers, investigator, judges
> Demands!
>   SHE
>   (With her arms around his neck
>   Whispers.)
> Herod had all the little children murdered!
>   It is dark
>   The floor is ice
>
> They stand on the edge of a hole singing –
>
> In Rama
> Rachel weeping for her children
>
> Refuses to be comforted
>
> Because they *are* not.

> Malice dominates the history of Power and Progress. History is the record of winners. Documents were written by the Masters. But fright is formed by what we see not by what they say.[75]

From the latter:

> On Sunday, December 7, 1941, I went with my father to the zoo in Delaware Park even now so many years after there is always for me the fact of this treasured memory of togetherness before he enlisted in the army and went away to Europe.[76]

Nicholls suggests that the 'hesitation' of Howe's writing plants 'a kind of violence at the heart of poetic language'.[77] I would argue that this kind of violence is more than figurative, is an expression of the 'fields of force' which mark all American subjects.[78] In this respect, the opacity of Howe's writing can be understood not just in terms of an intellectual response to modernism's failure to make history 'cohere' but also in relation to a range of personal experience in which people and events have not always been 'clear'. As a result, I am concerned not to generalize about her praxis but prefer to think of it, again, in terms of a border zone. Looking one way, the differences in grammar and typography that distinguish the instances of 'when next I looked he was gone' may be viewed as evidence for the claim that writing resolves the compulsion to repeat traumatic experiences. From this perspective, Howe's 'generation' is of the same stock as the creative, nurturing matrix. Looking the other way, the sightlines are made 'jagged' in the fields of force that no observer can entirely escape. In interview, Howe looked behind the mask of learning and propriety worn by Harvard, to see the violent history behind it:

> Behind the façade of Harvard University is a scaffold and a regicide. Under the ivy and civility there is the instinct for murder, erasure, and authoritarianism.[79]

As we have seen, Howe's personal history is bound up with this institution. Should it be a surprise that her praxis is marked by the coercive and aggressive characteristics that she believes have shaped that institution? Hence, perhaps, the hesitation and concern she expresses a little bit later in the same interview:

> I hope there is something ... I don't know ... I mean that's why I am concerned that so much of my work carries violence in it. I don't want to be of Ahab's party. I want to find peace.[80]

At stake here is Howe's fear that her Puritan origins may link her with the 'dark side' of Milton's poetics, with the 'rage to destroy and tear down' that contaminates his use of 'beautiful words borrowed from other traditions'.[81] For a writer who opens her page to the words of others, possession is a risk. In a letter to Lyn Hejinian, Howe refers to the 'terror I have always had – about words and their power'.[82] A few sentences on from the desire to find peace, she makes a similar point when she states that 'language taps an unpredictable power source in all of us'.[83] The risk here is not only that of being haunted by the malevolent discourses of others but also relates to that aspect of her own work that Nicholls describes as 'courting the non-cognitive'.[84] From one side of the border, the realm of the non-cognitive is sorely tempting, drawing the subject towards ineffable spiritual uplift, towards 'peace'. From the other side, however, insanity reaches, threatening to pull the subject into the isolation of wordlessness. In the letter to Hejinian, Howe records her affinity with Shakespeare and Swift, both of whom 'were also obsessed with words and reality and afraid at times of going mad'.[85] Threatening here is the captivity of the subject within an order of language that it is beyond comprehension. As she asks of her correspondent, do 'words have interlocked rules of their own – that we may not really understand?'[86]

Precursors

At this point, I would like to return Objectivism to the discussion. Howe's engagement with 'precursor' texts from the dark side of American history can be compared with Zukofsky's concern to work with 'historic particulars'. Her sensitivity to the ways in which these external materials are not, in fact, altogether external but have the power to unsettle the subject aligns her poetics with Michael Palmer's emphasis on 'subjective authenticity' as the unrelenting exposure of self (Chapter 5). At the same time, this aspect of her work is thoroughly historicized by the tradition of witness in American writing. Given the roots of this tradition in the captivity narrative of Mary Rowlandson, it should come as no surprise that Howe's version of witness entails risk. It occupies, after all, a threshold condition between inside and outside. Historically, some witnesses have had more to lose than others:

> Early narratives of conversion, and first captivity narratives in New England, are often narrated by women. A woman, afraid of not speaking well, tells her story to a man who writes it down. The participant reporters follow and fly out of Scripture and each other. All testimonies are bereft, brief, hungry, pious, *authorized*.[87]

Possession awaits on either side: in the light, one may have to yield one's particular testimony to the abstractions of the official order; in the dark, one may disappear altogether in the yawning maw of other.[88] On this threshold, as we have heard, 'How(e) you sound?' is a pressing question – sh(e) lodges the line between identity and silence. Howe's 'green' grid generates a further correspondence, between Symbolist and Objectivist constructions of music. While music represents a positive horizon for both Zukofsky and Baudelaire, there is surely a difference between the 'convergence' that it yields for the latter and the discriminating arrangement of the fugue preferred by the former. That said, Baudelaire might have some sympathy with the suggestion that 'Zukofsky utilizes the sound properties of words as an index of aesthetic autonomy in his attempts to formulate a poetics that resists commodifying appropriation'.[89] Howe, too, would approve of the attempt to keep poetry out of the hands of predatory discourses. But how easily does aesthetic autonomy sit on the ground of witness? The perfection of musical arrangement is tempting in a nation where language is guilty of repressing the violence done in the name of the fathers but to withdraw from history is to leave that violence intact – untouched, unsounded. As Howe spins it, spinet is spiked by briars of spinney.

Zukofsky's upper limit is also brought a little lower by Howe in this meditation on the lyric:

> Albert Dürer said 'For in truth art lies hidden with nature, he who can wrest it from her has it.' A lyric poet hunts after some still unmutilated musical wild of the Mind's world. Unconcealed consciousness out in pure Open must be acutely alert if *he* is feminine.[90]

The writing of lyric poetry had a contradictory profile in the nineteenth century. By many it was deemed a feminine activity, even when predominantly practised by men. This mixed identity could work against the male poet trying to make his mark in a market partitioned along gender as well as class lines. But Howe warns here against the lyric poet who would wear femininity to cloak *his* predatory intent.[91] To be alert in this situation is to realize the subordination, the entrapment that may attend the identification of the feminine with nature's purity, her lack of guile and her aesthetic perception. In this respect, when Baudelaire and Zukofsky celebrate music, they both overlook the fact that, historically, that realm has been for many women an enclosure kindred to silence. Witness the genteel lady as decorative tinkler, as caged bird singing. Dürer lets the cloak slip in the violence of his imagery, while Howe's alertness makes that slippage stick. Future readers may well ask what *kind* of man passes through the forest of symbols. In *her* Emily Dickinson, Howe has already proposed and argued for the kind of woman who escapes absorption into 'a shadowy and deep oneness'.[92]

The motif of the hunt also features in what I take to be one of the most compelling images in *My Emily Dickinson*. In a section headed 'ATTRACTION INITIATION AND MURDEROUS INTENTION', Howe revisits Timothy Flint's '"brief sketch of a night *fire* hunt"' (p. 95). This sketch comes from Flint's *The First White Man of the West, or the Life and Exploits of Col. Dan'l Boone*. Flint is described not as a historian but as 'the most popular interpreter of the West to the East during the first half of the nineteenth century' (p. 96). For Flint, the fire hunt is both an anthropological detail of pioneer life – in which a pair of hunters find deer at night by stupefying them with pine knot torches, and detecting them by the reflected gleam in their eyes – and a mythographic tactic whereby Boone mistakes his future wife for a deer, is especially attracted to her for that reason and is able thereby to symbolically wed the wilderness. Howe notes the way in which Flint deploys 'archetypical imagery' and comparisons of 'the hunter's quasi-mystical "calling" to that of a painter or poet', all to domesticate the violent character of frontier experience for readers in the east. As an easterner, Howe might wish to take shelter in the civilized fabric of this narrative. Instead, she evades 'Flint lock' by offering the poem as a fire hunt, tending tinder to his flimsy structure:

> The poem is a fire-hunt, the Poet an animal charmed in one spot, eyes fixed to the light. My precursor attracts me to my future. Fixed purpose is the free spirit of fire. Conversion of consciousness – metamorphosis, may be a flight into wordlessness. Creation was never possession. Daniel Boone willingly cut himself away from civilization's positive progress, in order to re-enter a clear morning of Nature's primeval measuring. To risk the game he married the game and was one with the Wild he roamed. Out of America's text-free past, sounds spelled *kain-tuck-kee* are an Indian place. (p. 97)

Whereas Flint rendered the dangerous aesthetic, Howe's parable returns the risk to poetry. 'Howe you sound' remains a vital question; survival itself is at stake.

Dickinson is the 'precursor' closest to the light in this passage but there are also echoes to be heard, I think, of Williams's wrestling with civilized forms of language in *The Great American Novel*. This hybrid text is his attempt to sever writing from 'civilization's positive progress', to break words free from the identity of 'possession' with 'acquisition'. From this perspective, despite the technological advances of the nation at the beginning of the twentieth century, words have precious little space to roam. The narrative of this 'great' American novel can speed its subject, in a Pullman car, through 'the great spaces of New Jersey, Pennsylvania, Ohio, Indiana' but he remains 'ground between two wheels'.[93] Add to this constriction the inherent belatedness of language – the status of words as 'the flesh of yesterday' – and the writer's passage seems mired in an equivocal medium. At this extreme, Williams contemplates his own version of 'wordlessness':

> Words are the flesh of yesterday. Words roll, spin, flare up, rumble, trickle, foam – Slowly they lose momentum. Slowly they cease to stir. At last they break up into their letters – Out of them jumps the worm that was – His hairy feet tremble upon them.[94]

Williams here construes creation in Dadaist terms, as always corresponding with destruction. The hairy-footed worm signals the primitivist bent of this construction, as well as its negation of the Christian creation myth. Whereas Williams seems to be applying a generalized, maybe even a romanticized, model of language's fate in the cycles of history,

Howe regards wordlessness as a particular element in the English settlers' experience of the New World. Given the traumatic character of this experience – and here I risk a generalization of my own – wordlessness is a *recurring* element, one that she encounters, too. Indeed, this is one way of interpreting the intervals between words in her verbal matrices. In 'Encloser', she draws attention to the fact that early Puritan accounts of the New World were tested by 'the threat of openness. Something quite new there might be *no* words for.'[95] The terms in which she describes the testimonial response of the Puritans to this threat suggest a continuity between their praxis and her own:

> Here is a kind of desperate dependency on biblical quotations. The quotations become a second voice. Often a paternal and a contra-dictory one. The syntax is choppy and nervous.[96]

Howe's outlook diverges from this Puritan line in important respects, however. Her version of the fire hunt illuminates a more promising horizon for American poetry. If the pioneer-poet is prepared to risk her self to the other of American civilization, she is not necessarily condemned to a recurring encounter with wordlessness but may at least reach towards a kind of clearing, where the relationship between settlers and natives, past and present has not been concluded. It is sound that measures what ground there is for this environment, unsettling familiar designations with a resonance which, although uncanny, is affirmative if allowed: 'Out of America's text-free past, sounds spelled *kain-tuck-kee* are an Indian place'. Again, the concept of deferred action seems relevant here. Howe the 'initiate' poet is 'attracted' back to her 'precursor', to find her own way forward. Similarly, sounding the oral culture of America's indigenous peoples might fracture the past of dividing into a future of communing. In this respect, Howe's 'articulation of sound forms in time' performs what Forrester describes as 'a transferential function in which the past dissolves the present such that the future becomes once again an open question' (see Chapter 2). I hope it is not predatory to suggest that this theoretical perspective is kin to Howe's liberating announcement that 'A poem is an invocation, rebellious return to the blessedness of beginning again, wandering free in pure process of forgetting and finding'.[97]

Williams has wandered in and out of my discussion of Howe's work but I want to end this chapter by considering in a little more depth the relationship between their respective paths. At issue here is not just a range of parallel themes and practices but a model of influence that might itself be considered in terms of deferred action. Howe surely points in this direction when she places the 'attraction' of her precursor in the present rather than the past. Unspecified, Howe's 'precursor' is open. In this respect, Boone's flight from civilization prefigures the contradictory interventions in American history initiated by both Howe and Williams. What qualifies this flight as intervention rather than withdrawal is its power to negate the ordered categories of reality-as-it-is. From this point of view, Boone, Dickinson and Howe meet in the 'imaginary community' of writers proposed by Michael Palmer (Chapter 5). A few sentences after the sounding of *kain-tuck-kee*, Howe makes a statement of poetics that resonates with Williams's avowal of 'a fantastic reality which is false' (Chapter 3) and with Palmer's 'other voice' (Chapter 5). 'Connections', she writes at the end of the paragraph, 'between unconnected things are the unreal reality of Poetry'.[98]

If influence is to be read under the rubric of deferred action, then the literary past must be open to re-articulation as well as the future. Howe's reading of Puritanism in *My Emily Dickinson* profiles, but never identifies, a Williams whose poetics were more closely aligned with his nation's English origins than is usually allowed. Again, the link is through negation. From the perspective of a new community struggling to sustain itself in a physically hostile environment, the nature of reality is not to be taken for granted. This is a disturbing situation which demands ideological input. Writing of the first Calvinist settlements on the eastern seaboard of America, Howe notes that 'the idea that our visible world is a whim and might be dissolved at any time hung on tenaciously' (p. 39). The doctrinal consequence of this belief was the renunciation of *this* world, in preparation for the next. In this respect, Calvinism negates worldly recognition and worldly accomplishments. Williams's disdain for the materialistic and the populist aspects of modernity sound familiar in this setting. Moreover, sheltered within Howe's meticulous delineation of a Dissenting community is a glowing affinity between Williams and the renegade Puritan minister Jonathan Edwards. Edwards was exiled from his congregation in 1750, banished 'by circumstance and choice' to the frontier zone of Stockbridge. It is precisely 'Edwards' negativity, his disciplined journey through conscious despair, humiliation, and the joy of submission to an arbitrary and absent ordering of the Universe' that qualifies him as a significant precursor for Dickinson. Howe goes on to suggest that it is in their shared negativity that 'these two' are both 'prophets of American Modernism' (p. 49).

The commitment Williams makes in his modernist history, his efforts in *In the American Grain* to 'rename things seen' are similarly foreshadowed in the connections that Howe draws between Edwards, Dickinson and John Locke's *Essay Concerning Human Understanding*. Williams would surely have felt sympathy for Locke's lesson to Edwards, that 'words are annexed to reality by sensation, facts charged with meaning by an intelligence behind them', and that the universe is 'organized around the act of perception' (pp. 49–50).[99] In this nexus, the modernist anxiety to 'make it new' has already been experienced by the Puritan minister:

> If language imposes on the understanding names which familiarity has deadened, how does a minister preach a sermon when words and images have become predictable? Ideas must be stripped to their essence, rhetorical embroidery torn off. (p. 50)

So is Williams's redesignation of American history articulated against custom's indiscriminate haul/hall of labels, in which 'things seen' have become 'now lost in chaos of borrowed titles, many of them inappropriate, under which the true character lies hid'.[100] A further bond links Williams's idea of the imagination as a sovereign force with 'the gift of grace'. Although hard to swallow for 'a struggling community at the edge of the mapped earth', Calvinism balanced the evil power of Satan with 'a mystical vision of grace as free imaginative force' (p. 46). When Grace visits, the Pilgrim is ushered into a realm of otherness that resembles the condition of 'imaginative suspense' towards which Williams aspires in *Spring and All*:

> Grace often visited the elect, with visionary intensity born in
> ecstasy and trance. Domain of creative immediacy and intellectual
> beauty, awakened before the finite front of time, Pilgrim arrives as
> in a dream. On this enchanted ground, weary of similitudes, weary
> of law, I might withdraw into distance beyond name. (p. 47)

This correspondence is not my discovery but Howe's: 'Through a forest of mystic meaning, Religion hunts for Poetry's freedom, while Poetry roams Divinity's sovereign source' (p. 55).

The 'forest of mystic meaning' overlaps with the 'forest of symbols' through which this discussion has already erred. A secret history of Surrealism and its reception in the United States is also on the line here. Howe's recuperation of the aesthetic dimension of Puritan ideology enables a conjunction between Grace and what Breton might call 'the Marvelous'. Both intervene in the subject's experience of reality; both release spontaneous expression. Where the Puritan 'pilgrim' enters the domain of 'creative immediacy', his Surrealist *confrère* yields to 'creation, spontaneous action'.[101] Furthermore, both states are compromised by language and, consequently, tempted by parallel yearnings. Breton aspires to the primal utterance of 'spoken thought'; Howe's speaker peeks at the possibility of withdrawing into 'a distance beyond name'. Williams's enthusiasm for Surrealism is also bound up in this nexus. The complex temporality of deferred action seems appropriate to express the relationship. For it could be said that Howe's careful scanning of the scorch marks of Puritanism have paved the way for Williams's typological interpretation – expressed in *A Novelette* – of Surrealism as an 'epidemic' that will return writing to the purity of the word.

CHAPTER SEVEN

'Just Rehashed Surrealism'?
The Writing of Barrett Watten

Tests of Zukofsky

Of those associated with the Language school, Barrett Watten is the writer who has engaged most directly with Surrealism. Watten was involved in Language writing from its early stages, editing *This* magazine between 1971 and 1982, as well as being co-editor of *Poetics Journal* from 1982 to 1998. In common with some other Language writers, he has more recently taken up academic positions and is, at the time of writing, Professor of English at Wayne State University. His first collection of critical writings, *Total Syntax*, includes an essay entitled 'The Politics of Poetry: Surrealism and $L=A=N=G=U=A=G=E$'.[1] This essay is important for my discussion but I will take as my point of departure one of Watten's more recent texts. 'Tests of Zukofsky' is part of an ongoing project to 'post' on Watten's homepage at Wayne State 'time-based writings on poetics, media, politics, and culture'.[2] Watten's decision to articulate critical positions via the web and on an apparently occasional basis chimes with his description, in that text of Zukofsky's poetics as 'a signal instance of "horizon work" – writing that attempts to write its way into the structures of its reception, even as those structures change' (p. 1). The shape of the future, the different ways in which it might be constructed, is a dominant concern for Watten and Zukofsky (an instructive precursor). Although Watten accepts that Zukofsky is now 'canonical', he is not content to see that status endlessly and uncritically conferred. Central to his discussion in 'Tests' is 'the notorious memorial evening for Zukofsky in November 1978'. This event, which Watten describes as 'a poetic watershed and a political disaster', was memorable for the clash between his 'Constructivist' reading of Zukofsky and Robert Duncan's 'expressivist' interpretation (pp. 3–4). According to Watten, Duncan was incensed both by his 'revival of the politics of the

1930s' and his neglect of Zukofsky's 'authorship' (p. 4). It is this second area of contention that most concerns me for the moment.

The focus of Watten's Constructivist reading of Zukofsky was the elder poet's work *Catullus*.[3] Instructive for Watten is Zukofsky's technique of allowing his 'translation' to be led by similarities in sound structure between English and Latin words, rather than by accuracy of meaning. 'What I saw Zukofsky doing', writes Watten, 'was refunctioning the original text into a new language, not through identification with the author' (p. 4). From this Constructivist perspective, Zukofsky becomes 'a critic of the "author function"' (p. 4). A fruitful comparison may be made at this point with Surrealism's critique of the author function, as elaborated through automatism. In 'The Automatic Message' of 1933, André Breton presents the involuntariness of automatism in a critical relation to the status of the author as the rational master of his or her material:

> Vile crossings-out afflict the written page more and more, with lines that are rusting barriers to life. All these 'sonnets' that still get written, this senile horror of spontaneity, all this rationalistic refinement, these stiff-lipped supervisors, all this incapacity for love, leave me convinced that escape is impossible from this ancient house of correction.... Correct, correct yourself, be corrected, polish, tell off, find fault, never plunge blindly into the subjective treasury purely for the temptation to fling here and there on the sand a handful of frothy seaweed and emeralds; that is the order we have for centuries been forced to comply with in art as in other spheres, by this ill-digested rigour and slavish prudence. It is also the order that has historically been broken in exceptional, fundamental circumstances. It is from there that Surrealism sets out.[4]

Surrealist method and beyond

But the aim of Surrealism is, of course, to re-integrate the self at a higher level. The prevalent author function hinders that goal to the extent that it represses the unconscious with all its 'crossings-out'. This is how Watten reads Surrealism in 'The Politics of Poetry', describing it succinctly as 'above all a defense of the self and its value in art' (p. 35). Addressing the issue of Surrealist method, he elaborates:

> This method begins with the representation of the self, the agency or efficacy of the writer thinking beyond categories, as absolute, expanded beyond and unimpeded by previous literary domains. (p. 38)

Further, the revolutionary potential of Surrealism lies in the 'predictive value' of technique, 'the ability of technique to construct a possible future' (p. 41). Watten's analysis is consistent here with the later preference for a 'Constructivist' reading of Zukofsky. *Catullus* is exemplary for the way it re-opens the horizon of the future, within a method that remains valid in contemporary practice: 'Poetry becomes the site of a critical construction of that which precedes it, and there is no sense that this process could not continue' ('Tests of Zukofsky', p. 4).

In relation to the historical avant-garde, however, Watten's emphasis on the 'material text' situates his perspective closer to that of the Soviet experience than to Bretonian Surrealism. In the introduction to his recent collection of essays *The Constructivist Moment* (2003), he makes it clear that 'the Soviet constructivists are the privileged example of the historical avant-garde'. Less privileged (along with the Italian Futurists and the German Dadaists) are 'the French surrealists (who rejected social construction as just another form of realism)'.[5] This stance continues Watten's earlier assessment of Surrealism, according to which Breton 'identified the revolution with his own psychic resources and intellectual discipline' ('Tests of Zukofsky', p. 4). On the other hand, the impetus of Constructivism to 'construct a new world within the ashes of the old' allows for a materialist version of 'deferred action', where a prior text takes the place of the traumatic event (p. 4). As practices governed by the same method, both poetry and criticism are constructive in this respect. At the same time, construction is also *re*construction, since both the poetic and the critical act re-inscribe the past as they open up the future. Hence, perhaps, Duncan's shock and resistance to Watten's non-canonical reading of Zukofsky. As an 'act of criticism', Watten's presentation intervened in both Zukofsky's reputation and the protocols of the 'memorial evening'. Against the traditional memorial mode, of rehearsing uncontroversial representations of the past, Watten's reading issued from a belief in criticism as 'a continual restaging in new historical circumstances, not a reinvestment of orders that had been there all along (like "American" or "literature")' (p. 4).

It is worth pausing to remember that 'deferred action' – or 'retrospective determination' as he calls it – has a place in Watten's own critical lexicon, appearing as it does in his definition of Constructivism:

> As a concept, the constructivist moment is informed by the historical experience of social construction ... just as it depends on the way that meaning is constructed through retrospective determination or *Nachträglichkeit*.[6]

The Constructivist moment is itself prefigured – Breton might say 'predicted' – in the essay on Surrealism and $L=A=N=G=U=A=G=E$ in *Total Syntax*, when Watten argues that Surrealism's 'defense of the self' must be superseded by a turn to reflexivity. As he puts it, 'the beginning for further extension of method is in the reflexiveness of "the self"' (p. 50). Reflexivity forges the link between Surrealism and $L=A=N=G=U=A=G=E$, amongst the early articles in which are to be found 'a series of reflexive positions' (p. 50). These positions both acknowledge the mediation of the self in language and seek to re-establish the 'dialectical frame' that had been lost from post-war American interpretations of Surrealism (p. 49).

Watten's approving account of specific instances of reflexivity in the pages of $L=A=N=G=U=A=G=E$ are consistent with his Constructivist reading of Zukofsky. In particular, he applauds Clark Coolidge's 'Larry Eigner Notes', reading them as a critique of the author function. As in Zukofsky's *Catullus*, the aim is to supersede subjective agency and control:

> Here, as in much of his criticism, Coolidge is looking for points of recognition or congruence. In so doing he transposes the reflexiveness of language and experience in Eigner into values seen in language 'as such.' 'I do not think of Eigner.' Coolidge's approach in general preserves a romance of language taken as a whole; there is useful exclusion of any interpretation in this stance. An operator in a language medium looks at others doing similar work; finally the operators disappear and one language looks at another. (p. 51)

Coolidge's approach to Larry Eigner's Language writing here offers a paradigm for the 'further extension of method', from the defence of self practised by Surrealists to the 'reflexive positions' offered in the early numbers of $L=A=N=G=U=A=G=E$ magazine. The agency that once belonged to the self as creator now belongs with language; the self as an artist is first reduced to a mere executor, and then disappears altogether. Watten's account of the means by which Language writing advances Surrealist method suggests that Peter Nicholls is wholly justified in his view that it is as a 'practice of writing' that the European movement informs 'an alternative non-image based poetics in America running from Gertrude Stein to the Language writers'.[7] While this claim can be successfully tested against a range of examples, it is open to qualification. To recognize the tension between the Surrealist aspiration to re-integrate the self and its fear that disintegration might be the result of its efforts is to discern a persistent reflexiveness within Surrealist poetics. Behind, or within, what Watten describes (p. 38) as 'an utter flamboyance of self-presentation' there lurks insecurity about self-possession. In an essay marked by the early influence on literary studies of Jacques Lacan, Michael Sheringham evaluates automatism in terms that recognize both Surrealist aspirations and the way in which they might be compromised by the 'values' of language 'as such':

> At the core of automatism is an experience of integration: the subject coincides symbiotically with the language by which he is traversed. But if, within the context of automatism as an experience, the freedom of language can seem to corroborate a parallel freedom in the realm of the psyche, the moment we move outside this context the freedom of words can begin to look dangerously like ... the freedom of words; and the new order of the subject can begin to seem like an illusion. In crude terms what is at issue is the possibility that automatism is primarily an experience within language and that therefore the products of this experience are at best partial embodiments of, and at worst no more than testaments to what was once alive in it.[8]

As William Carlos Williams puts it in *The Great American Novel*, 'Words are the flesh of yesterday'.[9]

As we have already seen, Nicholls also recognizes the conflicted character of the automatic technique. Undeveloped, perhaps, are the positive implications of this conflict for the life of Surrealism in twentieth-century American poetry. The qualification I am suggesting here can itself be viewed as a kind of 'retrospective determination', in Watten's terms, a restaging of a clash within an arena where the terms have changed. My discussion of 'Tests of Zukofsky' in relation to Watten's essay on 'The Politics of Poetry' anticipates this departure but it is important to note that Zukofsky is included in Watten's earlier piece, as another example of the modernist movement's engagement with Marxism. Zukofsky is ahead of the game, as far as subjectivity is concerned, since for him 'the self is corrected, reflexive to begin with' (p. 33). This reflexivity is surely conditioned in part by his social background as the son of immigrants to the United States, who spoke Yiddish at home. Hence, perhaps, Watten's description of his poetics as 'the poetics of assimilation' (p. 33). Indeed, 'Tests of Zukofsky' speaks back to this analysis. In 'The Politics of Poetry' (p. 34) Zukofsky is described as a '"noncanonized individual"'. In the more recent piece, Watten treats his subsequent canonization almost as a cause for lamentation: 'Zukofsky is "canonical"', he writes, 'this result may be subject to revision, but it cannot be undone' (p. 2). We might say, then, that Zukofsky's reflexivity has a secure material base, for want of which the Surrealists can only gerrymander an unconvincing hybrid of revolutionary politics and romantic lyricism. Or is this to forget too readily Breton's experience as a medical assistant during the First World War, from which his interest in automatism was partly derived? If so, the tensions within the poetics of automatism manifest as the trace of psychological disturbance experienced and witnessed as historical fact, outside the domain of poetry. Such a trace is not inert but actively resists sublimation into a poetics, as well as recuperation into revolutionary activism. The objectified form of Surrealist expression is, then, provoked by the continued agency of this trace. As far as it both produces and reacts to the objectified condition of its own mental processes, the Surrealist self can be considered a reflexive one. By the same token, as far as the Objectivist self fails to stabilize desire within the internal arrangements of the aesthetic object – the 'rested totality', as Zukfosky would have it (Chapter 4) – it is as mobile, as given to interpretation as its Surrealist counterpart.

When a modernist poetics seeks to address the relationship between subjectivity and objectivity, it often does so in the arena of the image. Relevant here is the shadow cast by Imagism over the second phase of Anglo-American modernism, as well as Breton's evaluation of 'verbo-aural' and 'verbo-visual' forms of automatism.[10] Important for my understanding of this often complex area is Walter Benjamin's invocation of 'the image sphere'. Articulated in his defence of Surrealism, this sphere presents a significant contrast to Imagist principles. As more than one critic has observed, Ezra Pound deploys the image within a poetics of mastery. At the level of the person, the economy, directness and precision of the image serve the poet in his attempt to control the flux of both the inner life and external phenomena. The relationship between language and meaning is also at stake in this poetics; as Tim Woods points out, 'Pound employs his Imagist principles ... essentially as an attempt to keep words under control and, thereby, to prevent the "dissemination" of meaning'.[11] At the level of culture, the image is an artistic instrument of redemption; as Nicholls puts it, 'Pound regarded art as the means by which to give structure and value to an otherwise formless modernity'.[12] Benjamin's formulation of the image sphere is also redemptive but it differs from Pound's in important respects. Whereas Pound's image manages flux in a process of diligent differentiation between subject and object, Benjamin's image *sphere* is altogether more inclusive and reconciliatory. It is to be understood as:

> the world of universal and integral actualities, where the 'best room' is missing – the sphere, in a word, in which political materialism and physical nature share the inner man, the psyche, the individual, or whatever else we wish to throw to them, with dialectical justice, so that no limb remains unrent.[13]

Moreover, if modernity is to be redeemed in the image sphere, it will be through the agency of the 'revolutionary intelligentsia' rather than by artistic means alone.[14] Writing in 1929, when the relationship between art and radical politics was vexed on both sides of the Atlantic, Benjamin begins his defence of Surrealism with an emphatic rejection of it as an 'artistic' or 'poetic' movement.[15]

Benjamin's enthusiasm for the revolutionary potential of Surrealism is valuable for anyone seeking to test the claims of those American writers who derogate the movement for its apparent commitment to the poetics of the inner life. Once again, however, this is not simply a question of the intentions of the Surrealists being lost in translation across the Atlantic. Benjamin's construction of the image is important for Paul Naylor's analysis of 'investigative' poetry, and he makes the point that Benjamin's writing on Surrealism 'offers a critique ... as well as an endorsement'.[16] As members of the revolutionary intelligentsia, the Surrealists must keep the image real by keeping it dialectical. Only images that 'originate in real rather than ideal conditions' have utopian potential and the Surrealists risk their revolutionary credibility if they lose sight of this materialist principle.[17] In his essay on Surrealism, Benjamin presents this challenge in the form of a distinction between the image sphere and the abuse of metaphor to be found in the poetic expressions of 'the bourgeois parties'. In the programme of these parties, metaphor is reduced to 'mere images' – representations of a deferred utopian future rather than agents of that future.[18] By contrast, the image sphere does not deal in representation but will be 'discovered in political action'. Consequently, those artists who would pledge their work to the revolution need to remember that the sphere of images 'can no longer be performed contemplatively'.[19] In Watten's terms, the Surrealists must advance beyond Hegel's notion of the image as a 'repressed act'.[20]

It is at least convenient for my discussion that Benjamin was exhorting the Surrealists to political action in 1929, that is, at the same time as a range of American writers were exercised over the future direction of modern experiments in the arts and literature. Crucial for my understanding of the Surreal-O-bjectivist nexus is Benjamin's belief that Surrealist praxis could have a genuine materialist element. The image sphere recognizes both the integrity of the world of objects and the political charge of that world. Indeed, the dialectical parity of subject and object, as Benjamin conceives it, has a kind of premonitory force for the legacy of Objectivism. As we have seen, contemporary writers such as Bob Perelman and Michael Palmer have, in their own readings, sought to tease out rather than exile the subjective dimension of Objectivist poetics. Had their modernist precursors had access to Benjamin's reading of Surrealism, they might have been more receptive to the objectification entailed by Surrealist practice.

Benjamin closes his essay by asserting that the utopian future will be a sphere not just of images but 'more concretely, of bodies'. Indeed, he envisages the ultimate transcendence of reality demanded by the *Communist Manifesto* as taking place only when the body and image 'so interpenetrate that all revolutionary tension becomes bodily collective innervation, and all the bodily innervations of the collective become revolutionary discharge'.[21] In Benjamin's judgement, only the Surrealists had come close to understanding the imperative of this revolutionary *physis*, exchanging 'to a man, the play of human features for the face of an alarm clock that in each minute rings for sixty seconds'.[22] The image is similar to some of the photo montages being published at the same time (1929) in *Variétés* magazine but the technological interpenetration of body and image also finds an application in automatic writing, wherein the hand rematerializes as a bodily mechanism that is much more than a mere instrument of the writer's creativity. For the degree of dissociation to be found in automatic texts depends, to a large extent, on the speed of the writing process. In the introduction to his translation of *The Magnetic Fields*, David Gascoyne asserts that this issue was 'of capital concern' to Breton and Soupault, and he points out that Breton developed a scheme of annotation whereby he could record the relative rapidity of different automatic experiments.[23] The relationship between this concern and Benjamin's aspiration for a revolutionary *physis* becomes clearer in the context of Tim Armstrong's account of automaticity in his book *Modernism, Technology and the Body*. In the chapter on 'Distracted Writing', Armstrong draws attention to a paradigm shift in discourses surrounding automaticity. What was in the nineteenth century 'evidence of a "secondary personality"' becomes a modernist 'focus' for explorations of 'modes of production – and, eventually, of reception' (p. 187). This shift was driven partly by the development of communicative technologies 'such as the typewriter, phonograph and film', all of which 'disconnected the production of language from time, distance, and the individual body' (p. 193). This breakage opens up a space for the critique of conventional literary representation. As 'a representative modernist moment', Armstrong offers the speech made by Louis Aragon's pen in his *Treatise on Style* (1928), a speech in which the pen laments its subordination to the physique of the writer, on the one hand, and the poverty of his expression, on the other (p. 194). Moreover, as writing becomes increasingly identified as a technological phenomenon, the greater is its capacity to 'distract' the 'attention' of the subject. For the Surrealists, as for Freud, the effects of distraction are 'creative', since they elude the censorship of the ego (p. 195).

Aragon's treatise is a touchstone for Benjamin's essay on Surrealism, since it points the way to the necessary distinction between metaphor and image. Armstrong's analysis provides significant cultural context for Benjamin's goal of a revolutionary *physis*. His hope that bodies will fuse with images in the technological realm expresses the desire to redeem dialectically the gap between the human subject and 'the production of language'. That automaticity also results in the lowering of social inhibitions to expression only improves its candidacy as means for 'revolutionary discharge'. From the point of view of Watten's critique of Surrealism, the preoccupation with writing as both a physical and a technological activity is further evidence that the Surrealist self was, to some extent, always reflexive, despite appearances to the contrary. Watten and other Language writers might have been more comfortable with the automatic texts of Surrealism if Breton had annotated the rapidity with which he registered unconscious promptings within the texts themselves. They might then have seemed closer in kind to more recent works, such as this, the beginning of Ron Silliman's *Tjanting*:

Not this.
What then?
I started over & over. Not this.
Last week I wrote 'the muscles in my palm so sore from halving the rump roast I cld barely grip the pen.' What then? This morning my lip is blisterd.
....

Wld it be different with a different pen?[24]

Complete Thought

As I read it, the Surreal-O-bjectivist nexus persists in the writing of Barrett Watten. One place to explore it is *Complete Thought*, a work from 1982, originally published by Tuumba Press.[25] Divided into four sections, this piece is composed almost entirely of direct statements in the present tense.[26] The units of composition vary but share the quality of discreteness. So, in the first section, the heading of which reproduces the title of the whole work, the statements are organized into fifty numbered couplets.[27] In subsequent sections, the model of organization appears to hover between poetic and prose structure. The writing is shaped to fit the margins of the prose page but, as there are never more than two sentences sequent upon each other, it looks more like poetry than it does prose. As paragraphs, these compositional units would have to be described as incipient, or fractured.

In what sense, then, can such a form articulate 'complete thought'? Joseph Conte's understanding of the work as 'postmodern meditation' is relevant here.[28] Conte describes the work as a 'meditative poem', the 'careful organization' of which points towards 'a system of thought, perhaps one that aspires to totality or universality'.[29] If so, then this aspiration is undercut by the formal arrangement of the poem:

> Each statement in 'Complete Thought' is bound by the sequence of words on the page, but these words don't 'follow' one another except in time. Thus the total syntax of the poem as art object in this case stands as a corrective, an undoing of the limited copular totality or surety of the individual statement.[30]

Conte's analysis implies that a postmodern meditation entails scepticism about systematic thought. This scepticism, I would suggest, is linked to Watten's call for reflexive positions in poetry. Here, reflexivity demands recognition and consideration of the 'materials' of thinking, as well as of the situation of the thinker. In this respect, it is not surprising to find that Conte discerns in Watten's text an argument for 'objectivist parity between mind and object'.[31] That said, he also describes the writing as 'dissociative', by virtue of the absence of explicit linkage between paired lines.[32] We might compare this assessment with the way in which the dissociation of Surrealist writing is understood by other Language writers. As we have seen (Chapter 2), when Ron Silliman argues for the distinctive character of the 'new sentence', he invokes Michael Davidson's conviction that the gaps in sense to be found in the Surrealist prose poem are 'expressive', that is, a representation of the subject's disturbed psychological state. The accurate rendition of mental imbalance is not the goal of Watten's 'uncoupled' expressions; Conte is emphatic that 'these are not the antic ravings of a madman but an investigation of that substantial portion of the mind's activity that lies beyond the systematic'.[33] Conte's reading chimes with Watten's advocacy of the reflexive self to the extent that he accepts the view that 'syntax offers the cleanest graph of "the act of the mind," of the meditative process'.[34]

In what follows, I want to pursue some of the possible outcomes of viewing *Complete Thought* through the overlapping lenses of Surrealism and Objectivism. As ever, I am looking for points of contact as well as difference. So far, my consideration of Objectivism has leaned heavily towards the poetry and poetics of Louis Zukofsky but the terms of Watten's poem suggest a correspondence with George Oppen's 1962 collection *The Materials* (discussed below). This correspondence reanimates the Surreal-O-bjectivist nexus and suggests the continued relevance of Benjamin's idea of the image sphere, as a tool for analysis if not as a social goal. To begin with an Objectivist perspective, the 'parity between mind and object' noted by Conte is relayed through a network of terms relating to construction. As these words recur in different local contexts, their connotations, as well as their grammatical possibilities, proliferate. Take, for example, the word 'work', which first appears in the fifth couplet (p. 87):

V

Work breaks down to devices.

All features present.

Here, the word is operating as a gerund. In the twelfth couplet (p. 89), it serves as a verb:

XII

False notes work on a staircase.

The hammer is as large as the sun.

Without narrative context, however, the meaning of the word oscillates between different possibilities. Are the 'False notes' 'labouring' on the 'staircase' or are they 'functioning properly'? Coming as the subsequent step to 'notes', 'work' is also coloured by aesthetic connotations. Indeed, it is tempting to cloak the whole couplet in musical vestments. Hammers assist in the building of staircases but they also make strings sound. The fact that the second statement raises a question of scale may prompt us to re-read the staircase as a metaphor for what is also a musical structure.[35] The musical frame is not exclusive, however, but shares the semantic space of the couplets with two visual images. For one, the relative sizes of hammer and sun are perceived by the eyes. Less explicitly, it may be that the first statement is proposing a contrast between the visual and the aural realms. In which case, notes that would *sound* 'false' when played *look* fine when written on the stave.[36]

It seems to me that this couplet provides a good example of what Conte means when he says that the 'total syntax' of the 'poem as art object' unpicks 'the limited copular totality or surety of the individual statement'. This syntax assumes the thorough imbrication of visual and aural stimulation – what Pound would call phanopoeia and melopoeia – within the image, such that attempts to differentiate between them may well lead to a 'false' abstraction. By contrast, the falsity of Watten's 'notes' (these couplets seem pretty fragmentary, after all) 'works' as a negation of the referential force of the copular. The disjunctive mode of composition leads us to consider the conditions in which it might be true that false notes work on a staircase. The fact that the poem makes us consider reference in this way ensures that its understanding of construction extends beyond the aesthetic work to include social engagement. The numerous references in the first section to the built environment then correct any temptation to believe that such engagement can be achieved by a turn inwards, by a withdrawal from the materials to the subjective interior. In this respect, *Complete Thought* is to be distinguished from 'complete dream'. Put another way, the poem gains social and political purchase only when it includes in its meditation the material realities that it shares with the rest of the world. This proposition provides one rubric under which to read the disjunction in the ninth couplet (p. 88) between a statement that could easily be taken as a self-conscious reflection on poetics and one that asserts the violent imperatives of a culture built on the uncritical reflex to dominate:

> IX
>
> Construction turns back in on itself.
>
> Dogs have to be whipped.

The formal regularity of the first section of *Complete Thought* foregrounds the poem's ontological status as a material object, as one thing amongst many. So much for the Objectivist credentials of Watten's poem but what of its links to Surrealism? When considered as an aspect of technique, the rigid formal structure of the first section can be understood to provide a kind of distraction from the writer's conventional modes of attention, since it inhibits the development of narrative, character or scene. The effect is not, however, to present writing as 'motor activity', or to produce the spontaneity of *spoken* thought. As we have seen, Watten's couplets do not open onto the 'subjective treasury' so prized by Breton, but yield reflexive positions. At the beginning of 'The XYZ of Reading' (1988, reprinted in *Frame*), Watten gives an incomplete citation suggesting that automatism is no longer an experimental resource for the contemporary writer but an unavoidable and burdensome feature of experience:

> The world is structured on its own displacement. 'We don't believe our senses. The level of automatism we have to deal with...' is functionally exact. (p. 151)

Here, the voice of the other does not arise out of the deliberate cultivation of the writer but interrupts the thesis unbidden. The dialectic is not between dream and reality or conscious and unconscious but between a literal self – as writer or speaker – and a literal reader or hearer. From this perspective, the quoted statement both makes the argument and is a concrete example of it. Watten's brief essay acknowledges a 'stricture' for writing that the Surrealists barely considered: 'that the work is only completed, apart from the writer's intentions, in a response' (p. 151). With Zukofsky in mind, perhaps, Watten argues that the writer should adapt to this stricture in a progressive way, by learning to 'transcend the writer's mind at work'. In this way will the writer resolve the opposition between conscious control of the materials and 'whatever dissociation participates in the original act'. Significantly, the movement is outward, towards 'the work in the world', not towards the self beyond the world (p. 154). Withdrawal from the world is not an option either. 'Romantic negativity', understood as 'the avoidance of any conditions that compromise the subject leading to the subject's lyrical denial of itself', is regarded by Watten as 'too easily symptomatic' of political inequality. Statements expressing 'lyrical horror' are examples of something tantamount to false consciousness. Ostensibly demonstrations of freedom of speech, such expressions signify the coerced passivity of citizens within a participatory democracy, a situation which is as 'violent' and contradictory as 'compulsory voting in El Salvador' (p. 153).

It is in this contemporary context of political agency that 'the medial space between the work and the world' is described as 'the aesthetic object or *act*' (p. 153, my emphasis). This space provides the ground for any agency that the writer has. In a vein similar to Benjamin's warning that the image sphere cannot be achieved through contemplation, Watten charges that 'in order to perceive the work this object or act must be made instantly concrete; there is no other choice' (pp. 153–54). The thirty-third couplet of *Complete Thought* (p. 92) provides the opportunity to witness and to participate in the kind of engaged Constructivism that Watten has in mind here:

XXXIII

A boot steps into an example.

Conviction is selected from space.

The opening statement brings together two particulars in a relationship that could be either cooperative or antagonistic. In the first case, the verbal expression is a metaphor derived metonymically from the subject. 'Translated' literally, the sentence could then be read as 'A boot is included as part of an example'. In the second case, such rhetorical finesse disappears as violence overwhelms rational discourse. In both cases, it has to be said, the subject is elided metonymically, since it is not the boot that takes steps but the person wearing the boot. The second statement is less figurative in its assertion that abstractions are derived from the concrete world. In terms of the 'medial space between the work and the world', it is the disclosure of rhetorical manipulation that makes the aesthetic object or act concrete. As social and political subjects, we are more often coerced by constructions in language than we are by physical violence. It is tempting to read the first statement of the next couplet (p. 92) as a commentary on this one:

XXXIV

Two unequal figures complete an act.

The wife turns out to be sane.

Figures of speech are 'unequal' in the sense that they cannot be sub-
stituted for one another without consequences that extend beyond the
realm of the aesthetic. To emphasize the metaphorical aspect of 'steps
into' is to privilege rational behaviour over physical force. To discern
only its metonymical aspect – the boot as image for violence – is to break
this rational world apart. To 'project' these options into the space that
will become the reader is to initiate an act that another (figure) will
complete.[37]

Taken as a whole, couplet XXXIII is active to the extent that it presents
a political arena in which the extremes of violence and rational discourse
are possibilities, dependent upon the beliefs of subjects. From the perspective of Benjamin's image sphere, Watten's poetics acknowledges that the
seeds of progress – if not revolution – lie in the 'real'. Indeed, the close
focus on the decay of the built environment that can be found at the
beginning of *Complete Thought* recalls Benjamin's fascination with the
dialectical potential of 'the outmoded' as a critique of the eternal newness promised by modernity.[38] The echo is particularly pronounced in the
fourth couplet (p. 87), where both statements combine positive and negative images of vulnerable constructions:

IV

Crumbling supports undermine houses.

Connoisseurs locate stress.

At the same time, the real is extended by Watten to include the materials
of language. Consequently, it is in the context of the technology of writing that his practice comes closest to the revolutionary *physis* proclaimed
by Benjamin. The case for considering Watten's poem in this light is
strengthened by reading it in relation to another work concerned with
construction, George Oppen's *The Materials*. Correspondences at the level
of both form and content justify the comparison. With regard to form,
Alan Golding's work on the 'serial' poetry of Oppen is particularly helpful
for establishing a link with *Complete Thought*. Following Joseph Conte –
who, as we have seen, has himself written about Watten – Golding argues
that Oppen's serial poems should be considered under the heading of
the American 'long poem'.[39] He adopts Conte's classification of the series
as separate from 'the modernist epic' and the 'neoromantic sequence'.
Characterized by 'discontinuity, incompleteness, and "accumulation"',
the series thus defined has something in common with parataxis. But the
disruption of standard literary forms *per se* is not so much at issue as the
significance for Oppen of poetry as 'a form of thinking'.[40] In this connection, Golding cites John Taggart's suggestion that the serial form is more
flexible in application and more tenacious of its object. 'More flexible
than what?', we might ask. In Benjamin's terms, seriality appears to resist
'contemplation', the tendency of which is to establish a train of thought
that departs particulars for the distant realms of abstraction.

From the perspective offered by Golding, Oppen's American 'long poem' seems to present a general model for the meditative cast of Watten's American 'long poem'. Oppen's understanding of poetic structure is also instructive. In a late interview, Oppen expressed the view that one of the functions of the poetic line is to separate 'the connections of the progression of thought'.[41] Watten's 'uncoupling' couplets would appear to fulfil this function admirably. Moreover, Golding emphasizes the 'formal dialectic' built into the 'very structure' of the serial poem. This dialectic is most concisely expressed in the title of Oppen's first collection, *Discrete Series* (1934). Golding's analysis suggests that the synthetic stage of this dialectic does not come easily for Oppen:

> Are Oppen's serial poems most usefully seen as a number of discrete pieces added together to make a whole? Or do they represent the remains of single, continuous poems that have been shattered into pieces?[42]

The serial accumulation of couplets in the first section of Watten's poem, as well as the fragmented/incipient paragraphs in subsequent sections, stage a similar dialectic between part and whole. Equivocation often features between and within statements, as in these two couplets (pp. 87 and 89, my emphasis):

V

Work *breaks* down to devices.

All features present.

XII

Connected pieces *break* into name.

Petrified trees are similar.

The use of the verb 'break' links these couplets, despite the root meaning of the word. As far as the different prepositions coordinate relations within and between the statements, they extend Oppen's commitment to poetry as a form of thinking. Thinking, however, which does not resolve its questions within the text. If 'Work breaks down to devices', we cannot be sure whether it can be reassembled. Are 'All features present' at the same time, or do they present themselves at specific times and in particular arrangements? When 'Connected pieces break into name', do they unite in identity or desecrate that sovereign state?

The individual text is, then, incomplete but the synthetic stage of the dialectic between part and whole ought to be covered by Watten's notion of 'total syntax'. This concept, which Watten has derived from the work of Clark Coolidge, Ron Silliman and Steve Benson, extends the function of arrangement beyond grammar to include 'a multiplicity of relations'.[43] My example foregrounds semantic relations but the field of total syntax includes spatial, temporal and social relations. As the tension between totality and completeness implies, however, such a synthesis is problematic if 'total syntax' is conceived as an abstraction. Significantly, Breton's thinking about arrangement is relevant to Watten's elaboration of total syntax; as with automatism, Breton's ideas represent a historical stage that must be superseded in contemporary writing. In citing a section from *Nadja*, Watten implies a criticism of Breton's tendency to regard mental arrangement as having greater priority over material arrangement:

> In *Nadja*, André Breton makes a curious statement, but one that indicates his own priorities: 'As far as I am concerned, a mind's arrangement with regard to certain objects is even more important than its regard for certain arrangements of objects, these two kinds of arrangement controlling between them all forms of sensibility.'[44]

By contrast, total syntax demands that 'the observer, rather than being ironic, is responsible to the contingencies of any *thing* that might compel him or her. The situation as a whole must be taken in'.[45] Articulated as it is, as a corrective to the perceived subjectivist bias of Surrealism, Watten's stance is exemplary for Woods's argument that Language writing continues the 'discourse of responsibility' begun in Objectivism (see Chapter 1).

In Watten's analysis, Breton's preference for the mind's arrangement results in a stalled image. In an expression that appears slightly tautological, he affirms that:

> Breton's surrealist image fixes the flux of automatism in static images, simple objects. Later, an object can be incorporated directly into the poem, which is essentially an oneiric form, without any loss in translation.[46]

Benjamin, we might imagine, would have been deflated to know that this was the future standing of the Surrealist image. The interpenetration that he discerned between subject and object has given way to the simple mastery of the former over the latter. The perception that the 'oneiric form' has priority suggests that the Surrealists have failed to convince subsequent generations of innovative writers that they were genuinely interested in keeping the dialectic 'real'. As Naylor's reading of Benjamin implies, a static image can be a virtuous image from the point of view of a radical politics. Naylor cites Benjamin's claim, made in 'N', that 'an image is dialectics at a standstill'. He goes on to quote 'Thesis 17' from 'Theses on the Philosophy of History', wherein the image is linked to a form of critical thinking that itself bears comparison with serial form:

> thinking involves not only the flow of thoughts, but their arrest as well. Where thinking suddenly stops in a configuration pregnant with tensions, it gives the configuration a shock.[47]

As far as Benjamin's own historical writing was concerned, shock could lead to 'awakening' only if an imagistic mode was juxtaposed with commentary.[48] The reflexivity engendered by this mixed form is certainly also to be found in Watten's poem but his answer to the problems of both the stalled image and the potential abstraction of total syntax is to open the text to the world in a constructive way that neither the Surrealists nor Benjamin considered. A 'multiplicity of relations' will not yield to the arrangement of a single mind, however magisterial that mind may be. Nor does that multiplicity ever cease to unfold and develop; in which case, 'the only solution for the poem is to keep going, to argue the work into a lived present that can take such multiplicity into account'.[49] It is its purchase in the 'lived present' that keeps total syntax from being merely a theoretical horizon. The commitment to the particulars of experience extends the poetics of Objectivism and returns us to a couplet (the thirty-third) already discussed: 'A boot steps into an example./Conviction is selected from space.' Golding interprets Oppen's claim that he perceived and wrote 'in isolated "moments of conviction"' as a sign of the ethical motivation of the 'disjunctive structure' of serial form. Watten's passive expression in the second statement is a reminder that such motivation applies to readers as well as to writers. Coming after the first statement, we might also pause to remember that the bond between writers and readers is only one of the multiplicity of relations in which we find ourselves.

The Constructivist Oppen

The case for reading *Complete Thought* in relation to the older poet's work is strengthened by Watten's own acknowledgement of the importance of Oppen in the development of his editorship of *This*. Along with Robert Creeley's *Pieces*, Oppen's serial poems were relevant, says Watten,

> [to] a construction of meaning using the freshly cast or broken down units of lyricism that were becoming available with the crisis of the expressive subject after the 1960s, reconfigured in new forms of organization.[50]

It is salutary that this disclosure comes in a 'polemic' framed by Watten in terms of a comparison between the development of radical poetics, on the one hand, and production-line technology, on the other.[51] For it seems to me that the first section of *Complete Thought* resonates with specific echoes of 'Image of the Engine', a short series of five poems from near the beginning of *The Materials* (quotations below are taken from Oppen's *Collected Poems*[52]). The poems are of varying length and follow an open form that plays lineation against syntax. Taken as a 'whole' and despite the title, the series offers more than the close observation of a material particular. The first poem does present the diagnostic observation of an engine but the technical expertise of the observer then gives way to the faculty of imagination. As a result of this shift, consciousness and its object become harder to distinguish. Here is the first poem in full:

1

Likely as not a ruined head gasket
Spitting at every power stroke, if not a crank shaft
Bearing knocking at the roots of the thing like a pile-driver:
A machine involved with itself, a concentrated
Hot lump of a machine
Geared in the loose mechanics of the world with the valves
    jumping
And the heavy frenzy of the pistons. When the thing stops,
Is stopped, with the last slow cough
In the manifold, the flywheel blundering
Against compression, stopping, finally
Stopped, compression leaking
From the idle cylinders will one imagine
Then because he can imagine
That squeezed from the cooling steel
There hovers in that moment, wraith-like and like a plume
    of steam, an aftermath,
A still and quiet angel of knowledge and of comprehension.
(p. 18)

I will return to this poem but note for now that shifting perspectives are a recurring element of the series. The second poem, which seems to begin tersely but end in yearning, abruptly challenges the power of metaphor to resolve the tensions between animate and inanimate features of the world:

2

Endlessly, endlessly,
The definition of mortality

The image of the engine

That stops.
We cannot live on that.
I know that no one would live out
Thirty years, fifty years if the world were ending
With his life.
The machine stares out,
Stares out
With all its eyes

Thru the glass
With the ripple in it, past the sill
Which is dusty – If there is someone
In the garden!
Outside, and so beautiful.
(p. 19)[53]

Given Watten's belief in the constructive potential of precursor texts, it does not seem unreasonable to suggest that, when he writes 'The materials' in two of the couplets from *Complete Thought*, he is allowing for the possibility of a return to Oppen's collection.[54] The reference to a 'pile driver' in the twenty-third couplet, albeit not a hyphenated one, suggests a specific correspondence between Watten's serial poem and 'Image of the Engine'. Like Watten, Oppen shows a concern for the built environment in his series. This concern is most in evidence in the fifth and final poem of the series. Hitherto, positive affection between subjects has offered the only possibility of redemption in a world that cannot be transcended. The quest for such contact is most to be prized amongst those who are young and deprived but even their efforts are compromised by the unavoidable decay of the material world:

5

Also he has set the world
In their hearts. From lumps, chunks,

We are locked out: like children, seeking love
At last among each other. With their first full strength
The young go search for it,

But even the beautiful bony children
Who arise in the morning have left behind
Them worn and squalid toys in the trash

Which is a grimy death of love. The lost
Glitter of the stores!
The streets of the stores!
Crossed by the streets of stores
And every crevice of the city leaking
Rubble: concrete, conduit, pipe, a crumbling
Rubble of our roots.
(p. 21)

Reading this passage from the point of view of the image sphere, we might speculate whether an alternative and dialectical redemption is possible, one in which the 'seeds' of the future lie in the 'lumps' and 'chunks' of now. Reading it as a precursor text to Watten's, we remember a similar equivocation in his use of the word 'crumbling' in the statement 'Crumbling supports undermine houses'. As a companion writer, Oppen is perhaps one of those 'Connoisseurs' who 'locate stress' in a world that would otherwise ignore its own contradictions.

Benjamin's concept of the image sphere seems even more pertinent to this discussion in the light of the first of the two epigrams that Oppen gives to *The Materials*. This epigram comes from the work of the French philosopher Jacques Maritain. His idea of 'critical realism', according to which 'what the mind knows is identical with what exists', sets up a parity between subject and object that clearly found favour with Oppen.[55] In the given citation (p. 91), Maritain suggests an illumination of which Benjamin is also likely to have approved:

> *We awake in the same moment to*
> *ourselves and to things.*

The quotation from Maritain is 'coupled' with a second, unattributed epigram:

> *They fed their hearts on fantasies*
> *And their hearts have become savage.*
> (p. 21)

As a pair, these two 'pieces' stage a conflict reminiscent of Benjamin's challenge to Surrealism to keep the image dialectical and not retreat into the inner life. In the context of the extension of Objectivist poetics into Language poetry, the choice is between 'unrelenting exposure of the self' and an irresponsible turn inward that is tantamount to barbarism. The first poem in 'Image of the Engine' points toward a simultaneous awakening to self and thing. Object and consciousness increasingly interweave as the poem progresses. Initially, the observer's attention is diagnostic but the technical mastery that this stance implies gives way to recognition of the integrity of the engine, as 'A machine involved with itself'. Integrity does not equal isolation, however; although 'concentrated', the machine is formally integrated with the 'world' at large. The parity between thing and self becomes more pronounced in the second period. The shift from the intransitive 'stops' in the eighth line to the copular form at the start of the ninth – 'Is stopped' – is an attempt to represent the transient moment between one state and another. Read reflexively, as a commentary on the poem as machine, this shift can also be understood as a change from active to passive voice.[56] In subsequent lines, 'stopping' and 'Stopped' raise the same alternative readings.

Up to this point, the technical scrutiny has been articulated directly by the poem but when the engine is 'finally / Stopped', a generalized subject is interposed between it and the poetic voice. This subject then constructs in his imagination an image that is only *of* the engine to the extent that it is derived *from* it. A more conventionally lyric poet might be tempted simply to convert the steam of the expired machine into a metaphor for the escaping soul but the unspecified subject of this poem is not seduced by this option. Instead, he formulates an image which does not wing it away from its constituent materials. At the material level, this is a question of hearing the similarity in sound between 'angel' and 'engine'. At the figurative level, what is required is a refusal to choose between a metaphysical and a physical frame of reference. The image is both 'aftermath' and 'angel', simultaneously 'wraith-like and like a plume / of steam'. This poised ambiguity might be compared with Benjamin's idea of the image as 'dialectics at a standstill'. Transcendence is doubly stalled: firstly, as it is displaced from the poetic voice onto the generalized subject; and secondly, as it is downgraded from epiphanic vision to an apparently unmotivated exercise of the imaginative faculty.

This poem is not an example of the revolutionary *physis* proposed by Benjamin but it does constitute an effort to think through the relationship of subject and object in the technological domain. In this respect, it bears comparison with Parker Tyler's poem 'Hymn' (discussed in Chapter 4) and it seems to me that, despite the gap in time, it shares with this poem the desire to go beyond the limitations of Imagism. This is certainly one way to read the 'leakaging' that results in the image of equivalence between aftermath and angel. From this perspective, despite controlled 'compression', subjectivity cannot be completely converted into an 'image of the engine'. This critique is advanced from a historical point where the modernist promise of an alliance between technological innovation and experimental poetry seems naïve at best. The Cold War was unusually hot in the early 1960s and *The Materials* includes two poems that explicitly address the possibility of nuclear holocaust. In a world where 'We are endangered/Totally at last',[57] redemption of any kind other than apocalypse is hard to posit. At a time when technological innovation is so clearly controlled by the military–industrial complex, both Benjamin's and Pound's hopes for the technological development of the image are hard to sustain.

If the community invoked in the second poem of Oppen's series cannot 'live on' an image of itself as an engine, what can it live on? As befits the meditative cast of serial form, 'Image of the Engine' does not seem to offer a single, secure alternative. As we have seen, the last poem in the series stands on the verge of a revelatory awakening to the physical decay of the environment to which this community belongs. At the point of revelation, however, this train of thought is blocked by an adversary proposition. Identity, it seems, is a question of bodies, after all. Not bodies conceived as machines, or bodies fused in technology, but bodies that share with natural elements a susceptibility to extreme changes in the physical environment. The poem cites examples of epic scale. Drawn from the Bible, perhaps, they gain fresh momentum in the nuclear age:

> But they will find
> In flood, storm, ultimate mishap:
> Earth, water, the tremendous
> Surface, the heart thundering
> Absolute desire.
> (p. 21)

The 'heart thundering' would seem to echo and displace the 'flywheel blundering' in the first poem of the series, just as a particular moment of cognition gives way to a libidinal longing that defies time. The poem appears to reach a Surrealist conclusion when it finds a state of 'Absolute desire' but, as the second epigram to the collection warns, this is not the kind of desire that will feed the heart with fantasy. Hence, perhaps, the significance of the 'tremendous/Surface', as the place where the interior becomes accessible to the exterior. The appositional structure of this section of the poem makes it unnecessary to discriminate between the surface of the world and that of the self. In this respect, the surface is also a threshold to awakening.

To return to the significance of Oppen's serial form for Language writing, there is a way in which 'Image of the Engine' invites the expanded notion of syntax developed by Watten. If the 'engine' is itself an image of the modernist conception of the poem as a machine, then Oppen gestures towards total syntax when he presents the engine as 'Geared in the loose mechanics of the world'. Perhaps 'loose' is used to indicate the questionability of that eminent modernist metaphor, and also to dissent from Imagism's faith in the absolute correlation between symbol and thing.[58] As we have seen, scepticism is well served by serial form, the loose mechanics of which are also apt for Watten's policy that 'the observer, rather than being ironic, is responsible to the contingencies of any *thing* that might compel him or her'. Just as the mechanic must attend to the contingent failure of the engine, so must the poet recognize the 'multiplicity of relations' in which the image might find a place. In this respect, Oppen's poem anticipates Watten's poetics in its acceptance of the engine as an actual machine, a metaphor for poetic organization and a 'definition of mortality'. Such responsibility clearly contributes to our simultaneous awakening 'to ourselves and to things'. However close this revelation is to Benjamin's hopes for the image sphere, it is quite distinct from Breton's view, expressed in *L'Amour Fou*, of the object as 'the solution, symbolic or other, of a problem you have with yourself'.[59] The sceptical cast of serial form militates against solutions. At the same time, the problem of the self, as proposed in *The Materials*, is that of its relations with others. Indeed, the *formal* equivocation between part and whole is also a question of social relations. *The Materials* presents a social fabric wrenched to the point of *dis*solution by 'ultimate mishap', a fabric in which it is impossible to represent secure bonds between even the closest of individuals.

Haunted by the global catastrophes of the early twentieth century, and pressed by the threat of contemporary stand-offs between the superpowers, the connotative possibilities of language represent one of the contingencies to which the poet will be responsible. As if to register that language is just as demanding as an engine in this respect, the shift from the third to the fourth poem in Oppen's series engineers a concrete spectacle from an abstract noun:

3

What ends
Is that.
    Even companionship
Ending.

'I want to ask if you remember
When we were happy! As tho all travels

Ended untold, all embarkations
Foundered.

4

On that water
Grey with morning
The gull will fold its wings
And sit. And with its two eyes
There as much as anything
Can watch a ship and all its hallways
And all companions sink.
(p. 20)

Here, the possible significations of a single word parallel the possible interpretations that might be placed on a letter sent by a loved one to another whose life is at risk. These two poems are emphatically not a word game. In time of war, companionship and the ship's company come to an end repeatedly. Similar to the introduction of the generalized subject in the first poem, the appearance of the gull as observer in the fourth is a reminder that the poet's responsibility to the contingencies of any thing will not be adequately fulfilled by their absorption into an eternal moment of recuperative 'vision'. The embodied, stereoscopic vision of the seabird is morally neutral, expressing no identification with those who are not its companions, in fact, not even discriminating between this spectacle and any other.

Through this concretization, Oppen's poem occupies the 'medial space' between work and world. Indeed, it is tempting to read couplet XXXII of Watten's *Complete Thought* (p. 92) as a commentary on this specific instance of correlation between the particulars of language and the particulars of history:

XXXII

The materials motivate storms.

Play is felt to be constructed.

If this suggestion is a fair one, then the second statement might also speak to Oppen's poem, acknowledging that word games, so called, do not escape the frame of social signification but are – in this case at least – generated in lived experience. In addition to recognizing how 'Image of the Engine' builds itself out of its own resources – even though the engine gives out in the first poem – Watten's couplet affirms a dual temporality. This is to say that the present of his response was the future of Oppen's open meditation. Indeed, the series seems to have built this future into its thinking.

Both the imaginings of the generalized subject in the first poem and the perceptions of the gull in the fourth are launched by the future tense. This future opens up to the reader in a way that the Surrealists never seemed to have cared much about. The only significant future reader envisaged by Breton is the self at a later stage of development. In this case the automatic text, like the found object, becomes legible not in terms of its contingencies but in terms of its absolute function as the site of self-revelation.

Watten's Constructivist fields

In the light of this discussion, it is ironic that George Oppen has been reported to have accused Watten of 'rehashed surrealism'. The disclosure is Watten's own, made in a footnote to his discussion of the relationship between Language writing and the historical avant-garde.[60] Oppen's view had appeared much earlier, in cryptic form, when Watten began his essay on Surrealism with the personal statement 'I, too, have been called a Surrealist'. The footnote gives some valuable context for Oppen's opinion. It was an occasional remark, overheard after Watten had given a reading at the Poetry Center at San Francisco State University. In full, it runs 'That's just rehashed surrealism'. Watten gives the date of his reading as 1979. The archives of the Poetry Center contain a recording of Watten reading there on 13 December 1978. If this was the reading at which Oppen passed his dismissive judgement, then the most likely prompt for it, in my view, would be *City Fields*.[61] Published in 1978, this work echoes in form and title the early automatic texts of Breton, Soupault and Eluard. The title, itself an image of contradiction, evokes the urban environment of Surrealist experience while also raising the possibility of a link with *The Magnetic Fields*. The text (quoted here from the *Frame* collection) bears the narrative form characteristic of automatic writing and presents the reader early on with the familiar surreal situation of a character in uncertain surroundings:

> Vague forms surround him, shapes more fearful each time he looks. They appear as dim lights, objects undetermined and of no consequence, not to be found. (p. 133)

This character's *paysage* is through a physical environment not specifically located and which refuses to attain a fixed arrangement. A minotaur, a potent Surrealist figure for hidden depths, appears towards the end of the seventh paragraph (p. 134).

The second section is particularly interesting from a Surrealist point of view. A window features strongly in the first paragraph, perhaps restaging Breton's initial automatic image, of the man cut in two by the material guardian of transparency between inside and outside.[62] Man and window are not so dramatically related in Watten's text but the scene is no more transparent for that. Notably, it ends with an expression of contradiction between reality and imagination:

A man is standing in front of a window. In possession of what
he sees. A person becomes a lens on a room inside. Then to walk
into the room on sequent occasions. The lights go down on the
buildings outside. The window is off of the kitchen, the room is
filled with people. Smoke coming out of the cracks. What can he
have. All words resolve this matter like a huge weight balancing on
a single point. That point is in motion, verging from one word to
the next. A cyclone covers the surface of the ceiling with wavering
lines. The room fills in with fragments of their talk. But a window
is an opening to the outside. He is contradicted in his rooms,
imagining a better place to live. (pp. 137–38)

This section also appears to imitate two of the generic modes employed
in Surrealist 'narratives'. Firstly, there is the parody of realism deployed in
'false novels':

His father and mother lived in a house on the edge of an industrial
park. One house was basically like any other, with the exception that half of them were the mirror image of the other half....
(pp. 138–39)

Secondly, there is a passage through an allegorical landscape of 'endless
plain', 'plateau', 'ravine' and 'mountain', wherein the subject encounters,
if not the minotaur, at least a 'mad bull'. As he makes his way through this
terrain, he cannot 'make out the place from which he had come' and the
paragraph literally ends in mid-air: 'Sloping away to one side was a rock
like a cement wall projecting into space' (pp. 139–40).

Despite such echoes, there is plenty to differentiate this text from
Surrealist models. From the beginning, the text takes pains to lay bare
the devices from which its 'fields' are composed. Repeatedly, its 'lines' of
construction are rendered concrete, fending off complete absorption into
the scene of representation. The identification that we might experience
in relation to the urgent and mysterious journey of the Surrealist hero
is blocked by expressions like 'These lines are what he is, and he looks
out to see them', or 'Any person is the image of what he sees' (p. 134).[63]
The objectification that is taking place here is clearly towards the realization of literary form. The same process is applied to the urban setting.
It would be a mistake, however, to think of this process as a one-way
street. More accurately, the reader's attention shifts between the material
surface of the text and its 'depths' of representation. As in the following
paragraph:

It's as if there were openings from field to field, but he is closed up
in the city. Walled to his approach, he moves within it. Rows of
houses, contained by gray wallpaper, become the pages of a book.
Streets contained within a line of print. And so compact, the pages
crowd upon each other. He opens the book and starts reading anywhere. Lines going out straight to the horizon, walls revealed and

close. Fenced-in areas hidden from the street, doors opening to houses. Every place he has already been, he is to encounter there again. (pp. 136–37)

Here, the first four sentences draw us out of an imaginary space measured by openness and closure to the material text. In the fifth sentence, the 'compact[ness]' reminds us that material texts occupy physical space. By virtue of the inversion of main and qualifying clauses, however, the pages barely have time to coordinate themselves in physical space before they are 'crowded' into the space of metaphor. In the second sentence, the subject starts again, with what for him is a material text and for us is the representation of a material text, from which a future of other possible scenes opens out. Except that this 'horizon' is extremely limited, the urban environment more like Weber's 'cage of modernity' than Breton's theatre of desire.[64] 'There' is hard to locate in the final sentence but, be it the built environment or the written one, 'encounter' is not charged with the erotic frisson or revolutionary spark that we might anticipate from a Surrealist *rendezvous*. Rather, it appears to represent simple repetition, about which there is nothing more to say.

City Fields further distances itself from Surrealist precursors when it introduces a direct statement of poetics. In the third section of the text, five paragraphs from the end (p. 146), Watten includes a declaration that bears both on serial form and total syntax. Indeed, *Complete Thought* seems to be anticipated in its pronouncement:

> The operative principle of this writing is now clear. Every sentence avoids the representation of a completed thought. No one expression can adequately include all that is the case. All the sentences taken as a whole might be enough to accomplish this. If they are taken completely, in the context of an even larger world. It is hard to tell where this logic will stop. There is more going on here than meets the eye. No one thing anyone does makes the slightest bit of difference. Any excuse is as good as any other. The problem is to find a situation in which this account makes sense.

From the Surrealist point of view, the ultimate integration of the self, as self, is not the goal. This writing would not express the perfect resolution of conscious and unconscious states, even if it could. Any text participates in a broader – 'looser' – arrangement that always exceeds the individual. The implications of this recognition are daunting, particularly when they are carried over into the 'field' of action. Far from being the agent of *all* change, the self appears to lose agency altogether. Threatening here, perhaps, is a lapse into the postmodern – Oppen's 'loose mechanics' transformed into an ironic 'design' of infinite, equivalent substitutions.[65] That said, the paragraph does not seem to end in *aporia* but suggests, I think, that as long as *aporia* can be represented and recognized as such, there remains some hope.

Nonetheless, when the 'problem' goes in search of a solution, it looks for a 'situation', not a person. An earlier paragraph (p. 143) has begun with the injunction that 'We must objectify our life. Is this the most from writing that we progressive citizens can hope for, then – the objectification of a predicament that we share with all other citizens? Bob Perelman's reading of Watten's work suggests not. Perelman is interested in 'self and mapping in language writing', a topic that he explores in relation to both Watten's and Susan Howe's poetry. The focus of his analysis of Watten's work is *Progress*, 'a book-length poem written in the early eighties'.[66] In Perelman's view, Watten's apparent intention to disavow 'any investment in the self' is belied by tensions between subject positions within the writing:

> Almost any passage will show self and external social materials engaged in a rapid, contradictory confrontation. Rather than a dispersed 'I' yielding unobstructed access to an unproblematic plane of discourse, the real-time self often reemerges, uncomfortably, into a material history that has precious little space for it.[67]

From this point of view, it is provocative that Watten's paragraph on poetics is followed by one that opens with a reference to 'The object of desire'. As it happens, the object is not so much a thing as a place: 'The object of desire is the intersection of two main streets, in a neighbourhood where no one lives' (p. 146). It is a contradictory place, at that, where 'things' both are and are not. At an intersection, both streets are there but who can tell them apart? Within a broader context, signalled by the reference to 'neighborhood', this place is utopian; just as the object of desire can never be attained, so it is a place where 'no one lives'. The closest we can get to this object, perhaps, is the concrete image of the intersection. But this suggests a life fully objectified, brought to a standstill in the impossible union of contradictory directions.

Or is this image a more positive one, a cousin to Benjamin's notion of 'dialectics at a standstill'? Not stalled indefinitely, it awaits future construction:

> The object of desire is the intersection of two main streets, in a neighbourhood where no one lives. Everyone is familiar with this place, though no one calls it home. But often he passes through that point. The place where all the traffic comes from. His home is an extension of such means. The problem is how to build it. The materials must be transported up a grade. (p. 146)

At the 'point' where the subject 'passes through' the objective environment, the Imagist might have called a halt, built a monument to Confucius or Mussolini in the middle of the road. The Surrealist might be seen looking to the sky, arms extended, waiting to absorb the passing cars into the traffic of his desire. By contrast, the subject of Watten's paragraph looks to a future in which subjective desire and objective conditions must accommodate each other if his 'home' is to be built in a better world.

Nevertheless, compared with the exuberant subjectivity of Surrealist explorations of the cityscape, Watten's image seems impersonal, didactic. Three paragraphs on, however, at the border between *City Fields* and the world beyond, the writing seems to come closer to home:

> This writing is actually about the intersection one block away. The situation there is entirely different, more difficult of approach. Multiple gas stations which are indistinguishable from each other. The traffic spreads out, large objects fill the sky. The body fills with annoyance. The relative openness invites one not to look. Only distance remains until the end of the line. The gray cement is a ceremonial occasion. This is where he lives his life. (p. 147)

The word 'actually' is a trigger for the 'real-time self' that Perelman discerns as everywhere disclosing itself in *Progress*. But the subject remains in the third person, while the deictic pronoun, 'this', implies the dispersal of the 'I' into discourse, be it the text in process or the magazine of which Watten was an editor. As *materials*, however, texts exist in the world, too. 'This' paragraph is then a further intersection between the place of writing and the physical place of living, a point where Watten engages in an 'honest' exposure of self, admitting the 'difficulty' of sustaining a refined poetic perspective. Here, the extraordinary organic sensibility of the poet, his visionary exceptionalism, is notably lacking. Discrimination is impossible; figures of speech are vague; description is limited to the broadest of categorical classifications. Here, visionary insight and profane illumination are displaced by physical irritation. *In extremis*, the poet is tempted to abandon the specific sense that confers his elections; he almost accepts the invitation not to look. But we should not forget that *City Fields* begins (nearly) with a compressed meditation on the first person: 'The first person, which is the eye – the person speaking or writing, at first sound complete' (p. 133). This statement falls short in the order of the sentence. Whether it is taken as a noun or a verb, 'sound' implies the homophonic relationship between 'I' and 'eye'. The grammatical failure of this sentence signals, I think, the limitations of making the first person co-terminous with the singular eye. In raising the possibility of difference between the two, he distances the poem from a poetics of sight. This is not to say that it stops looking at the world or the self at large in it, just that there are other materials with which to work. The ambiguity of the expression also yields a relationship between self and other that is crucial for the poem's Constructivist aspirations. If 'complete' is read as an adjective in apposition to 'the first person', the sentence proposes a sovereign and independent subject. But both 'sound' and 'complete' can be read as imperatives. Perhaps the second is addressed to the reader, as if discourse is instructing him or her how to participate in 'the person's' subjectivity, in the material realm of sound. Perhaps the first is addressed directly to the 'the person speaking or writing', thereby creating a reflexive moment in which the sovereign subject is revealed as an illusion.

We should not, perhaps, read too much into Oppen's apparently dismissive response to Watten's reading as 'just rehashed surrealism'.[68] But off-the-cuff remarks are not unmotivated. On the one hand, the fact that Surrealism is presented so readily as a negative exemplum is indicative of the generalized suspicion in which it has been held by American poets of a materialist persuasion.[69] On the other, Oppen's remark can be read as a pointer to the continuing exchange between Objectivism and Surrealism. Watten's critical treatment of the European movement makes it clear that he believes its aspirations for the sovereign self belong to a phase of revolution that no longer applies. The section that I have taken from his work, however, suggests that, in some specific instances, Language writers, Objectivists and Surrealists are linked by the ways in which they map 'the murky realms' between subject and object.

Notes

Notes to Chapter 1

1 Of the writers discussed in detail in this book, both Susan Howe and Barrett Watten have held professorships.

2 Hank Lazer, *Opposing Poetries. Volume 2: Readings* (Evanston: Northwestern University Press, 1996), pp. 6–18. 'Radical Collages' appeared in *The Nation*, 247 (2–9 July 1988).

3 Mark Wallace and Steven Marks (eds), *Telling It Slant: Avant-Garde Poetics in the 1990s* (Tuscaloosa: University of Alabama Press, 2002), pp. 1–2.

4 Bernstein is, with Hank Lazer, one of the editors of the 'Modern and Contemporary Poetics' series in which *Telling It Slant* appears.

5 Christopher Beach (ed.), *Artifice and Indeterminacy: An Anthology of New Poetics* (Tuscaloosa: University of Alabama Press, 1998).

6 Jerome J. McGann, 'Contemporary Poetry, Alternate Routes', *Critical Inquiry*, 13 (spring 1987), pp. 624–47; George Hartley, *Textual Politics and the Language Poets* (Bloomington: Indiana University Press, 1989).

7 Charles Bernstein, 'Stray Straws and Straw Men', reprinted in Bruce Andrews and Charles Bernstein (eds), *The L=A=N=G=U=A=G=E Book* (Carbondale: Southern Illinois University Press, 1984), p. 44.

8 For the full sample, see Ron Silliman (ed.), *In the American Tree* (Orono: National Poetry Foundation, 1986), pp. 336–340.

9 Recent discussions in the field have included a growing interest in the 'sounding' of poetry. See Charles Bernstein (ed.), *Close Listening: Poetry and the Performed Word* (New York: Oxford University Press, 1998), in particular part I.

10 Alex Preminger and T. V. F. Brogan, *The New Princeton Encyclopedia of Poetry and Poetics* (Princeton: Princeton University Press, 1993), p. 676.

11 Ken Edwards, 'Language: The Remake', *Fragmente*, 2 (autumn 1990), p. 57.

12 Amongst those who raise the question of reference are: Lee Bartlett, 'What is "Language Poetry"?', *Critical Inquiry*, 12 (summer 1986), pp. 741–752; Andrew Ross, 'The New Sentence and the Commodity Form: Recent American Writing', in Cary Nelson and Lawrence Grossberg (eds), *Marxism and the Interpretation of Culture* (Urbana: University of Illinois Press, 1988); Michael Greer, 'Language Poetry in America 1971–1991', *Meanjin*, 50:1 (1991), pp. 149–56; John Koethe,

'Contrary Impulses: On the Tension Between Poetry and Theory', *Critical Inquiry*, 18:1 (1991), pp. 64–75; Hank Lazer, *Opposing Poetries. Volume 1: Issues and Institutions* (Evanston: Northwestern University Press, 1996).

13 Marjorie Perloff describes the orthodoxy in question as 'a kind of neo-confessionalist, neo-realist poetic discourse, a discourse committed to drawing pretentious metaphors about failed relationships from hollandaise recipes'. Marjorie Perloff, 'After Language Poetry: Innovation and Its Theoretical Discontents', at http://epc.buffalo.edu/authors/perloff/after_langpo.html.

14 See Greer, 'Language Poetry in America', p. 150; Bartlett, 'What is "Language Poetry"?', p. 242; Lazer, *Opposing Poetries, Volume 1*, pp. 39–40.

15 Lazer, *Opposing Poetries, Volume 1*, p. 40.

16 Hartley, *Textual Politics*, p. 38.

17 And, in so doing, reminds the reader of Walt Whitman's 'Song of Myself'. Perelman's poem originally appeared in *Primer* (San Francisco: This Press, 1981). Perelman's poem also corresponds with a section of Louis Zukofsky's 'A'-6. I will return to this correspondence in Chapter 5.

18 Bernstein, 'Stray Straws and Straw Men', pp. 41–42.

19 Bernstein, 'Stray Straws and Straw Men', p. 39.

20 Reminding us that despite the parallelism in sound between 'rosy' and 'rasa', individual consciousness is not a pristine 'page' awaiting, through perception, nature's imprint and promptings.

21 The exalted state of the apostrophe is equally undermined by the echo in these two words of the comic idiom of a stereotypical mass (and, therefore, not Romantic) tourism.

22 The dominance here of the mediating technology of the automobile also undermines Romantic aspirations to 'direct' encounters with Nature. In this respect, the voices of both Ralph Waldo Emerson and William Carlos Williams can also be heard in the poem.

23 See Vernon Shetley, *After the Death of Poetry: Poet and Audience in Contemporary America* (Durham: Duke University Press, 1993), pp. 138ff. Shetley's positioning of Language writing is idiosyncratic. Acknowledging the differences in political allegiance, he nonetheless aligns the movement with New Formalism, since both, in his view, are defined by their participation in a 'technological determinism', according to which the most significant choice to be made by poets is whether to write in open or closed forms (p. 136).

24 His analysis of the reciprocal relationship between academy and literary movement seems to me reductive both in the way that it assumes a secure division between the two and in its failure to consider how such a relationship might operate to the benefit of a broader constituency, involving, for example, readers and students. That said, Shetley is not on his own in this cynical assessment. In the most extreme reaction against Language writing that I have yet come across, James Brook situates the 'language school' in 'the endless dialectic ... of period commodity art'. In this diatribe, Barrett Watten is likened to Ronald Reagan: both, we are told, are 'authoritarian' personalities, while neither is an author. See James Brook, 'Political Poetry and Formalist Avant-Gardes: Four Viewpoints', in Lawrence Ferlinghetti and Nancy J. Peters (eds), *City Lights Review 1* (San Francisco: City Lights Books, 1987). For a more nuanced analysis of the relationship between Language writing and the academy, see Alan Golding, *From Outlaw to Classic: Canons in American Poetry* (Wisconsin: University of Wisconsin Press, 1995).

25 Bob Perelman, *The Marginalization of Poetry: Language Writing and Literary History* (Princeton: Princeton University Press, 1996), p. 14. Wary of the lure of

origins, Perelman offers (p. 38) the opening issue of *This* magazine in 1971 as 'as much of an originary moment as language writing can be said to have'.

26 Hartley, *Textual Politics*, p. 76.

27 Perloff, 'After Language Poetry'. In this article, Perloff draws attention to the 'editorial disclaimer' that accompanied the printing of the proceedings of the symposium 'The Politics of the Referent' as Supplement 1 to the magazine *L=A=N=G=U=A=G=E* (1980), and to Steve McCaffery's subsequent statement that he had never been happy with the title of his own contribution to that symposium and supplement, 'The Death of the Subject'.

28 Peter Nicholls, 'An Interview with Bob Perelman', *Textual Practice*, 12:3 (1998), p. 539.

29 Koethe, 'Contrary Impulses', p. 73.

30 Peter Middleton, 'Language Poetry and Linguistic Activism', *Social Text*, 25/26 (1990), p. 250.

31 Middleton, 'Language Poetry and Linguistic Activism', p. 251.

32 Fredric Jameson, 'Postmodernism, or the Cultural Logic of Late Capitalism', *New Left Review*, 146 (1984), pp. 73ff.

33 Michael Davidson, 'Skewed by Design: From Act to Speech Act in Language Writing', *Fragmente*, 2 (autumn 1990), p. 48.

34 Davidson, 'Skewed by Design', p. 48. The role of the reader as co-producer has also been one focus for the exchange of views on Language writing between McGann and Charles Altieri. In a dialogue published in a collection of essays on politics and poetics, Altieri responds to McGann's claims with the charge that the 'focus on language per se' was itself a kind of reification, in relation to which 'audience freedom' might be understood in terms of 'neoconservative economics' rather than leftist opposition. In his response to the response, McGann suggests that Altieri's criticisms are possible because of his own inadequate representation of the Language movement. In returning to the question of 'audience freedom', he concedes that his discussion was 'too abstractly presented'. Nonetheless, his attempt to put the record straight is not entirely convincing. From the point of view of the reader, 'L=A=N=G=U=A=G=E texts' are to be distinguished from advertising copy by virtue of the fact that they 'hold out nothing but problems'. The reader first enters this contract through the 'recognition' that 'the surfaces, the appearances' of these texts are 'disaffected'. This recognition itself prepares the reader for the 'complex and ramifying networks of difficulty' in store. The problem here is with the word 'recognition', which presupposes a particular kind of audience, one already familiar with the defamiliarization that lies ahead. In this respect, McGann's description embraces the possibility of an uninitiated reader only in a limited fashion, as one who may not have encountered Language writing specifically but who is probably well versed in both poetic and theoretical schools of 'complexity' and 'difficulty'. For the reader who has not received such schooling, the first response is not necessarily one of 'recognition'. Deprived of this preparation for the 'reading experience' outlined by McGann, total novices may be unable to resituate themselves as self-reflexive participants in the construction of meaning. The 'consequence' then appears much closer to Jameson's pessimistic outlook. For this exchange, see Charles Altieri, 'Without Consequences Is No Politics: A Response to Jerome McGann', and Jerome J. McGann, 'Response to Charles Altieri', both in Robert von Hallberg (ed.), *Politics and Poetic Value* (Chicago: University of Chicago Press, 1987), p. 305, and pp. 311–12.

35 Nicholls's work on modernism sets the stage in crucial ways for the present

work, in particular his book *Modernisms: A Literary Guide* (Houndmills: Macmillan, 1995).

36 Barrett Watten, *The Constructivist Moment: From Material Text to Cultural Poetics* (Middletown: Wesleyan University Press, 2003), p. xviii.

37 Rachel Blau DuPlessis and Peter Quartermain (eds), *The Objectivist Nexus: Essays in Cultural Poetics* (Tuscaloosa: University of Alabama Press, 1999), p. 20.

38 Tim Woods, *The Poetics of the Limit: Ethics and Politics in Modern and Contemporary American Poetry* (Houndmills: Palgrave Macmillan, 2002).

39 DuPlessis and Quartermain, *The Objectivist Nexus*, p. 22. The editors include 'poet-critics' in this relation, a designation that fits Watten admirably. We might look forward to the day when it is also possible to talk about the critic-poet.

40 Watten, *The Constructivist Moment*, pp. 103 and 118. The essay is called 'The Bride of the Assembly Line: Radical Poetics in Construction'.

41 Watten, *The Constructivist Moment*, p. 118. Watten is quoting from Charles Altieri, 'What Is Living and What Is Dead in American Postmodernism: Establishing the Contemporaneity of Some American Poetry', *Critical Inquiry*, 22:4 (1996), pp. 764–89.

42 Watten's work is the exception here, as we shall see.

43 This claim is repeated throughout Nicholls's work on American poetry. This instance of it comes from his essay 'Beyond *The Cantos*: Pound and American Poetry', in Ira B. Nadel (ed.), *The Cambridge Companion to Ezra Pound* (Cambridge: Cambridge University Press, 1999), p. 152.

44 See Nicholls, 'Beyond *The Cantos*', p. 152.

45 Nicholls, 'Beyond *The Cantos*', p. 152.

46 For a developed account of Surrealism's impact on the arts in the United States, see Dickran Tashjian's, *A Boatload of Madmen: Surrealism and the American Avant-Garde 1920–1950* (New York: Thames and Hudson, 1995).

47 Margaret Cohen, *Profane Illumination: Walter Benjamin and the Paris of Surrealist Revolution* (Berkeley: University of California Press, 1993).

48 Cohen, *Profane Illumination*, p. 27.

49 Charles Borkhuis, 'Writing from Inside Language: Late Surrealism and Textual Poetry in France and the United States', in Mark Wallace and Steven Marks (eds), *Telling It Slant: Avant-Garde Poetics in the 1990s* (Tuscaloosa: University of Alabama Press, 2002), pp. 237 and 245. Against Breton's magistracy, Borkhuis ranks Batailles, Artaud, Leiris, Michaux, Celan and Paz.

50 Borkhuis, 'Writing from Inside Language', p. 241.

Notes to Chapter 2

1 Bernstein, 'Stray Straws and Straw Men', pp. 42–43.

2 Charles Bernstein, 'An Interview with Tom Beckett', *Content's Dream: Essays, 1975–1984* (Los Angeles: Sun and Moon Press, 1986), pp. 385–410.

3 Ron Silliman, 'The New Sentence', reprinted and revised in Ron Silliman, *The New Sentence* (New York: Roof Books, 1987).

4 For a list of qualities which characterize the 'new sentence', see Silliman, 'The New Sentence', p. 91.

5 In the version that appeared in *The New Sentence*, Silliman dropped the reference to European and American 'varieties'.

6 Ron Silliman, 'The New Sentence', *Talks: Hills*, 6/7 (1980), excerpted in Ron Silliman (ed.), *In the American Tree* (Orono: National Poetry Foundation, 1986), p. 570.

7 Michael Davidson, 'After Sentence, Sentence', *American Book Review* (September–October 1982), p. 3.

8 Davidson, 'After Sentence, Sentence', p. 3. Silliman himself refers to this passage in 'New Prose, New Prose Poem', in Larry McCaffery (ed.), *Postmodern Fiction: A Bio-Bibliographical Guide* (New York: Greenwood Press, 1986), p. 159.

9 André Breton, *What Is Surrealism? Selected Writings*, ed. Franklin Rosemont (London: Pluto Press, 1978), p. 105.

10 Lyn Hejinian, 'The Rejection of Closure', reprinted in Lyn Hejinian, *The Language of Inquiry* (Berkeley: University of California Press, 2000), p. 200. This important text was first published in Bob Perelman (ed.), *Writing/Talks* (Carbondale: Southern Illinois University Press, 1985).

11 Malcolm Bowie, *Lacan* (Cambridge: Harvard University Press, 1991), p. 82. 'High' though his theory is, Lacan did not spurn Surrealism. Elizabeth Roudinesco suggests that the 'Surrealist experiment' with automatic messages was inspirational for him as a young man, precisely to the extent that it forced 'an encounter between the Freudian unconscious, language and the decentering of the subject'. Similarly, David Macey claims that what is at stake for Lacan in Surrealism 'is language itself, the symbolic, and therefore the status of the individual subject'. Elizabeth Roudinesco, *Lacan & Co. A History of Psychoanalysis in France 1925–1985*, trans. Jeffrey Mehlman (London: Free Association Books, 1990), p. 26; David Macey, *Lacan in Contexts* (London: Verso Books, 1988), p. 55.

12 This distinction is crucial to ecocritical reformulations of subjectivity. See, for example Patrick D. Murphy, 'Anotherness and Inhabitation in Recent Multicultural American Writing', in Richard Kerridge and Neil Sammells (eds), *Writing the Environment: Ecocriticism and Literature* (London: Zed Books, 1998), pp. 40–52.

13 Fredric Jameson, *Marxism and Form* (Princeton: Princeton University Press, 1971).

14 For the primary texts of the debate between Benjamin and Adorno, see Ernst Bloch, Georg Lukacs, Bertolt Brecht, Walter Benjamin and Theodor Adorno, *Aesthetics and Politics: The Key Texts of the Classic Debate Within German Marxism*, trans. R. Taylor (London: Verso, 1980), pp. 110–41.

15 Hal Foster, *Compulsive Beauty* (Cambridge: MIT Press, 1993). For Nicholls on the segregation of the unconscious from therapy, see *Modernisms*, p. 281.

16 The departure of Breton from Freudian models of the unconscious is central to Foster's argument. The difference is partly due to the fact that Breton first encountered Freud's work indirectly. The 'Janetian orientation' which formed part of the context of Breton's reception of psychoanalysis enabled him to develop 'a conception of the unconscious at a remove from Freudian models of conflictual forces, a conception of a *champ magnétique* of associations registered through automatist means, an unconscious based on originary unity rather than primal repression'. Foster, *Compulsive Beauty*, p. 3.

17 John Forrester, *The Seductions of Psychoanalysis: Freud, Lacan and Derrida* (Cambridge: Cambridge University Press, 1990).

18 André Breton, 'Manifesto of Surrealism', in *Manifestoes of Surrealism* (1969), trans. Richard Seaver and Helen R. Lane (Ann Arbor: University of Michigan Press, 1972), p. 11.

19 Breton, 'Manifesto of Surrealism', p. 11.

20 Quoted in Hartley, *Textual Politics*, p. 35.

21 Cited in David Gascoyne's introduction to André Breton and Philippe Soupault, *The Magnetic Fields*, trans. David Gascoyne (3rd edn) (London: Atlas Press, 1985), p. 11.

22 Breton, 'Manifesto of Surrealism', p. 34.

170

23 Distraction is key to Tim Armstrong's cultural analysis of Surrealism, in *Modernism, Technology and the Body: A Cultural Study* (Cambridge: Cambridge University Press, 1998).

24 André Breton, Paul Eluard and Philippe Soupault, *The Automatic Message*, trans. David Gascoyne, Antony Melville and Jon Graham (London: Atlas Press, 1997), p. 49. David Gascoyne makes reference to this comment in his useful introduction to his own translation of *Les Champs Magnétiques*.

25 André Breton and Philippe Soupault, *Les Champs Magnétiques* (Paris: Gallimard, 1968), p. 53.

26 Breton and Soupault, *The Magnetic Fields*, pp. 50–51.

27 Breton and Soupault, *Les Champs Magnétiques*, p. 53.

28 Breton and Soupault, *The Magnetic Fields*, p. 51.

29 Silliman, 'The New Sentence', p. 89.

30 Breton and Soupault, *The Magnetic Fields*, p. 51.

31 Silliman, 'The New Sentence', p. 90.

32 Bruce Andrews, 'Writing Social Work and Political Practice', reprinted in Bruce Andrews and Charles Bernstein (eds), *The L=A=N=G=U=A=G=E Book* (Carbondale: Southern Illinois University Press, 1984), p. 134.

33 In *gravité*, Breton may also be punning on the word's Latin root, *gravidus*, which is used to denote the pains of childbirth.

34 Surrealism was committed from the outset to a rejection of French colonial enterprises. Also echoing in this spatialized juxtaposition of social harmony and military conflict is, of course, the civil strife of the Paris Commune.

Notes to Chapter 3

1 Hank Lazer, 'Language Writing; or Literary History and the Strange Case of the Two Dr. Williamses', in *Opposing Poetries. Volume 2: Readings* (Evanston: Northwestern University Press, 1996), p. 19. Lazer first delivered this paper at the 1989 University of Louisville Twentieth Century Literature conference. His account of the Williams constructed by Language writers draws on two important interventions in the narrative of American literary modernism. The first is Ron Silliman's 'Z-Sited Path', reprinted in Ron Silliman, *The New Sentence* (New York: Roof Books, 1987); the second is Charles Bernstein's 'The Academy in Peril: William Carlos Williams Meets the MLA', reprinted in Charles Bernstein, *Content's Dream: Essays, 1975–1984* (Los Angeles: Sun and Moon Press, 1986).

2 Lazer, 'Language Writing', p. 21.

3 Lazer, 'Language Writing', p. 25.

4 Silliman, 'Z-Sited Path', p. 132.

5 Silliman, 'Z-Sited Path', p. 135.

6 Bernstein, 'The Academy in Peril', p. 244.

7 Bernstein, 'The Academy in Peril', pp. 249 and 245.

8 Stephen Fredman, *Poet's Prose: The Crisis in American Verse* (2nd edn) (Cambridge: Cambridge University Press, 1990).

9 Fredman selects for special mention two talks given in a series hosted by Bob Perelman in the spring of 1997. The first was 'The Prose of Fact' by Michael Davidson; the second was Silliman's 'The New Sentence'. Fredman's account of the fierce debate that took place during the course of Davidson's talk is interesting for the way in which the disputants are aligned according to either

their Objectivist or their post-structuralist leanings. See Fredman, *Poet's Prose*, pp. viiff.

10 Michael Benedikt, *The Poetry of Surrealism: An Anthology* (Boston: Little, Brown, 1974).

11 Receptivity distinguishes poet's prose from an alternative, Emersonian stance, as Fredman defines it. Vying with poet's prose in the representation of experience is the American 'long poem'. Exemplified by Ezra Pound's *Cantos*, this form eschews receptivity for 'the heroic imposition of the verse epic'. See Fredman, *Poet's Prose*, p. 7.

12 Gerald L. Bruns, 'De Improvisatione', *Iowa Review*, 9:3 (1978), pp. 66–69.

13 'Contact' was a key word for Williams during this phase of his career. Signifying the direct relation between the work of art and its local environment, it was used by him and Robert McAlmon as the title of the magazine that they co-edited between 1920 and 1924.

14 Paul Mariani, *William Carlos Williams: A New World Naked* (New York: W. W. Norton, 1990), p. 186.

15 William Carlos Williams, *Imaginations* (New York: New Directions Books, 1970).

16 Mariani, *William Carlos Williams*, p. 186.

17 Fredman, *Poet's Prose*, p. 19.

18 The juxtaposition is even more extreme if we read the dot between the two 'words' as the marker of petroleum's abbreviation.

19 In fact, the list is a series of juxtapositions of positive and negative terms. Nor are the pairs fixed: 'food-grease' is a juxtaposition in itself but works equally well when it rubs along with 'hair'.

20 Tzvetan Todorov, *The Fantastic: A Structural Approach to a Literary Genre* (Cleveland: Case Western Reserve University, 1973), p. 25.

21 Mariani, *William Carlos Williams*, p. 187.

22 Breton, *Manifestoes of Surrealism*, pp. 31–32.

23 Breton, *Manifestoes of Surrealism*, p. 31.

24 Breton, *Manifestoes of Surrealism*, pp. 89–90.

25 Armand Hoog, 'The Surrealist Novel', *Yale French Studies*, 8 (1951), p. 17.

26 Hoog, 'The Surrealist Novel', p. 18.

27 The trip back from the Extermination Commission is based in fact, as is the bedroom scene. See Mariani, *William Carlos Williams*, p. 187.

28 Breton, *Manifestoes of Surrealism*, p. 31.

29 Michael Riffaterre, *Semiotics of Poetry* (London: Methuen, 1978), p. 140.

30 Riffaterre, *Semiotics of Poetry*, p. 140. The 'given' is the first sentence of the 'text' that Riffaterre is analysing. Text 27 begins with the sentence 'Il y avait une fois un dindon sur une digue', or, in English, 'Once upon a time there was a turkey on a dike'. Riffaterre goes on to point out that this sentence derives from a children's rhyme from the nineteenth century, in which the words are run together and 'scrambled' – *diguedondaine diguedindon* – to produce 'a sound-symbolization of bells ringing' (p. 140). While Breton scrambles rhyme with tale, he actually unscrambles the words themselves.

31 Riffaterre, *Semiotics of Poetry*, p. 141.

32 Williams had, in fact, been translating Soupault's book at the same time as working on *A Novelette*. For a brief discussion of the circumstances surrounding the translation, and Williams's flagging enthusiasm for the project, see Mariani, *William Carlos Williams*, pp. 286–87.

33 William Carlos Williams and Robert McAlmon, Editorial, *Contact*, 1 (1920), p. 1.

34 In the discussion of the work of Juan Gris which follows the section on Surrealism, Williams continues the theme of revolution in language, noting that 'the aberrant is the classic' (p. 283).

35 Tyrus Miller talks in terms of a 'metaphorics of contagion' that is linked to the 'nonspecialization' and 'generic transgressions' of Surrealism. See Tyrus Miller, 'Poetic Contagion: Surrealism and Williams's *A Novelette*', *William Carlos Williams Review*, 22 (spring 1997), pp. 19–20.

36 See Marjorie Perloff, '"Barbed-Wire Entanglements": The "New American Poetry," 1930–32', in *Poetry On and Off the Page: Essays for Emergent Occasions* (Evanstown: Northwestern University Press, 1998), pp. 51–82.

37 Perloff, 'Barbed-Wire Entanglements', p. 53.

38 Perloff, 'Barbed-Wire Entanglements', p. 53.

39 Perloff, 'Barbed-Wire Entanglements', p. 64.

40 Perloff, 'Barbed-Wire Entanglements', pp. 66–67.

41 Mike Weaver, *William Carlos Williams: The American Background* (Cambridge: Cambridge University Press, 1971), p. 135. Perloff includes Dahlberg in the new aesthetic.

42 Weaver, *William Carlos Williams*, p. 137. Weaver notes that Williams recommended the article to Zukofsky. The original article can be found in *Fifth Floor Window*, 1:3 (1932), pp. 1–6.

43 Weaver, *William Carlos Williams*, p. 137. This analysis does not map exactly onto Perloff's. In her discussion of proletarian poetry, she suggests that in aesthetic terms it was derived not from naturalism but 'the genteel tradition of a previous generation'. See Perloff, 'Barbed-Wire Entanglements', p. 80. Nevertheless, both accounts assume a limited terrain in which Surrealism might take root in the US.

44 Cited in Weaver, *William Carlos Williams*, p. 138.

45 Arguably, this critique reappears in the criticism of the 'twin deconstructors' of Williams's writing, J. Hillis Miller and Joseph N. Riddel. For this designation of these two major interpreters of Williams, see Steven Gould Axelrod and Helen Deese (eds), *Critical Essays on William Carlos Williams* (New York: G. K. Hall, Macmillan, 1995), p. 44 n24.

46 Perloff, 'Barbed-Wire Entanglements', p. 67.

47 For Tashjian's discussion of *Blues*, see Tashjian, *A Boatload of Madmen*, pp. 155–57.

48 Steven C. Tracy, 'William Carlos Williams and *Blues: A Magazine of New Rhythms*', *William Carlos Williams Review*, 15:2 (1989), p. 20.

49 The poem was 'simplex sigilum veri: a catalogue', which appeared in *Blues*, 2:7 (1929), p. 9.

50 William Carlos Williams, 'For a New Magazine', *Blues*, 1:2 (1929), p. 30.

51 Williams, 'For a New Magazine'. Ford directly encouraged Williams in the role of mediator, to the point of suggesting what and how he might contribute to its pages. In a letter on the magazine's stationery (dated July 1929), Ford states his wishes for a future article by Williams, noting that he would like him 'to convey to the young artist who is fascinated by "word revolt" and modernistic techniques that now of all moments when he can be reassuringly a la mode [sic] is the time for him to reflect upon the essential nature of his art'. The anxiety about Imagism identified by Perloff seems well illustrated by Ford's wish that readers be told that *Blues* has no desire to elevate form over subject matter, even though that impression is sometimes given 'by accident'. In delivering the message, Williams is urged to 'use "hard" language without seeming to ignore critical precision'. This letter (F684) is held in the William

Carlos Williams papers, at the Poetry and Rare Books Collection, University Libraries, State University of New York at Buffalo. Ford's remarks seem to echo Williams's concern about the public perception of contemporary writing and it is worth noting that Williams pretty much followed the editor's instructions in a piece that also seeks to distance the role of the artist from negative caricatures based on ill-founded applications of Freud. So, in 'Caviar and Bread Again: A Warning to the New Writer', Williams begins with a discussion of 'substance', and moves on to note that 'technique is a part of it – new technique; technique is itself substance, as all artists much know; but it is the substance under that, forming that, giving it its reason for existence which must be the final answer and source of reliance'. See William Carlos Williams, 'Caviar and Bread Again: A Warning to the New Writer', *Blues*, 2:9 (1930), p. 47.

52 Williams, 'For a New Magazine', p. 30.
53 William Carlos Williams, 'A Note on the Art of Poetry', *Blues*, 1:4 (1929), p. 77.
54 Williams, 'A Note on the Art of Poetry', p. 79.
55 William Carlos Williams, 'Introduction to a Collection of Modern Writings', *Blues*, 2:7 (1929), p. 3.
56 Williams, 'For a New Magazine', p. 30. For Surrealism's 'living defense of literature', see Williams, *Imaginations*, p. 281. This thread of critical estimation extends to 1938 and the preface that Williams wrote for Ford's *The Garden of Disorder*. Here he approves of Ford's verbal juxtapositions as 'a counterfoil to the vague and excessively stupid juxtapositions commonly known as "reality"'. Cited in Tashjian, *A Boatload of Madmen*, p. 162. Tashjian finds in Williams's commentary on Ford's poetics an allusion to Breton's account (made in the First Manifesto) of the first time he experienced the automatic image but makes much of the difference between the 'contactual' character of Ford's composition and the allegedly isolated experience recounted by Breton.
57 William Closson Emory, 'Miner Away', *Blues*, 1:3 (1929), p. 53.
58 It is interesting to note that Emory also experimented with a Blues format. See, for example, 'Theme for a Blues Song', *Blues*, 1:4 (1929), p. 95.
59 Charles Henri Ford, 'The Room', *Blues*, 1:3 (1929), p. 75.
60 William Carlos Williams, 'The Work of Gertrude Stein', reprinted in *Imaginations*, p. 348.
61 Williams, *Imaginations*, p. 351.
62 Williams, *Imaginations*, p. 348.
63 Marjorie Perloff, 'Late Late Modern', at http://wings.buffalo.edu/epc/authors/perloff/parker.html. This essay was originally published in the *William Carlos Williams Review*.
64 Parker Tyler, *Fantasy*, 6:4 (1940), p. 44, cited in Perloff, 'Late Late Modern'.
65 See *Blues*, 1:2 (1929), pp. 49–51.
66 Parker Tyler, 'This Dreaming Image', *Blues*, 1:2 (1929), pp. 49–50.
67 The polar motif that opens and closes the poem seems to be in close communication with the Surrealist trope of *Les Champs Magnétiques* (see Chapter 2).
68 Perloff, 'Late Late Modern'.
69 These remarks are made in 'Paris, Capital of the Nineteenth Century'. My citation is from Cohen, *Profane Illumination*, p. 27.
70 Cohen, *Profane Illumination*, p. 27.
71 Parker Tyler, 'Sonnet', *Blues*, 1:2 (1929), pp. 50–51.
72 The chase involves going upstairs but also seems to remain inside the door.

Notes to Chapter 4

1 Perloff, 'Barbed-Wire Entanglements', p. 51.
2 Perloff concludes that this 'matrix ... may well be more telling than the usual placement of that poetry in the Pound–Williams tradition'. See 'Barbed-Wire Entanglements', p. 68. My own discussion implies that Williams's improvisational writing fits this matrix more comfortably than it does the contours of Imagism.
3 DuPlessis and Quartermain, *The Objectivist Nexus*, p. 19.
4 Richard R. Frye, 'Scrying the Signs: Objectivist Premonitions in Williams' *Spring and All*', *Sagetrieb*, 8:3 (1989), pp. 77–95.
5 See Jenny Penberthy, *Niedecker and the Correspondence with Zukofsky 1931–1970* (Cambridge: Cambridge University Press, 1993), pp. 20–28.
6 See Peter Nicholls, 'Lorine Niedecker: Rural Surreal', in Jenny Penberthy (ed.), *Lorine Niedecker: Woman and Poet* (Orono: National Poetry Foundation, University of Maine Press, 1996).
7 In some important ways, I am setting up here a false distinction between poet and critic, one that could not be applied to first- or second-wave modernists and which is even more misleading in the case of Language writing. The best example here is the man who has probably had more to say about Surrealism than any other Language writer, Barrett Watten. Watten is not just a critic but also holds the position of Professor of English at Wayne State University. The title of his prize-winning collection of essays, *The Constructivist Moment*, echoes that of Perloff's scholarly monograph *The Futurist Moment*.
8 Take, for example, Charles Bernstein's comments on Charles Reznikoff, that 'perhaps he understood the nature, the social structure, of obscurity better than his contemporaries. Neglect, disregard – the socially obscure, the forgotten and repressed, the overlooked – this was his subject.' See 'Reznikoff's Nearness', reprinted in Charles Bernstein, *My Way: Speeches and Poems* (Chicago: University of Chicago Press, 1999), p. 221. Bernstein also draws parallels between the experience of Reznikoff's immigrant forebears and his own.
9 In his essay on Zukofsky and political radicalism, Mark Scroggins notes that 'the economic disaster ... worked to destroy a large proportion of the network of little magazines that had sprung up during the 1920s to publish avant-garde and experimental work'. See Mark Scroggins, 'The Revolutionary Word: Louis Zukosky, *New Masses*, and Political Radicalism in the 1930s', in Mark Scroggins (ed.), *Upper Limit Music: The Writing of Louis Zukofsky* (Tuscaloosa: University of Alabama Press, 1997), p. 56.
10 Writing in 1930, against the detractors of Surrealism, Breton spurns a critical method that picks up on isolated instances of the Surrealist image: 'One will not have succeeded in sanctioning neo-naturalistic procedures at the expense of ours, that is, in deprecating everything which, since naturalism, has contributed to the most important conquests the mind has made'. See André Breton, 'Second Manifesto of Surrealism', *Manifestoes of Surrealism*, trans. Richard Seaver and Helen R. Lane (Ann Arbor: University of Michigan Press, 1972), pp. 153–54.
11 Walter Benjamin, 'Surrealism: The Last Snapshot of the European Intelligentsia', *One-Way Street and Other Writings*, trans. Edmund Jephcott and Kingsley Shorter (London: Verso, 1985), p. 239.
12 Louis Zukofsky, 'American Poetry 1920–1930', *The Symposium*, 2:1 (January 1931), reprinted in Louis Zukofsky, *Prepositions: The Collected Critical Essays* (New York: Horizon Press, 1967), pp. 129–43.
13 Charles Altieri, 'The Objectivist Tradition', in Rachel Blau DuPlessis and Peter

Quartermain (eds), *The Objectivist Nexus: Essays in Cultural Poetics* (Tuscaloosa: University of Alabama Press, 1999), pp. 25–36; Rosalind Krauss, *The Originality of the Avant-Garde and Other Modernist Myths* (Cambridge: MIT Press, 1986).

14 See Armstrong, *Modernism, Technology and the Body*, pp. 187ff.

15 For a discussion of the mechanical character of Surrealist automatic writing, see Armstrong, *Modernism, Technology and the Body*, pp. 202–3.

16 For a translation of Breton's return to his 'Sunflower', see André Breton, *Mad Love*, trans. Mary Ann Caws (Lincoln: University of Nebraska Press, 1987), pp. 53ff. In her introduction, Caws describes the original as itself 'an object-book, in the classic surrealist style, interleaved with photographs … and with letters from Breton stuck between the pages' (p. xvi).

17 Zukofsky, *Prepositions*, p. 21.

18 Zukofsky, *Prepositions*, p. 21, my emphasis.

19 Zukofsky, *Prepositions*, p. 140.

20 The photograph of the abandoned locomotive was first published in *Minotaure* in 1937.

21 Zukofsky, *Prepositions*, p. 20.

22 Breton, *Mad Love*, p. 15.

23 *Blues*, 2:9 (February 1929), p. 42. Serly was a student of Béla Bartók. In the context of the Blues aesthetic, it is worth noting his influence on Manny Albam, a jazz composer who taught composition at the Manhattan School of Music in New York City. The other dedication – 'D.R.' – is to Diego Riviera; unlike 'Tibor Serly', it is explicitly political in its mode of address, prompting speculations about its non-appearance in *Blues*.

24 'Not much more than being' becomes the second poem in '29 Poems' and 'Tibor Serly' is the twenty-eighth. See Louis Zukofsky, *Complete Short Poetry* (Baltimore: Johns Hopkins University Press, 1991), pp. 22 and 37.

25 The first poem of the four, which begins 'Not much more than being', is revisited by Zukofsky in his 1969 interview with L. S. Dembo. This interview is reprinted in Carroll F. Terrell (ed.), *Louis Zukofsky: Man and Poet* (Orono: National Poetry Foundation, University of Maine Press, 1979), pp. 265–81.

26 As I have already indicated, 'diurnal' is a key word for my reading of this group of poems. In itself, it signals the contrasting contexts of ecclesiastical temporality – in the form of the book of canonical hours – and the measurement of modern time by the issue of daily newspapers.

27 Zukofsky, *Prepositions*, p. 20.

28 Zukofsky, *Prepositions*, pp. 23–24.

29 Zukofsky, *Prepositions*, p. 22.

30 For their translation, in which the Zukofskys sought to preserve not just the meaning but the sound, the rhythm and the syntax of the Latin, see Zukofsky, *Complete Short Poetry*, pp. 272–79.

31 The reference to Mormonism adds an extra twist to this subversion of conventional chronology. The Book of Mormon seeks to establish the migration of the Hebrews to the United States in 600 BC, before the ascendancy of Athens.

32 Likewise does the subversive potential of literary Latin haunt the pieties of liturgical Latin.

33 In seeking to bring into balance different traditions, Zukofsky's method contrasts with the direct challenge of the Book of Mormon to Christian orthodoxy.

34 This assertion raises provocative questions in relation to the animal 'kingdom'.

35 Zukofsky, *Prepositions*, p. 24.

36 Zukofsky, *Prepositions*, p. 24.

37 Altieri, 'The Objectivist Tradition', p. 30.
38 I am invoking here Krauss's discussion of the importance of doubling for Surrealist photography. In her account, the double establishes a kind of 'formal rhythm' of rupture, which 'banishes the unitary condition of the moment, that creates *within* the moment an experience of fission'. Against this formal rhythm, Zukofsky tries to take more material measures, broadening the threshold between the second 'hey' and the first, lest 'through duplication, it opens the original to the effect of difference, of deferral, of one-thing-after-another, or within another: or of multiples burgeoning within the same'. See Krauss, *The Originality of the Avant-Garde*, p. 109.
39 For the 'sensational' response to the first issue of *Blues*, see Tashjian, *A Boatload of Madmen*, pp. 137–38.
40 Cited in Tashjian, *A Boatload of Madmen*, p. 138.
41 For the 'full' story of Iphis, see Ovid, *Metamorphoses*, Book IX, ll. 666–797. Ovid emphasizes the foreign origins of Isis through reference to her Egyptian origins and the symbolic accoutrements of her rituals: moon-shaped horns and the sistra.
42 Space forbids my discussion of the poem, 'Ferry'; it, too, takes place on the border between water and land. Like Williams's poem XX, it uses the word 'plash' to describe the motion and the sound of the sea. See Zukofsky, *Complete Short Poetry*, p. 24.
43 Even without the shadow of Shakespeare's 'dark lady', this poem keeps faith with Williams in crossing the colour line. Whereas Williams refers explicitly to race, however, in poem XIX, Zukofsky's gesture is, paradoxically, both more cryptic and more graphic. The distinction between black and white hides within the reference to sunburn but once this allusion is disclosed, torture and violence 'stand naked' in the final stanza.
44 Williams, *Imaginations*, p. 281.
45 Williams, *Imaginations*, p. 136.
46 Zukofsky, *Prepositions*, p. 141. He is referring to *The Tempers, Al Que Quiere, Sour Grapes* and *Kora in Hell*.
47 Another Classical reference seems germane here. *The Aeneid* begins 'arma virumque cano' ('Of arms and the man, I sing'). The rest of the epic explores the complexities of this specific conjunction.
48 Krauss, *The Originality of the Avant-Garde*, p. 109.
49 See *Poetry*, 37:5 (February 1931), pp. 285–89.
50 Ford's piece, 'Left Instantly Designs', seems to resonate with 'The sun—' in several specific ways:

> describe the circles
> first; terror
> will stay and
> the moon displace
>
> them and control
> the rain; –
> then walk away
> in the rain's disgrace;
>
> the blood's obedience
> will follow
> instantly designs
> left in the sky's hollow;

once fearful often
each ear then
accepts its
rightful coffin;

if the dream
cries, let
the moon mother
it, encircled

with goodbyes
mist
cannot
smother;

explain your circles
to the sun
and, but for the dark,
run.

'Circles' describe the shape of Zukofsky's 'sign on the wave', while 'terror' may pick up on 'tortured'. Most suggestive, however, is the final stanza. Here, the verbal echoes are clear; thematically, a contrast is offered. 'Run' defies the rest of 'dun', while the status of the sun as emblematic for the rational mind is tested by the 'dark' power of the moon, guardian of 'dream / cries'.

51 Burton Hatlen, 'Objectivist Poets in Context', in Rachel Blau DuPlessis and Peter Quartermain (eds), *The Objectivist Nexus: Essays in Cultural Poetics* (Tuscaloosa: University of Alabama Press, 1999), p. 40.
52 Tashjian's account suggests that the engagement of Ford and Tyler with Surrealism took time to develop. Ford did not meet Breton, for example, until the late 1930s. See *A Boatload of Madmen*, pp. 156ff.
53 Hatlen, 'Objectivist Poets in Context', p. 32.
54 Hatlen, 'Objectivist Poets in Context', p. 32.
55 *Poetry*, 37:5, p. 287.
56 *Poetry*, 37:5, p. 288.
57 *Poetry*, 37:5, p. 287.
58 Foster, *Compulsive Beauty*, p. 126.
59 Foster, *Compulsive Beauty*, p. 127.
60 *Poetry*, 37:5, p. 288.
61 F. S. Flint, 'Imagisme', reprinted in Peter Faulkner (ed.), *A Modernist Reader* (London: Batsford, 1986), p. 41.
62 Ezra Pound, 'A Few Don'ts for Imagistes', reprinted in Peter Faulkner (ed.), *A Modernist Reader* (London: Batsford, 1986), p. 60.
63 Tyler's poem can be read fruitfully as a response to the second section of Pound's *Hugh Selwyn Mauberley* (1920).
64 Perloff, 'Barbed-Wire Entanglements', p. 75.
65 In this respect, my analysis is very much in sympathy with Cary Nelson's reading of Ford's work during the period. He carefully notes that Ford 'is mostly identified with surrealism' but takes pains to stress that this affiliation does not preclude the writing of 'socially conscious poetry'. Discussing a poem – 'Plaint' – which protests against segregational violence, Nelson discerns 'surrealism … articulated to political outrage'. See Cary Nelson, *Repression and Recovery: Modern American Poetry and the Politics of Cultural Memory 1919–1945* (Madison: University of Wisconsin Press, 1989), p. 116.

Notes to Chapter 5

1 *VVV* ran from 1942 to 1944, while *View* appeared between 1940 and 1947. For discussions of these magazines see Weaver, *William Carlos Williams*, and Tashjian, *A Boatload of Madmen*, pp. 209–14, 188–90. Catrina Neiman and Paul Nathan have also compiled a very useful anthology, *View: Parade of the Avant-Garde* (New York: Thunder's Mouth Press, 1992).

2 Williams recorded his version of the meeting in notes he made for the publication of Zukofsky's collection *Anew*: 'Being curious and talking a few words of French (he seemed to know nothing of my language) we said a few words to each other by way of greeting; when, thinking he might want to know something of my mind I told him I was much interested in new concepts of the structure of the poetic line – just as, perhaps, the physio-chemist might take an interest in the structure of the molecule or, even more radically, the atom. His reply was drastic and final, "Rien da ça!"'.

3 Bernstein, 'The Academy in Peril'.

4 Nicholls, 'An Interview with Bob Perelman', p. 534.

5 Charles Bernstein, 'Words and Pictures', in *Content's Dream: Essays, 1975–1984* (Los Angeles: Sun and Moon Press, 1986), p. 149.

6 Bernstein, 'Words and Pictures', p. 151.

7 Bernstein, 'Words and Pictures', p. 153.

8 Bob Perelman, *The Trouble with Genius: Reading Pound, Joyce, Stein and Zukofsky* (Berkeley: University of California Press, 1994), p. 186.

9 Perelman, *The Trouble with Genius*, p. 187. As we have seen in Chapter 1, Perelman has responded to this section of 'A'-6 in poetic form.

10 Perelman, *The Trouble with Genius*, p. 187.

11 Perelman, *The Trouble with Genius*, p. 188.

12 Silliman, 'Z-Sited Path', p. 127.

13 Michael Palmer, 'Some Notes on Shelley, Poetics and the Present', *Sulfur*, 33 (1993), p. 273.

14 Woods, *The Poetics of the Limit*, p. 8.

15 Palmer, 'Some Notes on Shelley, Poetics and the Present', p. 281.

16 Peter Gizzi, 'Interview with Michael Palmer', in Peter Gizzi (ed.), *Exact Change Yearbook 1* (Manchester: Carcanet, 1995). The editors of the one and (sadly) only *Exact Change Yearbook* had in mind an annual anthology that might fill the gap left when New Directions Books discontinued its annual in 1991. Gizzi did not just provide the interview with Palmer but edited the whole collection, finding what the publishers describe as 'a range of contemporary work that draws on the tradition we publish in our books of Surrealist and other early twentieth-century experimentation'. The selection included work by Gertrude Stein, Hugo Ball, Giorgio de Chiroco and Susan Howe. The anthology also represents poetic voices emerging from countries or regions historically marginalized in the Western literary canon.

17 Gizzi, 'Interview with Michael Palmer', p. 173. Palmer had set the series up himself, after he had discovered that Harvard's Adams House 'had money from the Ford Foundation for cultural purposes' (p. 172).

18 Michael Palmer, 'On Objectivism', *Sulfur*, 26 (spring 1990), pp. 121–22.

19 Palmer, 'On Objectivism', p. 122.

20 Palmer, 'On Objectivism', p. 123.

21 Palmer, 'On Objectivism', p. 122.

22 Nicholls, *Modernisms*, p. 288.

23 Nicholls, *Modernisms*, p. 288.

24 Palmer, 'On Objectivism', p. 123.
25 Palmer, 'On Objectivism', p. 123.
26 Michael Palmer, 'Autobiography, Memory and Mechanisms of Concealment', in Bob Perelman (ed.), *Writing/Talks* (Carbondale: Southern Illinois University Press, 1985), pp. 227–28.
27 Andrew Crozier, 'Zukofsky's List', in Rachel Blau DuPlessis and Peter Quartermain (eds), *The Objectivist Nexus: Essays in Cultural Poetics* (Tuscaloosa: University of Alabama Press, 1999), p. 275.
28 Crozier, 'Zukofsky's List', p. 275.
29 As someone whose scholarly training felt the brunt of the post-structuralist orthodoxy, I am gratefully sensitive to Palmer's remarks.
30 As indicated in Chapter 1, Vernon Shetley is critical of what he sees as the reciprocal relation of support between Language writing and academics. Participating in the 'ethical turn' of criticism that has emerged in recent years, Woods's is a good example of a thesis that returns to the 'critical' potential of deconstruction. The current work shares this aspiration.
31 Peter Bürger, *Theory of the Avant-Garde* (Minneapolis: University of Minnesota Press, 1984).
32 Palmer's comments on the inadequacy of the 'poetic sign' recall Adorno's haunting claim that poetry is impossible after the holocaust. Palmer's expression, perhaps clear in the original dialogue, is (ironically) ambiguous when written down. Poems of witness entail 'facing something that may even overwhelm the poetic sign in its multiplicity of meanings, sometimes often horrible' (Gizzi, 'Interview with Michael Palmer', p. 167). Does the horror of events create a multiplicity of meanings that the poetic sign is unable to capture, or is it the case that, even in its multiplicity of meanings, the poetic sign cannot contain the horror of events?
33 Zukofsky, *Prepositions*, p. 143.
34 Zukofsky, *Prepositions*, pp. 140–42.
35 See Chapter 1, p. 23.
36 Jean Baudrillard, *The Gulf War Did Not Take Place*, trans. Paul Patton (Sydney: Power Publications, 1995), p. 39.
37 Zukofsky, *Prepositions*, p. 25.
38 Zukofsky, *Prepositions*, p. 21.
39 *The New Shorter Oxford Dictionary*, ed. Lesley Brown (Oxford: Clarendon Press, 1993), vol. I, p. 1716.
40 *The New Shorter Oxford Dictionary*, p. 1716.
41 *The New Shorter Oxford Dictionary*, p. 1716.
42 I think of Williams here, of Zukofsky's Williams who achieved 'vision amid pressure', and of the Williams whose responsibility as a doctor and family man often collided with his desire to write.
43 Michael Palmer, *At Passages* (New York: New Directions, 1995).
44 There is a reference to 'The difficulties with burying the dead' two stanzas earlier on (p. 16).
45 These two lines must qualify as one of the tersest elegies ever composed. The memorial vein running through the sequence opens into a more personal and more literary place with 'Twenty-Four Logics in Memory of Lee Hickman'. Hickman was the editor of *Temblor*, a small magazine that published some of Palmer's writing. Marjorie Perloff describes Hickman as 'one of the great unsung heroes of the so-called innovative poetry scene'. His publication, she implies, lay outside the matrices of power in which poetry is usually produced. Hickman was not affiliated either to an academic or to a publishing institution,

and his magazine did not receive any grant money until the final issues. Added to which, he lived in 'the much despised San Fernando Valley above Hollywood'. See Marjorie Perloff, 'After Language Poetry'. Hickman died of AIDS. Palmer's elegy is characteristically at odds with the emphasis on sensibility of much elegiac poetry. He offers 'Logics in Memory' rather than feelings. The poem has twenty-four lines, suggesting that each line is in itself a logic. If it is meet to interpret one man's memory of another, it is tempting to invoke here logic's 'matrix'. The end of the poem can be read as a critique of commemoration as an accumulation of expressions so removed from their context that they almost become variables. The poem has no full stops, so it is difficult to quote from it (*At Passages*, p. 24) without beginning *in medias res*:

> and coloring nights the yellow of hay,
> scarlet of trillium, blue of block ice
> Words appear, the texture of ice,
>
> with messages etched on their shells:
> *Minna 1892, Big Max and Little Sarah,*
> *This hour ago*
>
> *Everyone watched as the statue fell*
> Enough of such phrases and we'll have a book
> Enough of such books
>
> and we'll have mountains of ice
> enough to balance our days with nights
> enough at last to close our eyes

46 Palmer, 'Some Notes on Shelley, Poetics and the Present', p. 281.
47 Palmer, 'Some Notes on Shelley, Poetics and the Present', p. 274.
48 Walter Benjamin, *Theses on History*, cited in Palmer, 'Some Notes on Shelley, Poetics and the Present', p. 273.
49 Palmer, 'Some Notes on Shelley, Poetics and the Present', p. 273.
50 Palmer, 'Some Notes on Shelley, Poetics and the Present', p. 274.
51 Palmer, 'Some Notes on Shelley, Poetics and the Present', p. 274.
52 Palmer, 'Some Notes on Shelley, Poetics and the Present', p. 281.
53 Palmer, 'Some Notes on Shelley, Poetics and the Present', p. 281.
54 Palmer, 'Some Notes on Shelley, Poetics and the Present', p. 277.
55 The alphabet will also have had a hand in the prominence of this body part beginning with 'h'.
56 Michael Palmer, 'The Site of the Poem', in Peter Gizzi (ed.), *Exact Change Yearbook 1* (Manchester: Carcanet, 1995), p. 190.
57 The recurrence of Osiris in Palmer's writing – he appears later in *At Passages* and in the preamble to the talk on Shelley – invites an understanding of the past that is mythological, disjunctive and literal in its re-membering.
58 The shadbush grows in North America; its name derives from its habit of flowering when the migratory shad fish appear in the rivers.
59 Later in the poem, we come across what might be veiled images of bodily mutation resulting from exposure to nuclear fall-out: 'that simply, as a poem / Have you heard the angels with sexed tongues, / met the blind boy who could see with his skin' (*At Passages*, p. 21). If the angels are of poetry, the potential for redemption remains, perhaps. The polysemous figure of the *Angelus Novus* is a fertile matrix, offering the generative tissue of language – 'sexed tongues' – 'for' physical regeneration now tragically compromised. As the first line of the

stanza implies, however, it is important to take care of the difference between the potential for poetic redemption and the need for practical assistance for people affected by nuclear experimentation in the American south-west. For a provocative account of the ongoing effects of such activity, see Mike Davis, *Dead Cities* (New York: New Press, 2002), pp. 33–63.

60 Michael Palmer, 'Period (Sense of Duration)', at http://www.english.uiuc.edu/maps/poets/m_r/palmer/period.html, p. 9.

61 Palmer, 'Period (Sense of Duration)', p. 9.

62 Palmer, 'Period (Sense of Duration)', p. 2.

63 Palmer, 'Period (Sense of Duration)', p. 1.

64 Cited in Palmer, 'Period (sense of duration)', p. 2. Kubler's remarks come in *The Shape of Time*.

65 Palmer, 'Some Notes on Shelley, Poetics and the Present', p. 273.

66 Palmer, 'Period (sense of duration)', p. 3.

67 Although he does, of course, assume a broad community of exposure to mediated images of the 'conflict'.

68 Michael Palmer, *The Danish Notebook* (Penngrove: Avec Books, 1999), p. 37. I hear this quotation voiced in the gothic tones of William Burroughs.

69 Michael Palmer, *Notes for Echo Lake* (Berkeley: North Point Press, 1981), p. 74.

70 Alan Soldofsky, 'Notes for Reading Palmer', *Ironwood*, 10(1):19 (1982), p. 154.

71 Palmer, *Notes for Echo Lake*, p. 4.

72 Palmer, *Notes for Echo Lake*, p. 3.

73 The cover of the collection suggests a link between visual and verbal instances of doubling. Not one but two apparitional figures reach from a green obscuring ground towards a fluid surface where their shapes may sound.

74 Palmer, 'Some Notes on Shelley, Poetics and the Present', p. 273.

75 Palmer cites Benjamin, along with Jakobson, Blanchot and Irigaray, as examples of symbiotic writers. See Keith Tuma, 'An Interview with Michael Palmer', *Contemporary Literature*, 30:7 (1959), p. 5.

76 Michael Palmer, 'NUAGES – or Further Notebook Selections', *Ironwood*, 24 (1984), p. 174.

77 I have run a section across this constellation from page 15 to page 19 of Palmer, *The Danish Notebook*.

78 Palmer indicates the naïvety or, at least, the straightforwardness of the dancer by drawing attention to his 'embarrassment' at the 'pretentiousness' with which he replied to her question 'Why poetry?' This brief dialogue is also a fable about embodiment. Palmer's embarrassing reply is 'Because we're made of language'. When he turns the question back on her, asking 'Why dance', she replies 'Because we're made of legs and arms!' Palmer, *The Danish Notebook*, p. 17.

Notes to Chapter 6

1 See, for example, Susan Howe, *My Emily Dickinson* (Berkeley: North Atlantic Books, 1985) and *The Birth-mark: Unsettling the Wilderness in American Literary History* (Middletown: Wesleyan University Press, 1993).

2 In an interview to which several commentators have had recourse, she describes Shakespeare as 'a miracle'. See Howe, *The Birth-mark*, p. 155. This interview was conducted by Edward Foster for *Talisman* in 1990.

3 A focal point for Howe's interest in Ireland is Susan Howe, *The Liberties* (Los Angeles: Sun and Moon Press, 1980). Written in 1980, it was dedicated to her maternal grandmother, Susan Manning.

4 See the *Talisman* interview in Howe, *The Birth-mark*, p. 160.

5 Howe, *The Birth-mark*, p. 160.

6 Excerpt from *The Difficulties* interview (1989), at http://www.english.uiuc. edu/maps/poets/g_l/howe/autobio.htm. Although her father believed in the partition of careers along gender lines, Howe has described him tenderly: 'Considerate and reasonable with a streak of radicalism, he was a man of common sense, a lover of learning, able and good'. Indeed, although a patriarch of the legal institution, and close to the workings of the New Deal, through his association with Professor Felix Frankfurter, Mark DeWolfe Howe appears to have shared with his daughter a sense of being oppressed by official discourses. In the essay 'Frame Structures', Howe gives an account of her father's involvement with Holmes's biography, disclosing that the task was passed on to him by Frankfurter, and suggesting that it may not have been gratefully received. See Susan Howe, *Frame Structures: Early Poems 1974–1979* (New York: New Directions, 1996), pp. 16–17.

7 In relation to this controversy, Howe has suggested 'the issue of editorial control is directly connected to the attempted erasure of antinomianism in our culture'. See *The Birth-mark*, p. 1.

8 Susan Howe, *The Europe of Trusts* (New York: New Directions, 1990).

9 These two expressions form a couplet that occurs twice in quick succession at the beginning of Howe's 1990 work 'Thorow'. Coordinated only by their lineation, they may be read as equivalents or alternatives. See Susan Howe, *Singularities* (Middletown: Wesleyan University Press, 1990), p. 46.

10 This risk also applies to the documents of the Mistresses. In the essay 'Frame Structures', Howe relates how the representation of her grandmother, Fanny Quincy Howe, was reduced to that of 'a standardized version of a "proper Bostonian"' by the editors of a feminist book who wanted to highlight by this reduction the '"multi-dimensioned" persona' of a reformed prostitute with whom Fanny corresponded. See Howe, *Frame Structures*, pp. 23–24.

11 Forrester, *The Seductions of Psychoanalysis*, p. 205.

12 Charles Bernstein, '"Passed by Examination": Paragraphs for Susan Howe', reprinted in *My Way: Speeches and Poems* (Chicago: University of Chicago Press, 1999), p. 101.

13 Peter Quartermain, *Disjunctive Poetics: From Gertrude Stein and Louis Zukofsky to Susan Howe* (Cambridge: Cambridge University Press, 1992), p. 183.

14 See Lynn Keller, *Forms of Expansion: Recent Long Poems by Women* (Chicago: University of Chicago Press, 1997), pp. 187–238; and Ann Vickery, *Leaving Lines of Gender: A Feminist Genealogy of Language Writing* (Hanover: Wesleyan University Press, 2000), pp. 179–90.

15 In discussing the importance of changes in the social and economic structure of England for migration to the New World, Howe has suggested that 'Many of the emigrants were traumatized before they got here'. See the published version of her talk 'Encloser', reproduced in Charles Bernstein (ed.), *The Politics of Poetic Form: Poetry and Public Policy* (New York: Roof Books, 1998), p. 191. Both 'THERE ARE NOT LEAVES ENOUGH' and 'Frame Structures' address the breach in representation that follows an enforced break in family relations.

16 Both these prefaces have titles. 'THERE ARE NOT LEAVES ENOUGH TO CROWN TO COVER TO CROWN TO COVER' begins *The Europe of Trusts*. *Frame Structures* begins with a 'Preface' of the same name.

17 Howe, *The Birth-mark*, p. 30.

18 Martin Jay notes that Calvin's hostility to the visual was so intense that he believed 'physical blindness ... was spiritually valuable because it forced one

to listen to the voice of God'. See Martin Jay, *Downcast Eyes: The Denigration of Vision in Twentieth-Century French Thought* (Berkeley: University of California Press, 1993), p. 43.

19 In 'Encloser', she notes that, even if they could not read, the settlers 'were used to hearing the written words spoken. They knew the structure of the words in the Bible.' See Bernstein, *The Politics of Poetic Form*, p. 190.

20 Howe, *The Birth-mark*, p. 172.

21 Woods, *The Poetics of the Limit*, p. 50.

22 Howe, *Singularities*, p. 50.

23 Howe, *Singularities*, p. 42.

24 William Carlos Williams, *In the American Grain* (Harmondsworth: Penguin Books, 1971), p. 121. Howe, 'Encloser', in Bernstein, *The Politics of Poetic Form*, p. 180.

25 Howe, *My Emily Dickinson*, p. 11.

26 The motif of the hunt is a recurring one in Howe's writing.

27 Lazer, *Opposing Poetries. Volume 2*, p. 65.

28 Rachel Tzvia Back, *Led by Language: The Poetry and Poetics of Susan Howe* (Tuscaloosa: University of Alabama Press, 2002), p. 5.

29 Back, *Led by Language*, p. 6.

30 Cited in Back, *Led by Language*, p. 5.

31 Bernstein, '"Passed by Examination": Paragraphs for Susan Howe', p. 101. The phrase in italics is a quotation from Howe's text *Defenestration of Prague*.

32 Charles Bernstein, 'Revenge of the Poet-Critic', in *My Way: Speeches and Poems* (Chicago: University of Chicago Press, 1999), p. 7.

33 Bernstein, 'Revenge of the Poet-Critic', p. 7.

34 Bernstein, 'Revenge of the Poet-Critic', p. 7.

35 Howe, *The Birth-mark*, p. 158.

36 Bernstein, 'Revenge of the Poet-Critic', p. 8.

37 Bernstein, '"Passed by Examination": Paragraphs for Susan Howe', p. 100. Bernstein borrows the term 'exophoric' (literally, 'carrying to the outside') from Quartermain's *Disjunctive Poetics*.

38 Howe, *The Birth-mark*, pp. 158–59.

39 Bernstein, '"Passed by Examination": Paragraphs for Susan Howe', p. 102. It should be noted that about three-quarters of Bernstein's paragraphs for Howe are preceded by brief, italicized quotations from her work. Links between her words and his are not made explicit but exist as a potential articulation in which the reader will participate. The quotation in this instance comes from *Secret History of the Dividing Line*: '*quintessential clarity of inarticulation*'.

40 Bernstein, '"Passed by Examination": Paragraphs for Susan Howe', p. 100.

41 See Peter Nicholls, 'Unsettling the Wilderness: Susan Howe and American History', *Contemporary Literature*, 37:4 (winter 1996), pp. 586–601. A condensed version of this discussion is to be found in Peter Nicholls, 'Beyond *The Cantos*', pp. 139–60.

42 Nicholls, 'Beyond *The Cantos*', p. 155.

43 Nicholls, 'Beyond *The Cantos*', p. 155.

44 *Frame Structures* includes work that appeared between 1974 and 1979: *Hinge Picture* (1974), *Chanting at the Crystal Sea* (1975), *Cabbage Gardens* (1979) and *Secret History of the Dividing Line* (1978).

45 Freud wrote 'A Note Upon "The Mystic Writing Pad"' in 1925.

46 Howe, *The Europe of Trusts*, p. 14.

47 Nicholls, 'Beyond *The Cantos*', p. 155.

48 The difference is, as I hope to indicate, one of degree rather than kind. The page frames syntax, just as syntax stalks the page.

49 Back, *Led by Language*, p. 56.
50 In this respect, it seems odd that Back should refer to the 'collision' of two words – 'canon' and 'canoes' – that are at a remove from each other on the page but not address areas of the page where words literally touch.
51 Howe, *Singularities*, pp. 56–57.
52 From the middle of the sixteenth century, 'sere' signalled a catch on a gunlock, part of the mechanism for keeping the firearm at half or full cock. 'Tent' is, in one derivation, related to the Latin *temptare*, 'to touch, feel, try'. Howe's line may gesture obliquely in the direction of this one from *Macbeth*: 'My way of life / Is fall'n into the sear, the yellow leaf'.
53 For a reading of this text as a whole, see Back, *Led by Language*, pp. 19–37. My contextualization of the 'green' grid relies on hers.
54 Back, *Led by Language*, p. 23.
55 Howe, *My Emily Dickinson*, p. 13.
56 This poem was published in *Les Fleurs du mal* in 1857.
57 The first stanza of Baudelaire's poem runs:

> La Nature est un temple où de vivants piliers
> Laissent parfois sortir de confuses paroles;
> L'homme y passe à travers des forêts de symbols
> Qui l'observent avec des regards familiers.

This can be translated as 'Nature is a temple, where living pillars sometimes speak confused words; man traverses it through forests of symbols, that watch him with knowing looks.' For the text of Baudelaire's poem, I have used Francis Scarfe (ed.), *Baudelaire* (Harmondsworth: Penguin, 1961), pp. 36–37. Back notes how difficult it was for Byrd's team to read the landscape; their efforts were particularly hampered by a swamp that they christened 'The Dismal'. Bogged down in 'thickets and underbrush', they gave up trying to map the line through it when they emerged. See Back, *Led by Language*, p. 190.

58 Scarfe, *Baudelaire*, p. 37, my emphasis.
59 'Comme de longs échos qui de loin se confondent / Dans une ténébreuse et profonde unité'.
60 Nicholls, *Modernisms*, p. 26.
61 Back uses these words, not to describe one of Howe's 'airy grids' but in relation to one of the 'monologues' from *The Liberties*. See Back, *Led by Language*, p. 95.
62 In the section of *In the American Grain* where Williams discusses the Jesuit missionary Père Sebastian Rasles, he laments that the Puritans 'must have closed all the world out'. 'Purity', which appears as the fourth word in Howe's matrix, is a key word in Williams's account. See Williams, *In the American Grain*, p. 124.
63 Breton, *Mad Love*, p. 15.
64 Breton, *Mad Love*, p. 15.
65 Howe, *Singularities*, p. 45.
66 Nicholls, 'Beyond *The Cantos*', p. 155, my emphasis.
67 The word 'mark' is, in fact, the first one of the work, after the title. See Howe, *Frame Structures*, p. 89. It appears again, this time in capital letters, in the second matrix on the same page.
68 Back, *Led by Language*, p. 28.
69 Back, *Led by Language*, p. 23.
70 Back, *Led by Language*, p. 28, my emphasis.
71 Howe, *Frame Structures*, p. 90.
72 Holmes is referring to 'the sudden death of a fellow officer whom he had just saluted before battle'. See Back, *Led by Language*, p. 23.

73 Howe, *Frame Structures*, p. 90.
74 Back notes that the first version of *Secret History* did not acknowledge its sources, whereas the version published in *Frame Structures* includes a conventional list of acknowledgments. See Back, *Led by Language*, 190.
75 Howe, *The Europe of Trusts*, pp. 10–11.
76 Howe, *Frame Structures*, p. 3.
77 Nicholls, 'Beyond *The Cantos*', p. 155.
78 Howe's preface, 'Frame Structures', written in 1995, gives an account of the involvement of Dutch businessmen in the settlement of 'undeveloped tracts' of land in central and western areas of New York and Pennsylvania: 'Their plan was to sell the wild lands to multitudes of German, Scottish, and Irish settlers, many of them poor and desperate, who were also rushing, under nobody's auspices, crossing from one field of force to another field of force'. See Howe, *Frame Structures*, p. 4.
79 Howe, *The Birth-mark*, pp. 176–77.
80 Howe, *The Birth-mark*, p. 177.
81 Howe, *The Birth-mark*, p. 177.
82 Cited in Vickery, *Leaving Lines of Gender*, p. 179.
83 Howe, *The Birth-mark*, p. 177.
84 Nicholls, 'Beyond *The Cantos*', p. 156.
85 Vickery, *Leaving Lines of Gender*, p. 180.
86 Vickery, *Leaving Lines of Gender*, p. 180.
87 Howe, 'Encloser', in Bernstein, *The Politics of Poetic Form*, p. 182.
88 We might also discern here an allegory of the sexual politics of modernism.
89 Woods, *The Poetics of the Limit*, p. 25.
90 Howe, *My Emily Dickinson*, p. 105. As with many of the paragraphs in *My Emily Dickinson*, this one corresponds with a stanza from Dickinson's poem 'My Life had stood – a Loaded Gun –'. The stanza in question is the fourth; it is cited, in italics, immediately before the passage I have just cited. The stanza runs:
    And when at Night – Our good Day done –
    I guard My Master's Head –
    'Tis better than the Eider-Duck's
    Deep Pillow – to have shared –
91 The cautionary aspects of Little Red Riding Hood seem germane here and it is interesting to note that Howe's family includes some fiercely predatory 'wolfs': 'Lustful and manifest in action, men in the early d'Wolf and Howe families were generally sea captains, privateers, slave traders'. See Howe, *Frame Structures*, p. 20. Howe's 'murderous ancestor' James d'Wolf was charged in 1791 with the offence of throwing a female African slave overboard. D'Wolf evaded trial until 1795, when 'a more lenient district attorney nol-prossed the case'. Howe, *Frame Structures*, p. 20.
92 The gendered nature of the French language makes this enclosure more explicit: 'Dans une ténébreuse et profonde unité'.
93 Williams, *Imaginations*, p. 192.
94 Williams, *Imaginations*, p. 160.
95 Howe, 'Encloser', in Bernstein, *The Politics of Poetic Form*, p. 190.
96 Howe, 'Encloser', in Bernstein, *The Politics of Poetic Form*, p. 190.
97 Howe, *My Emily Dickinson*, p. 98.
98 Howe, *My Emily Dickinson*, p. 97.
99 Gary Grieve-Carlson notes how Williams 'repeatedly stresses the sensory' in his praise of the historical figures who have shaped the American grain. See Gary Grieve-Carlson, 'Getting the News from Poems: History in *In the American*

Grain, and *Paterson'*, in Ian D. Copestake (ed.), *The Rigor of Beauty: Essays in Commemoration of William Carlos Williams* (Bern: Peter Lang, 2004), p. 342.
100 Williams, *In the American Grain*, preface.
101 Breton, *Mad Love*, p. 11.

Notes to Chapter 7

1 Barrett Watten, *Total Syntax* (Carbondale: Southern Illinois University Press, 1985), pp. 31–65.
2 'Tests of Zukofsky' was posted on 25 September 2004 and can be found at http://www.english.wayne.edu/fac_pages/ewatten.
3 Between 1958 and 1969, Zukofsky worked with his wife, Celia, to produce a homophonic translation of Catullus' lyric poetry. See Zukofsky, *Complete Short Poetry*, pp. 241–320.
4 Breton, Eluard and Soupault, *The Automatic Message*, p. 12.
5 Watten, *The Constructivist Moment*, p. xx. The Italian Futurists are suspect for their tendency to 'protofascist politics', the German Dadaists for their equivocal response to 'alienation affects in modernity'.
6 Watten, *The Constructivist Moment*, p. xix. The preference for 'retrospective' over 'deferred' perhaps reflects the emigration of the concept from its original context of trauma.
7 This claim is repeated throughout Nicholls's work on American poetry. This instance of it comes from his essay 'Beyond *The Cantos*', p. 152.
8 Michael Sheringham, 'Breton and the Language of Automatism: Alterity, Allegory, Desire', in Ian Higgins (ed.), *Surrealism and Language* (Edinburgh: Scottish Academic Press, 1986), p. 47.
9 Williams, *Imaginations*, p. 160.
10 See Breton, Eluard and Soupault, *The Automatic Message*, p. 20. For a detailed – and reflexive – reading of the relationship between Objectivist and Imagist poetics, see Woods, *The Poetics of the Limit*, pp. 17ff.
11 Woods, *The Poetics of the Limit*, p. 25.
12 Nicholls, *Modernisms*, p. 173.
13 Translated as 'Surrealism: The Last Snapshot of the European Intelligentsia', the essay from which this quotation is drawn appears in Benjamin, *One-Way Street and Other Writings*, p. 239.
14 Benjamin, 'Surrealism', p. 226.
15 Benjamin believes that it is his specifically German perspective that grants him access to the political import of Surrealism. As a German, he is 'long acquainted with the crisis of the intelligentsia'. See Benjamin, 'Surrealism', p. 225.
16 Paul Naylor, *Poetic Investigations: Singing the Holes in History* (Evanstown: Northwestern University Press, 1999), p. 24.
17 Naylor, *Poetic Investigations*, p. 21.
18 Benjamin, 'Surrealism', p. 237.
19 Benjamin, 'Surrealism', p. 238.
20 Watten, *Total Syntax*, p. 45.
21 Benjamin, 'Surrealism', p. 239.
22 Benjamin, 'Surrealism', p. 239.
23 Breton, Eluard and Soupault, *The Automatic Message*, p. 48.
24 Ron Silliman, *Tjanting* (Great Barrington: The Figures, 1981), p. 11.
25 Along with five other works by Watten, *Complete Thought* has been republished in *Frame (1971–1990)* (Los Angeles: Sun and Moon Press, 1997).

26 The sections are headed: 'Complete Thought', 'Universals', 'Artifacts' and 'Relays'.

27 In a work for which the formal organization is so important, it is worth noting that the couplets are numbered in roman numerals.

28 Joseph Conte, '*Complete Thought*: The Language of Postmodern Contemplation', in Ron Smith (ed.), *Aerial 8: Barrett Watten* (Washington, DC: Edge Books, 1995), pp. 209–14.

29 Conte, '*Complete Thought*', p. 209.

30 Conte, '*Complete Thought*', p. 212.

31 Conte, '*Complete Thought*', p. 210.

32 Conte, '*Complete Thought*', p. 214.

33 Conte, '*Complete Thought*', p. 214.

34 Conte, '*Complete Thought*', p. 211.

35 Staircase and scale are also linked in the Italian word *scala*. I am grateful to Ralph Pite for this suggestion.

36 Some notes may also resemble hammers when written down.

37 In 'The XYZ of Reading', Watten says 'The writer is faced with adjusting himself to what accurately is the medium, a missing person that is a space for projections, the ground for what wants to be perceived' (*Frame*, p. 151). Given the reference to automatism with which the essay begins, it is tempting to read Watten's argument for the new medium as a constructivist restaging of the debates surrounding Surrealist and spiritualist applications of the technique.

38 For a valuable reading of the outmoded in a Surrealist context, see Foster, *Compulsive Beauty*, pp. 157–92.

39 Alan Golding, 'Oppen's Serial Poems', in Rachel Blau DuPlessis and Peter Quartermain (eds), *The Objectivist Nexus: Essays in Cultural Poetics* (Tuscaloosa: University of Alabama Press, 1999), p. 88.

40 Golding, 'Oppen's Serial Poems', p. 89.

41 Cited in Golding, 'Oppen's Serial Poems', p. 327n.

42 Golding, 'Oppen's Serial Poems', p. 89.

43 Barrett Watten, 'Total Syntax: The Work in the World', reprinted in Christopher Beach (ed.), *The Artifice of Indeterminacy: An Anthology of New Poetics* (Tuscaloosa: University of Alabama Press, 1998), p. 65.

44 Watten, 'Total Syntax', p. 49.

45 Watten, 'Total Syntax', p. 49.

46 Watten, 'Total Syntax', p. 49.

47 Naylor, *Poetic Investigations*, p. 22.

48 Naylor, *Poetic Investigations*, p. 24. Naylor draws on Susan Buck-Morss's book *The Dialectics of Seeing* in this section of his discussion. Susan Buck-Morss, *The Dialectics of Seeing. Walter Benjamin and the Arcades Project* (Cambridge: MIT Press, 1991).

49 Watten, 'Total Syntax', p. 65.

50 Watten, *The Constructivist Moment*, p. 134.

51 The full title of this 'blast' is 'The Bride of the Assembly Line: Radical Poetics in Construction'. See Watten, *The Constructivist Moment*, p. 103.

52 George Oppen, *Collected Poems* (New York: New Directions, 1975).

53 The juxtaposition between a cultural interior and a natural exterior chimes with the structure of the first poem in the collection, 'Eclogue', the scene of which is also divided by a window. In neither poem, however, is the division secure.

54 The first instance is in the second couplet, which runs 'Things fall down to create drama./The materials are proof.' See Watten, *Frame*, p. 87. The second instance will be discussed subsequently. *The Materials* stages a number of scenes

of disaster and mishap. For example, a ship sinks in the fourth poem of 'Image of the Engine', while an impassive gull looks on. See Oppen, *Collected Poems*, p. 20. The second instance comes in couplet XXXII: 'The materials motivate storms./Play is felt to be constructed.' See Watten, *Frame*, p. 92.

55 See William Sweet, 'Jacques Maritain', in Edward N. Zalta (ed.), *The Stanford Encyclopedia of Philosophy* (spring 2004 edition), at http://plato.stanford. edu/archives/spr2004/entries/maritain.

56 Theoretically, there is another possible reading, namely that the observer intervenes to stop the engine. I find this reading less preferable, as it seems an assault on the integrity of a machine that, hitherto, has been allowed to follow its own fate.

57 This statement is addressed directly to 'My love' in 'Time of the Missile'. See Oppen, *Collected Poems*, p. 49. 'The Crowded Countries of the Bomb' also faces the fact that 'we can destroy ourselves/Now'. See Oppen, *Collected Poems*, p. 57.

58 Not to mention the aesthetic formalism to which Imagist poetics were welded by the New Critics.

59 Breton, *Mad Love*, p. 15.

60 Watten, *The Constructivist Moment*, p. 357 n10.

61 On this occasion, Watten also read from *Plasma, Silence* and *Non-Events*. See www.sfsu.edu/~poetry/archives/w.html. In the context of total syntax, the relationship between Oppen's remark and *City Fields* would not be annulled if Oppen had been talking about another of Watten's works.

62 See Breton, *Manifestoes of Surrealism*, p. 21. We might also hear an echo here of Oppen's 'Eclogue', *Collected Poems*, p. 17.

63 These sentences begin and end, respectively, the paragraph in which the minotaur appears.

64 The pen-penultimate paragraph of *City Fields* appears to reconstruct Weber's famous image in a concrete environment. In a description of an intersection of city streets, we learn that 'Black elastic wires press down over the street, crossing in a thick net supported by aluminum poles. An open environment seeming like a cage.' The final statement inverts Weber's image, as a means to expose how that image, despite its best intentions, slides from particular into abstraction.

65 Francis Picabia's machine drawings might serve as a modernist precursor in this respect.

66 Perelman, *The Marginalization of Poetry*, p. 122.

67 Perelman, *The Marginalization of Poetry*, p. 124.

68 Watten himself has suggested that the remark was second-hand and subject to interpretation. (Personal communication.)

69 Watten himself interprets Oppen's comment as a criticism that the writing 'was not grounded in "things" or experience in a responsible way' (personal communication). The 'discourse of responsibility' identified by Woods is clearly in evidence here.

Bibliography

Altieri, Charles (1987) 'Without Consequences Is No Politics: A Response to Jerome McGann', in Robert von Hallberg, ed., *Politics and Poetic Value* (Chicago: University of Chicago Press), pp. 301–22.

Altieri, Charles (1996) 'What Is Living and What Is Dead in American Postmodernism: Establishing the Contemporaneity of Some American Poetry', *Critical Inquiry*, 22:4, pp. 764–89.

Altieri, Charles (1999) 'The Objectivist Tradition', in Rachel Blau DuPlessis and Peter Quartermain, eds, *The Objectivist Nexus: Essays in Cultural Poetics* (Tuscaloosa: University of Alabama Press), pp. 25–36.

Andrews, Bruce (1984) 'Writing Social Work and Political Practice', reprinted in Bruce Andrews and Charles Bernstein, eds, *The L=A=N=G=U=A=G=E Book* (Carbondale: Southern Illinois University Press).

Armstrong, Tim (1998) *Modernism, Technology and the Body: A Cultural Study* (Cambridge: Cambridge University Press).

Axelrod, Steven Gould and Deese, Helen, eds (1995) *Critical Essays on William Carlos Williams* (New York: G. K. Hall, Macmillan).

Back, Rachel Tzvia (2002) *Led by Language: The Poetry and Poetics of Susan Howe* (Tuscaloosa: University of Alabama Press).

Bartlett, Lee (1986) 'What is "Language Poetry"?', *Critical Inquiry*, 12 (summer), pp. 741–52.

Baudrillard, Jean (1995) *The Gulf War Did Not Take Place*, trans. Paul Patton (Sydney: Power Publications).

Beach, Christopher, ed. (1998) *Artifice and Indeterminacy: An Anthology of New Poetics* (Tuscaloosa: University of Alabama Press).

Benedikt, Michael (1974) *The Poetry of Surrealism: An Anthology* (Boston: Little, Brown).

Benjamin, Walter (1985) 'Surrealism: The Last Snapshot of the European Intelligentsia', *One-Way Street and Other Writings*, trans. Edmund Jephcott and Kingsley Shorter (London: Verso), pp. 225–39.

Bernstein, Charles (1984) 'Stray Straws and Straw Men', reprinted in Bruce Andrews and Charles Bernstein, eds, *The L=A=N=G=U=A=G=E Book* (Carbondale: Southern Illinois University Press).

Bernstein, Charles (1986) *Content's Dream: Essays, 1975–1984* (Los Angeles: Sun and Moon Press).

Bernstein, Charles (1986) 'An Interview with Tom Beckett', in *Content's Dream: Essays, 1975–1984* (Los Angeles: Sun and Moon Press), pp. 385–410.

Bernstein, Charles, ed. (1998) *The Politics of Poetic Form: Poetry and Public Policy* (New York: Roof Books).

Bernstein, Charles, ed. (1998) *Close Listening: Poetry and the Performed Word* (New York: Oxford University Press).

Bernstein, Charles (1999) *My Way: Speeches and Poems* (Chicago: University of Chicago Press).

Bloch, Ernst, Lukacs, Georg, Brecht, Bertolt, Benjamin, Walter and Adorno, Theodor (1980) *Aesthetics and Politics: The Key Texts of the Classic Debate Within German Marxism*, trans. R. Taylor (London: Verso).

Borkhuis, Charles (2002) 'Writing from Inside Language: Late Surrealism and Textual Poetry in France and the United States', in Mark Wallace and Steven Marks, eds, *Telling It Slant: Avant-Garde Poetics in the 1990s* (Tuscaloosa: University of Alabama Press), pp. 237–53.

Bowie, Malcolm (1991) *Lacan* (Cambridge: Harvard University Press).

Breton, André (1969) *Manifestoes of Surrealism*, trans. Richard Seaver and Helen R. Lane (Ann Arbor: University of Michigan Press).

Breton, André (1978) *What Is Surrealism? Selected Writings*, ed. Franklin Rosemont (London: Pluto Press).

Breton, André (1987) *Mad Love*, trans. Mary Ann Caws (Lincoln: University of Nebraska Press).

Breton, André, Eluard, Paul and Soupault, Philippe (1997) *The Automatic Message*, trans. David Gascoyne, Antony Melville and Jon Graham (London: Atlas Press).

Breton, André and Soupault, Philippe (1968) *Les Champs Magnétiques* (Paris: Gallimard).

Breton, André and Soupault, Philippe (1985) *The Magnetic Fields*, trans. David Gascoyne (3rd edn) (London: Atlas Press).

Brook, James (1987) 'Political Poetry and Formalist Avant-Gardes: Four Viewpoints', in Lawrence Ferlinghetti and Nancy J. Peters, eds, *City Lights Review 1* (San Francisco: City Lights Books).

Bruns, Gerald L. (1978) 'De Improvisatione', *Iowa Review*, 9:3 (summer), pp. 66–69.

Buck-Morss, Susan (1991) *The Dialectics of Seeing. Walter Benjamin and the Arcades Project* (Cambridge: MIT Press).

Bürger, Peter (1984) *Theory of the Avant-Garde* (Minneapolis: University of Minnesota Press).

Cohen, Margaret (1993) *Profane Illumination: Walter Benjamin and the Paris of Surrealist Revolution* (Berkeley: University of California Press).

Conte, Joseph (1995) '*Complete Thought*: The Language of Postmodern Contemplation', in Ron Smith, ed., *Aerial 8: Barrett Watten* (Washington, DC: Edge Books), pp. 209–14.

Crozier, Andrew (1999) 'Zukofsky's List', in Rachel Blau DuPlessis and Peter Quartermain, eds, *The Objectivist Nexus: Essays in Cultural Poetics* (Tuscaloosa: University of Alabama Press), pp. 275–85.

Davidson, Michael (1982) 'After Sentence, Sentence', *American Book Review* (September–October), p. 3.

Davidson, Michael (1990) 'Skewed by Design: From Act to Speech Act in Language Writing', *Fragmente*, 2 (autumn), pp. 44–49.

Davis, Mike (2002) *Dead Cities* (New York: New Press).

DuPlessis, Rachel Blau and Quartermain, Peter, eds (1999) *The Objectivist Nexus: Essays in Cultural Poetics* (Tuscaloosa: University of Alabama Press).

Edwards, Ken (1990) 'Language: The Remake', *Fragmente*, 2 (autumn), pp. 57–60.

Emory, William Closson (1929) 'Miner Away', *Blues*, 1:3, p. 53.

Emory, William Closson (1929) 'Theme for a Blues Song', *Blues*, 1:4, p. 95.

Flint, F. S. (1986) 'Imagisme', reprinted in Peter Faulkner, ed., *A Modernist Reader* (London: Batsford), pp. 40–41.

Ford, Charles Henri (1929) 'The Room', *Blues*, 1:3, p. 75.

Forrester, John (1990) *The Seductions of Psychoanalysis: Freud, Lacan and Derrida* (Cambridge: Cambridge University Press).

Foster, Hal (1995) *Compulsive Beauty* (Cambridge: MIT Press).

Fredman, Stephen (1990) *Poet's Prose: The Crisis in American Verse* (2nd edn) (Cambridge: Cambridge University Press).

Frye, Richard R. (1989) 'Scrying the Signs: Objectivist Premonitions in Williams' *Spring and All*', *Sagetrieb*, 8:3, pp. 77–95.

Gizzi, Peter (1995) 'Interview with Michael Palmer', in Peter Gizzi, ed., *Exact Change Yearbook 1* (Manchester: Carcanet), pp. 161–79.

Golding, Alan (1995) *From Outlaw to Classic: Canons in American Poetry* (Wisconsin: University of Wisconsin Press).

Golding, Alan (1999) 'Oppen's Serial Poems', in Rachel Blau DuPlessis and Peter Quartermain, eds, *The Objectivist Nexus: Essays in Cultural Poetics* (Tuscaloosa: University of Alabama Press), pp. 84–103.

Greer, Michael (1991) 'Language Poetry in America 1971–1991', *Meanjin*, 50:1, pp. 149–56.

Grieve-Carlson, Gary (2004) 'Getting the News from Poems: History in *In the American Grain*, and *Paterson*', in Ian D. Copestake, ed., *The Rigor of Beauty: Essays in Commemoration of William Carlos Williams* (Bern: Peter Lang), pp. 339–64.

Hartley, George (1989) *Textual Politics and the Language Poets* (Bloomington: Indiana University Press).

Hatlen, Burton (1999) 'Objectivist Poets in Context', in Rachel Blau DuPlessis and Peter Quartermain, eds, *The Objectivist Nexus: Essays in Cultural Poetics* (Tuscaloosa: University of Alabama Press), pp. 37–55.

Hejinian, Lyn (1985) 'The Rejection of Closure', in Bob Perelman, ed., *Writing/Talks* (Carbondale: Southern Illinois University Press).

Hejinian, Lyn (2000) 'The Rejection of Closure', *The Language of Inquiry* (Berkeley: University of California Press), pp. 40–58.

Hoog, Armand (1951) 'The Surrealist Novel', *Yale French Studies*, 8, pp. 17–25.

Howe, Susan (1980) *The Liberties* (Los Angeles: Sun and Moon Press).

Howe, Susan (1985) *My Emily Dickinson* (Berkeley: North Atlantic Books).

Howe, Susan (1990) *The Europe of Trusts* (New York: New Directions).

Howe, Susan (1990) *Singularities* (Middletown: Wesleyan University Press).

Howe, Susan (1993) *The Birth-mark: Unsettling the Wilderness in American Literary History* (Middletown: Wesleyan University Press).

Howe, Susan (1996) *Frame Structures: Early Poems 1974–1979* (New York: New Directions).

Howe, Susan (1998) 'Encloser', reproduced in Charles Bernstein, ed., *The Politics of Poetic Form: Poetry and Public Policy* (New York: Roof Books), pp. 175–89.

Jameson, Fredric (1971) *Marxism and Form* (Princeton: Princeton University Press).

Jameson, Fredric (1984) 'Postmodernism, or the Cultural Logic of Late Capitalism', *New Left Review*, 146, pp. 54–92.

Jay, Martin (1993) *Downcast Eyes: The Denigration of Vision in Twentieth-Century French Thought* (Berkeley: University of California Press).

Keller, Lynn (1997) *Forms of Expansion: Recent Long Poems by Women* (Chicago: University of Chicago Press).

Koethe, John (1991) 'Contrary Impulses: On the Tension Between Poetry and Theory', *Critical Inquiry*, 18:1, pp. 64–75.

Krauss, Rosalind (1986) *The Originality of the Avant-Garde and Other Modernist Myths* (Cambridge: MIT Press).

Lazer, Hank (1988) 'Radical Collages', *The Nation*, 247 (2–9 July).

Lazer, Hank (1996) *Opposing Poetries. Volume 1: Issues and Institutions* (Evanston: Northwestern University Press).

Lazer, Hank (1996) *Opposing Poetries. Volume 2: Readings* (Evanston: Northwestern University Press), pp. 6–18.

Macey, David (1988) *Lacan in Contexts* (London: Verso Books).

Mariani, Paul (1990) *William Carlos Williams: A New World Naked* (New York: W. W. Norton).

McCaffery, Steve (1977) 'The Death of the Subject', *Open Letter*, 3:7.

McGann, Jerome J. (1987) 'Contemporary Poetry, Alternate Routes', *Critical Inquiry*, 13 (spring), pp. 624–47.

McGann, Jerome J. (1987) 'Response to Charles Altieri', in Robert von Hallberg, ed., *Politics and Poetic Value* (Chicago: University of Chicago Press), pp. 311–12.

Middleton, Peter (1990) 'Language Poetry and Linguistic Activism', *Social Text*, 25/26, pp. 242–53.

Miller, Tyrus (1997) 'Poetic Contagion: Surrealism and Williams's *A Novelette*', *William Carlos Williams Review*, 22 (spring), pp. 17–27

Murphy, Patrick D. (1998) 'Anotherness and Inhabitation in Recent Multicultural American Writing', in Richard Kerridge and Neil Sammells, eds, *Writing the Environment: Ecocriticism and Literature* (London: Zed Books), pp. 40–52.

Naylor, Paul (1999) *Poetic Investigations: Singing the Holes in History* (Evanstown: Northwestern University Press).

Neiman, Catrina and Nathan, Paul (1992) *View: Parade of the Avant-Garde* (New York: Thunder's Mouth Press).

Nelson, Cary (1989) *Repression and Recovery: Modern American Poetry and the Politics of Cultural Memory 1919–1945* (Madison: University of Wisconsin Press).

Nicholls, Peter (1995) *Modernisms: A Literary Guide* (Houndmills, Macmillan).

Nicholls, Peter (1996) 'Lorine Niedecker: Rural Surreal', in Jenny Penberthy, ed., *Lorine Niedecker: Woman and Poet* (Orono: National Poetry Foundation, University of Maine Press).

Nicholls, Peter (1996) 'Unsettling the Wilderness: Susan Howe and American History', *Contemporary Literature*, 37:4, pp. 586–601.

Nicholls, Peter (1998) 'An Interview with Bob Perelman', *Textual Practice*, 12:3, pp. 525–43.

Nicholls, Peter (1999) 'Beyond *The Cantos*: Pound and American Poetry', in Ira B. Nadel, ed., *The Cambridge Companion to Ezra Pound* (Cambridge: Cambridge University Press).

Oppen, George (1975) *Collected Poems* (New York: New Directions).

Palmer, Michael (1981) *Notes for Echo Lake* (Berkeley: North Point Press).

Palmer, Michael (1984) 'NUAGES – or Further Notebook Selections', *Ironwood*, 24, pp. 174–82.

Palmer, Michael (1985) 'Autobiography, Memory and Mechanisms of Conceal-ment', in Bob Perelman, ed., *Writing/Talks* (Carbondale: Southern Illinois University Press), pp. 227–28.

Palmer, Michael (1990) 'On Objectivism', *Sulfur*, 26 (spring), pp. 121–22.

Palmer, Michael (1993) 'Some Notes on Shelley, Poetics and the Present', *Sulfur*, 33, pp. 273–81.

Palmer, Michael (1995) 'The Site of the Poem', in Peter Gizzi, ed., *Exact Change Yearbook 1* (Manchester: Carcanet), p. 190.

Palmer, Michael (1995) *At Passages* (New York: New Directions Books).

Palmer, Michael (1999) *The Danish Notebook* (Penngrove: Avec Books).

Palmer, Michael (undated) 'Period (Sense of Duration)', at http://www.english. uiuc.edu/maps/poets/m_r/palmer/period.html.

Penberthy, Jenny (1993) *Niediecker and the Correspondence with Zukofsky 1931–1970* (Cambridge: Cambridge University Press).

Perelman, Bob (1981) *Primer* (San Francisco: This Press).

Perelman, Bob (1994) *The Trouble with Genius: Reading Pound, Joyce, Stein and Zukofsky* (Berkeley: University of California Press).

Perelman, Bob (1996) *The Marginalization of Poetry: Language Writing and Literary History* (Princeton: Princeton University Press).

Perloff, Marjorie (1998) '"Barbed-Wire Entanglements": The "New American Poetry," 1930–32', in *Poetry On and Off the Page: Essays for Emergent Occasions* (Evanstown: Northwestern University Press), pp. 51–82.

Perloff, Marjorie (not dated) 'After Language Poetry: Innovation and Its Theoretical Discontents', at http://epc.buffalo.edu/authors/perloff/after_ langpo.html.

Perloff, Marjorie (not dated) 'Late Late Modern', at http://wings.buffalo.edu/epc/ authors/perloff/parker.html.

Pound, Ezra (1986) 'A Few Don'ts for Imagistes', reprinted in Peter Faulkner, ed., *A Modernist Reader* (London: Batsford), p. 60.

Preminger, Alex and Brogan, T. V. F. (1993) *The New Princeton Encyclopedia of Poetry and Poetics* (Princeton: Princeton University Press).

Quartermain, Peter (1992) *Disjunctive Poetics: From Gertrude Stein and Louis Zukofsky to Susan Howe* (Cambridge: Cambridge University Press).

Riffaterre, Michael (1978) *Semiotics of Poetry* (London: Methuen).

Ross, Andrew (1988) 'The New Sentence and the Commodity Form: Recent Ameri-can Writing', in Cary Nelson and Lawrence Grossberg, eds, *Marxism and the Interpretation of Culture* (Urbana: University of Illinois Press).

Roudinesco, Elizabeth (1990) *Lacan & Co. A History of Psychoanalysis in France 1925–1985*, trans. Jeffrey Mehlman (London: Free Association Books).

Scarfe, Francis, ed. (1961) *Baudelaire* (Harmondsworth: Penguin).

Scroggins, Mark (1997) 'The Revolutionary Word: Louis Zukosky, *New Masses*, and Political Radicalism in the 1930s', in Mark Scroggins, ed., *Upper Limit Music: The Writing of Louis Zukofsky* (Tuscaloosa: University of Alabama Press), pp. 44–64.

Sheringham, Michael (1986) 'Breton and the Language of Automatism: Alterity, Allegory, Desire', in Ian Higgins, ed., *Surrealism and Language* (Edinburgh: Scot-tish Academic Press), pp. 46–62.

Shetley, Vernon (1993) *After the Death of Poetry: Poet and Audience in Contemporary America* (Durham: Duke University Press).

Silliman, Ron (1980) 'The New Sentence', *Talks: Hills*, 6/7.

Silliman, Ron (1981) *Tjanting* (Great Barrington: The Figures).

Silliman, Ron (1986) 'New Prose, New Prose Poem', in Larry McCaffery, ed., *Postmodern Fiction: A Bio-Bibliographical Guide* (New York: Greenwood Press), pp. 157–74.

Silliman, Ron, ed. (1986) *In the American Tree* (Orono: National Poetry Foundation).

Silliman, Ron (1987) *The New Sentence* (New York: Roof Books).

Soldofsky, Alan (1982) 'Notes for Reading Palmer', *Ironwood*, 10(1):19, p. 154.

Sweet, William (2004) 'Jacques Maritain', in Edward N. Zalta, ed., *The Stanford Encyclopedia of Philosophy* (spring edition), at http://plato.stanford.edu/archives/spr2004/entries/maritain.

Tashjian, Dickran (1995) *A Boatload of Madmen: Surrealism and the American Avant-Garde 1920–1950* (New York: Thames and Hudson).

Terrell, Carroll F., ed. (1979) *Louis Zukofsky: Man and Poet* (Orono: National Poetry Foundation, University of Maine Press).

Todorov, Tzvetan (1973) *The Fantastic: A Structural Approach to a Literary Genre* (Cleveland: Case Western Reserve University).

Tracy, Steven C. (1989) 'William Carlos Williams and *Blues: A Magazine of New Rhythms*', *William Carlos Williams Review*, 15:2, pp. 17–29.

Tuma, Keith (1959) 'An Interview with Michael Palmer', *Contemporary Literature*, 30:7, p. 5.

Tyler, Parker (1929) 'Sonnet', *Blues*, 1:2, pp. 50–51.

Tyler, Parker (1929) 'This Dreaming Image', *Blues*, 1:2, pp. 49–50.

Vickery, Ann (2000) *Leaving Lines of Gender: A Feminist Genealogy of Language Writing* (Hanover: Wesleyan University Press).

Wallace, Mark and Marks, Steven, eds (2002) *Telling It Slant: Avant-Garde Poetics in the 1990s* (Tuscaloosa: University of Alabama Press).

Watten, Barrett (1985) *Total Syntax* (Carbondale: Southern Illinois University Press).

Watten, Barrett (1997) *Frame (1971–1990)* (Los Angeles: Sun and Moon Press).

Watten, Barrett (1998) 'Total Syntax: The Work in the World', reprinted in Christopher Beach, ed., *The Artifice of Indeterminacy: An Anthology of New Poetics* (Tuscaloosa: University of Alabama Press).

Watten, Barrett (2003) *The Constructivist Moment: From Material Text to Cultural Poetics* (Middletown: Wesleyan University Press).

Weaver, Mike (1971) *William Carlos Williams: The American Background* (Cambridge: Cambridge University Press).

Williams, William Carlos (1929) 'A Note on the Art of Poetry', *Blues*, 1:4, p. 77.

Williams, William Carlos (1929) 'For a New Magazine', *Blues*, 1:2, p. 30.

Williams, William Carlos (1929) 'simplex sigilum veri: a catalogue', *Blues*, 2:7, p. 9.

Williams, William Carlos (1929) 'Introduction to a Collection of Modern Writings', *Blues*, 2:7, p. 3. Williams, William Carlos (1930) 'Caviar and Bread Again: A Warning to the New Writer', *Blues*, 2:9, p. 47.

Williams, William Carlos (1970) *Imaginations* (New York: New Directions Books).

Williams, William Carlos (1971) *In the American Grain* (Harmondsworth: Penguin Books).

Williams, William Carlos (1974) *The Embodiment of Knowledge*, Ron Loewinsohn, ed. (New York: New Directions Books).

Williams, William Carlos and McAlmon, Robert (1920) Editorial, *Contact*, 1, p. 1.

Woods, Tim (2002) *The Poetics of the Limit: Ethics and Politics in Modern and Contemporary American Poetry* (Houndmills: Palgrave Macmillan).

Zukofsky, Louis (1929) 'Group from Ten Poems (1924–26)', *Blues*, 2:9, p. 42.

Zukofsky, Louis (1931) 'American Poetry 1920–1930', *The Symposium*, 2:1.

Zukofsky, Louis (1967) *Prepositions: The Collected Critical Essays* (New York: Horizon Press).

Zukofsky, Louis (1991) *Complete Short Poetry* (Baltimore: Johns Hopkins University Press).

Index

The letter n indicates a note number